D0094171

Fun Is Not Enough

Also by Francis Canavan, S.J.

The Political Reason of Edmund Burke

Freedom of Expression: Purpose as Limit

The Light of Faith

Edmund Burke: Prescription and Providence

Pins in the Liberal Balloon

The Political Economy of Edmund Burke

*The Pluralist Game: Pluralism, Liberalism,
and the Moral Conscience*

By the Grace of God

Fun Is Not Enough
The Complete *catholic eye* Columns

Francis Canavan, S.J.

Edited by Dawn Eden Goldstein
Introduction by Stephen M. Fields, S.J.

a *catholic eye* book
Published by
The National Committee of Catholic Laymen, Inc.
New York

Anne Conlon, managing editor of the *Human Life Review*, put great dedication and warm enthusiasm into this project of publishing a (nearly)* complete edition of Father Canavan's *catholic eye* columns in time for the one hundredth anniversary of his birth. It is a blessing to have the written contributions of Father Stephen M. Fields, S.J., and Dr. Kenneth Grasso. The *Human Life Review*'s staff, particularly production manager Christina Angelopoulos and longtime senior editor Ellen Wilson Fielding, worked hard to prepare the essays for publication. Dr. Sebastian Mahfood of En Route Books and Media provided invaluable assistance, including engaging the services of master cover artist T. J. Burdick. I am heartily grateful to them, to the anonymous donor who co-funded the publication of this book, and to the divine providence that brought us all together. — D.E.G.

* A small handful of columns have been omitted because they repeated a significant amount of material or themes from other columns in the volume.

Published in the United States by
The National Committee of Catholic Laymen, Inc.
271 Madison Avenue, Suite 1005
New York, New York 10016

©2017 by The National Committee of Catholic Laymen, Inc.
All rights reserved. Published 2017

ISBN: 978-1-64136-648-9

Cover design by T. J. Burdick

Contents

Introduction ix
Editor's Foreword xiii

On Being Personally Opposed 1
Okay Clerics for Okay Kids 5
A Pluralist Church 7
Preaching by Silence 10
The Real World 13
The New Sacraments 16
Nearer to the Heart's Desire 19
The Loyal Opposition 22
Standing at Armageddon 25
Tadpoles and Babies 28
The Sermon on the Mount 31
The New Skepticism 34
The Hierarchy of Beings 37
Infanticide 40
Liberty, Equality, and Order 43
The Law Unbound 46
The Pope's Dutch Treat 49
Losing the Faith 52
Vive la Différence 55
Liberalism and the Catholic University 58
Liberalism and the Catholic University II 61
Rights as the Beginning and End 64
The Americanization of Catholics 67
Stooping to Folly 70
How to Kill Freedom of Speech 73
Dissolving the Norms 76
Slogans for All Seasons 79
Intrinsically Evil Acts 82
The Logic of Contraception 85
Argument Stoppers 88
A Divorce Culture 91

The Methodology Is the Message	94
Order in the Soul	97
Going to Hell	100
Ladies in Writing	103
Lost in the Cosmos	106
"Imposing" Moral Beliefs	109
Selective Listening	112
Why Anything Goes	115
Sunset of the Enlightenment	118
Meaning in a Meaningless World	121
Equal—and Separate	124
Not Tea for Two	127
The Severed Link	130
Christian Freedom	133
Those Who Care, Govern	136
A Disintegrating Culture	139
Ordered Liberty	142
The Feminine Touch	145
Plastic People	148
All of This for Me	151
Dying for Mama	154
The Problem of Evil	157
The Rot in Liberal Politics	160
Good Old Edmund Burke	163
How to Read a Newspaper	166
An Uncertain Trumpet	169
Papal Social Thought	172
"Reason" and Abortion	175
The Family Issue	178
Taking Christmas Seriously	181
Doing Better for Lent	184
Civilization Is for the Civilized	187
The Devil We Know	190
Handling the Easy Cases	193
Our Liberal Censors	196
To Whom Shall We Go?	199
Temporary Popularity	202
The Customer's Rights	205
"Man-Made Laws"	208

How to Write Libspeak 211
Why Squirrels Can't Sing 214
Downhill Passions 217
Salvation One by One 220
Celibacy and Contempt 223
Just a Matter of Taste 226
The Prophet Motive 229
Family Is as Family Does 232
When the Magic Is Gone 235
Anything Goes, Almost 238
A God to Live For 241
The Court of First Resort 244
The Sex Taboo Teens Need 247
The Culture of Death 250
Faith as a Burden 253
A Veto on Morality? 256
What Dr. Freud Knew 259
Madness in the Courts 262
Paying Our Dues 265
Middle-School Sex Mess 268
Home Swede Home 271
The Ideological Mind 274
"Does New York Believe Anything?" 277
Happy Family Ties 280
Our Pluralist Sea 283
Seen and Unseen 286
Democracy's Disease 289
"Tell Us What You Want!" 292
"Catch-22"? 295
Is There Golf in Heaven? 298
The Scandal Racket 301
The (Democratic) Party's Over 304
Deep Weariness 307
The Real Crisis 310
The Primacy of Choice 313
Catholic Individualism 316
The Linchpin of Sexuality 319
Modern Superstition 322
Who Says So? 325

The Faith of Liberals	328
Political Thinking	331
The Basis of Society	334
Laughing at the Court	337
What's Your Worldview?	341
Rot in the Soul	345
The Hearts of the Faithful	348
Women's Hearts	351
Believing Anything	353
The Idea of the Good	355
Something New and Different	358
The Rock of Culture	360
The Spiritual Solution	363
Getting It All Here	366
Community	368
Growing Into	371
About the Author	373
Index	375

Introduction

This new and timely edition of the essays of Francis Canavan, S.J., will be welcomed by everyone who heeds the prophecies of recent popes that our age is marked by a crisis of reason.

Benedict XVI sees the "dictatorship of relativism" as "the gravest problem of our time."[1] It holds, especially in religion and morality, "that mutually opposed points of view" can be equally legitimate.[2] It thus elevates the will of individual subjects over the objective order of reality long ago vindicated when Greece's golden age discovered the very nature of the human mind. John Paul II reminds us in his 1998 encyclical *Fides et Ratio* that reason nostalgically yearns for God, whose "infinite riches" make us inescapable seekers of truth. If reason flees from submitting to universally valid claims, it is not because reason is incapable, but because the choices that we make impede it.[3] John Henry Newman diagnoses the sophistry used to justify this flight. It becomes lauded as the healthy development of human maturation, not censured as an aberration.[4]

Like the pontiffs, Father Canavan robustly confronts this aberration. He renews our confidence in the power of rational argument to deconstruct the superficially captivating shibboleths of our time. He employs, for instance, a dialectic reminiscent of Socrates to pose probing questions to those who, although "personally opposed" to abortion, nonetheless approve of its legality. Would the same constraint to imposing their conscience on others apply, he asks, to infanticide and suicide? To torturing prisoners in jail? To genocide, should it become public policy? In showing that those "personally opposed" lack consistent moral principles, he also uncovers the irony in their hidden agenda: the advocacy of partisan politics that actually finds nothing wrong with what they purport to oppose.

Canavan presciently foretells the unraveling of the inevitable consequences entailed in abortion's legality, as subsequently evinced by the Clinton veto of the partial-birth abortion ban, Abu Ghraib and waterboarding, and by several states' recent permission of euthanasia. Are we now, he incites us to ask, but a small step from countenancing full-fledged genocide, despite more than seventy years of pledging "Never again!" to the Holocaust? Similarly, he reminds us that to endorse contraception even within marriage "pulls out the linchpin that holds" sexual morality intact. When this morality hinges only on the circumstances of the act and the intention of the agent, neglecting its intrinsic purpose, even the most "exotic" things can be deemed to cement "the bonds of love." Now that in *Obergefell* the Supreme Court "protects people's ability to define and express their [own] gender identities," we are left wondering whether the bonds of marital love need remain restricted even to human beings.[5] Canavan thus admonishes us more bluntly today than when he wrote — vindicating the poet's epigram: "Vice is a monster of so frightful mien, / As to be hated, needs but to be seen; / Yet seen too oft, familiar with her face, / We first endure, then pity, then embrace."[6]

Furthermore, Canavan's vigorous defense of the articles of faith echoes John Paul's rejecting reason ordered to utilitarian ends and his locating it within "the religious impulse innate in every person."[7] For Canavan, a "Liberal Christianity" that, for instance, turns the resurrection into a vaguely imagined metaphor for spiritual life divorced from the living flesh of Jesus may satisfy a scientifically biased mind, but it takes Christ "out of history altogether."[8] It makes reason our god rather than rejoicing in the utter divine gift that cleanses history of its all-too-real scourges felt squarely in the body: sin, suffering, and death. He also offers practical advice about the Beatitudes. Although they are not meant as a set of rules to guide our dealings with "panhandlers, grifters, and confidence men," much less any nation's foreign policy, still they do exhort us to set aside what our reason often demands as justice for the civilizing sake of mercy.[9] Otherwise, we turn our relations with each other into hell, "where no one takes the Sermon on the Mount seriously."[10]

In the midst of Canavan's rapier-like wit in service of truth, his essays disclose the gentler heart of a priest. He advises bringing boys, for example, to Marian devotions so that they can learn to "esteem womanhood as something more than mere femaleness." And he takes the sting out of the nihilism of

Nietzsche and of Beckett's *Waiting for Godot* by consoling us that the sheer hardness of life has already been lovingly embraced by Christ's own "'dire poverty,' 'labors, hunger, and thirst,' 'injuries and insults,' and death."[11] In sum, if as St. Paul tells us, in this world we see heavenly realities dimly as in a clouded lens (1 Cor. 13:12), then the writings of this noble-souled Jesuit help to make our vision of them brighter and more clearly focused.

Stephen M. Fields, S.J.
Georgetown University
Washington, D.C.
August 9, 2017

Stephen M. Fields, S.J., is Associate Professor of Theology at Georgetown University.

Notes

1. Joseph Cardinal Ratzinger, Homily *Pro Eligendo Papa*, April 18, 2005, cited in John L. Allen, Jr., "Pope Benedict XVI, One Year On," *National Catholic Reporter*, April 21, 2006, 12-14; Ratzinger, *Truth and Tolerance: Christian Belief and World Religions*, trans. Henry Taylor (San Francisco, CA: Ignatius, 2004), 72.

2. Avery Cardinal Dulles, S.J., "On Relativism," in *Symposium: In Honor of Pope Emeritus Benedict XVI's 90th Birthday*, ed. Stephen M. Fields, S.J., *Nova et Vetera: The English Edition of the International Theological Journal* 15 (Summer 2017): 729-43, at 730.

3. Pope John Paul II, *Fides et Ratio*, Encyclical Letter, September 14, 1998, *Acta Apostolicae Sedis* 91 (1991), 5-88, pars. 17, 24, 28; English trans. from www.vatican.va.

4. John Henry Cardinal Newman, *Apologia Pro Vita Sua* (New York: Doubleday, 1989), 336.

5. David B. Cruz, "Transgender Rights after Obergefell," *University of Missouri-Kansas City Law Review* 84/3 (2016): 693-705, at 693.

6. Alexander Pope, *An Essay on Man* (1733-34), Epistle II, ll. 217-20. See *Alexander Pope: Selected Poetry and Prose*, ed. William K. Wimsatt (New York: Holt, Rinehart and Winston, 1972), 208.

7. *Fides et Ratio*, pars. 47, 81.

8. *Infra.*, 182.

9. *Infra.*, 31.

10. *Infra.*, 33.

11. *Infra.*, 152, quoting *The Spiritual Exercises of St. Ignatius*; see trans. and ed. Louis J. Puhl (Chicago, IL: Loyola University Press, 1951), section 116.

Editor's Foreword

Readers such as James V. Schall, S.J., have called attention to the prophetic quality of Francis Canavan, S.J.'s observations on faith, philosophy, politics, and culture.[1] I too see Canavan as a prophet, but for reasons that are more personal.

In April 2006, one of Canavan's former students, Dimitri Cavalli, gave me a copy of *Pins in the Liberal Balloon*, the collection of the Jesuit's early *catholic eye* columns. The book sat untouched on my shelf for some weeks; I was too busy reading a collection of G. K. Chesterton's *Illustrated News* columns to bother exploring the work of an author I had never heard of. When I finally cracked its covers, I was surprised to discover a voice both new and familiar. It was almost as though someone had told me that G. K. was alive and well and living at Fordham. Between Chesterton and Canavan, there was a shared common sense, a shared faith, a shared gift for keen observation of the signs of the times, and — not least of all — a shared wit.

At about the same time, I was contacted by Faith Abbott McFadden, of blessed memory. The senior editor of *catholic eye* and the *Human Life Review*, who — if memory serves — had read in the *National Catholic Register* about my entrance into full communion with the Catholic Church, Faith invited me to lunch so she could wish me a hearty "welcome home."

Over our meal, I told Faith that I admired Canavan's work and wanted to meet him. She kindly arranged for me to be seated by him at the Human Life Foundation's upcoming Great Defender of Life Award dinner.

I found Canavan to be everything in person that he was in his columns. He possessed a rare combination of wit and humility; in this too, he reminded me of Chesterton, who was reputed to have no enemies.

In the wake of the dinner, I sent Canavan a copy of my first book, *The Thrill of the Chaste*. I cannot now locate the note he sent me in gratitude, but I remember that it gave me the confidence to contact him by telephone and begin a true friendship. What I particularly recall was that he told me that the book reminded him of the work he did as a chaplain for the Calix Society, a Catholic association for alcoholics who are maintaining their sobriety through participation in Alcoholics Anonymous. He said that I, like him, was promoting personal recovery, and he impressed upon me the need for laborers in that field. His message was akin to what I would later read in Paul VI's *Evangelii Nuntiandi* (no. 41): "Modern man listens more willingly to witnesses than to teachers, and if he does listen to teachers, it is because they are witnesses."

I cannot adequately express how much Father Canavan's response to *The Thrill of the Chaste* affected me. Where others simply saw a "chastity book," he saw the beginning of a writing career that could help people heal. He read beneath the surface, recognizing and understanding my desire to open readers to Christ's transformative grace. More than that, he believed I could actually accomplish that desire. It is no exaggeration to say that my subsequent apostolate as an author on healing from trauma is the outgrowth of his encouragement and prayers.

But Canavan's prophetic inspiration in my life did not stop there. He became a spiritual father to me — not in the manner of a spiritual director but rather in the manner of a father who seeks to help his child gain the confidence to attain his or her dreams. He understood my dreams long before I understood them myself. In June 2008, when I showed him an article I had written for a Catholic website, he told me I was capable of doing academic-level writing. Six months later, when I sent him the first paper I had written for a theology M.A. program, he told me I was capable of doctoral work.

I was going to add an additional compliment: that Father Canavan, in guiding and encouraging me toward college teaching, was always gentle and never pushy. But that is not entirely true. He was indeed gentle, but, to be honest, he did not merely tell me I could attain a doctorate. He told me I *had* to.

During the immediate aftermath of the Second Vatican Council, he said, Catholic theology faculties were eroded by dissent. Today, a small but growing number of faithful Catholic colleges were seeking to buck the tide. But, Canavan said, "faithful Catholic colleges need faithful Catholic professors." More than that, he said, the Church needed me personally to accept the vocation of a university professor. It needed *my* faith, *my* talent.

Father Canavan was then ninety-one years old and beginning to lose his short-term memory. When he first telephoned to tell me of my teaching vocation, I thought it would suffice to answer that I had neither the ability to do doctoral-level study nor any interest in teaching; then he would forget the whole thing.

Except he didn't. For two weeks, he phoned me every day asking me to reconsider. After the first week, he started offering to put me in touch with former students of his who could tell me what it was like to teach at Catholic colleges: "I called Bill Luckey at Christendom and he said you could call him. Here's his phone number. . . ." A professional lobbyist could not have worked harder.

I remember those weeks so well. There was the night I was in the audience at a noisy Theology on Tap event and my phone showed a message from Father Canavan. I took my phone to the doorway of the pub and called back to make sure he was all right.

His voice was so faint I had to strain to hear it. "Have you thought about getting a doctorate?"

"Father," I sighed, trying to think of a new excuse. "To tell you the truth, I'm scared of teaching. It's like being a parent of thirty kids with no spouse."

"I was scared too when I first started out," he replied. "When I was a scholastic . . ."[2]

This meddlesome priest, so dear to me, finally wore me down to the point that I told him I would *try* to attain a doctorate in hope of teaching.

That was all he wanted. My "yes" remained in his memory. The daily nudging stopped. Six weeks later, he went to his eternal reward.

Today, Father Canavan's prophetic spirit—unstintingly honest in discerning the signs of the times, yet unwaveringly hopeful of the power of faithful people to transform the culture—lives on in the essays in this volume. I hope this holy Jesuit will inspire you as he has me.

Dawn Eden Goldstein, S.T.D.
Holy Apostles College and Seminary
Memorial of the Queenship of the Blessed Virgin Mary
August 22, 2017

Notes

1. See James V. Schall, S.J., "On Merely Being Intelligent: Canavan's Views and Reviews," in *A Moral Enterprise: Politics, Reason, and the Human Good: Essays in Honor of Francis Canavan* , ed. Kenneth L. Grasso and Robert P. Hunt (Wilmington: ISI Books, 2002), 321-38.
2. Scholastic is the Jesuit term for seminarian.

On Being Personally Opposed

July 1983

Last spring, the name of Sister Agnes Mansour was much in the news. A member of the Sisters of Mercy, she had been appointed by the governor of Michigan to administer an important state agency. In May, confronted with an order from the pope himself either to quit the state post or leave the Sisters of Mercy, she chose to give up membership in her religious community. The *New York Daily News* reported her reason for leaving the community in these words:

> It was inevitable. Agnes Mansour, as she is known now, is head of the Michigan welfare and social services agency, which among other things paid 5.7 million last year . . . for 19,500 abortions for women too poor to afford them. Personally, Sister Agnes said, she opposed abortions. But, she also said, it was not fair to deny abortions to poor women as long as other women could afford them.

Since her sense of fairness triumphed over her personal opposition to abortion, Agnes Mansour departed from the Sisters of Mercy. There is no point in reviving discussion of her case now. But there is one sentence in the above report that is worth reflecting upon because so many other people have expressed the same sentiment as Miss Mansour. That is, she said she was personally opposed to abortions but thought it unfair to deny abortions to poor women when other women could afford them.

Now that is a very puzzling statement. At a first and rapid glance, it may seem to make sense. But when one pauses to think about it, the sentence becomes obscure. What does "personally opposed" mean in this context? Does it and can it mean anything at all?

A few hypothetical questions may serve to illustrate the

1

difficulty in rendering the statement intelligible. What would be implied, for example, by saying that I am personally opposed to infanticide and suicide (or voluntary euthanasia), but if they are made legal, I consider it unfair to deny the poor the right to have these operations performed by professional medical staff in antiseptic and properly equipped facilities? To up the ante a bit, could one coherently say, I am personally opposed to torturing prisoners in jails, but if the law were to allow it, I would be willing to serve as warden of a prison in which it was done? Would it make sense to say that I am personally opposed to genocide, but if it becomes public policy to achieve racial purity through the extermination of certain ethnic groups, I will not impose my conscience on the public and will even administer the extermination program?

One can answer these questions by calling them unfair, because genocide, torture, suicide, and infanticide are not morally the same thing as abortion. Precisely. One is saying that genocide, etc., are moral crimes even when the law allows them, and that no one with a conscience can approve of them or take part in them; abortion, however, is different. But what, then, does it mean to say, I am personally opposed to abortion, but will approve, vote money for, or administer an abortion program?

It could mean that because of family upbringing or the teaching of a church, one regards abortion as a personal no-no, but not as something wrong in itself. The Catholic Church once forbade its members to eat meat on Fridays, not because there was anything inherently wrong in eating meat, but as an obligatory act of penance on the day of the week on which Jesus Christ died. It was an external law which the Church had made and could unmake. A Catholic politician could therefore honestly have said, I personally do not eat meat on Fridays because my church, for religious reasons, tells me not to, but I certainly will not try to impose this prohibition on the rest of the population—after all, eating meat on Friday is not something wrong in itself. Similarly, when a public officeholder tells us that he is personally opposed to abortion but considers it his duty to make it readily available to the poor, he may mean that he sees nothing morally wrong with abortion.

Or perhaps he would agree that abortion is morally wrong because, to his mind, morality is something idiosyncratic and subjective, a kind of hang-up that some people have but others do not. ("Baptists are against the strangest things, but I am a Baptist, so I go along with them.") In this view of the matter, genocide and torture are *really* wrong and we simply may not engage in them, but abortion is only *morally* wrong and we must not impose our morality on those who do not share it.

What about suicide and infanticide? Well, of course, they are morally wrong too, or at least most churches say they are, but in this day and age one hesitates flatly to pronounce them really wrong. They pose a delicate question for the holder of or candidate for public office. Let us not, however, be unfair to him. He devoutly believes that some things are really and truly wrong — racial and sexual discrimination spring to mind — and should be banned by law. But in our pluralistic society, he is deeply concerned to keep merely moral issues out of politics and law.

This is a public stance that we can admire (though not without a little effort) for its courage and sincerity, but it does beg certain questions. For instance, how do we tell the difference between those actions, like genocide, that are really wrong and those, like abortion, that are only morally wrong? It is an important question and one that our society must ultimately answer. The issues that arise and will continue to arise in public policy will force us to decide what, if anything, we collectively judge to be really wrong. But I doubt if we can expect an answer, or even serious thought about an answer, from people whose chief concern is to keep "moral issues" out of politics.

To return, however, to where we began, what does it mean to say that one is personally opposed to abortion but feels that in fairness abortion must be equally available to rich and poor? Only the person who says that knows what it means, and perhaps even he or she doesn't know for lack of having thought about it. The one thing of which we may be sure is this: the person who makes this statement does not see anything really wrong with abortion.

He does not consider abortion an evil thing to inflict on the unborn child who is killed or an evil for the persons who take part in killing him. Otherwise, he would be saying that it is unjust to deprive the poor of the equal opportunity to commit the real and genuine evils in which the well-to-do can afford to indulge. But that would be to lapse into incoherence and, while incoherence is a mode of speech that has certain obvious attractions for persons engaged in the difficult art of politics, we should be slow to attribute it to anyone as his internal state of mind. We must therefore take the man or woman who is "personally opposed to abortion, but . . ." as meaning "opposed, but not really." Rightly understood, "personally opposed" is a code word and a signal to the elect among the electorate. Unless the sender of the signal is himself simply confused, it means, "I'm with you; I don't see anything really wrong in abortion, either."

Okay Clerics for Okay Kids

November 1983

Some years ago a woman came to see me because she had heard that I "knew something about law." Her son, it seemed, was coming up for trial in a federal court on a drug charge and she wanted legal advice about his chances. With some effort I succeeded in persuading her that she needed a real lawyer, not me. She finally accepted that but kept on talking, as distraught mothers do about their wayward children.

One of the stories she told me about her son was that once, when he was a child and had done something wrong, she told him to go into the bedroom, where there was a crucifix hanging on the wall, and "tell God what you did." The kid disappeared into the bedroom and, after a while, came out again.

"Did you tell God what you did?" his mother asked.

"Yeah."

"And what did God say?"

"He said: 'It's okay, kid, forget it!'"

I hope you do not find the child's report of his conversation with God too amusingly outrageous, for it describes perfectly the mission of the modern minister of the gospel. People have problems, you see, and our function as apostles of the gospel of love is to relieve them of those problems by telling them that what they are doing or thinking of doing is okay, and not to worry about it. A remote and unfeeling clerical bureaucracy in Rome has laws against these things, but the God of love wants mercy, not sacrifice, and understanding of people's problems, not demands for obedience.

It is true, too, that in the gospel we find much about mercy and the forgiveness of sins, for God is a God of mercy, and there is more rejoicing in heaven over one sinner who repents than over ninety-nine just who do not need repentance. The gospel, however, seems to be talking about the forgiveness of

5

real sins, of which sinners really repent. "Unless you repent, you will all likewise perish" (Luke 13:3), for example, evidently assumes that there is something of which to repent.

Repentance is also understood to include a purpose of amendment. The most scandalously merciful passage in the four gospels (John 8:3-11) concludes with the words, "Neither do I condemn you. Go and sin no more."

There is a difference, then, between forgiving sins and solving problems, even though we Americans, as a nation of problem solvers, do not like to admit it. To define a situation as a problem is implicitly to assert that it can be solved and must be solved, and this assertion is congenial to the pragmatic American way of thinking. We resent the notion that some situations can only be lived with until God in his good time enables us to change them without sinning against him—or to abandon them in order to cease sinning.

To the problem-solving mind there are no sins, only problems to be solved. I remember once taking part in a panel discussion of abortion. Afterwards a little boy, the son of one of my opponents on the panel, came up to me and kept pressing the question, "But suppose it isn't *feasible* for people to have another child?" There are, sad to say, a lot of people whom it isn't "feasible" to keep alive, and it makes a lot of difference in what you are willing to do about that fact whether you regard it as a problem or as an occasion of possible sin.

It is also now commonly alleged in the press that about half the marriages in the United States break up and that the rate of divorce and remarriage among Catholics is about the same as in the rest of the population. I sometimes wonder how much this last statistic owes to clerics who see their mission as telling troubled souls, "It's okay, kids, forget it."

A Pluralist Church

January 1984

Pluralism today is an "in" word. America, we are constantly told, is a pluralistic society in which no group may impose its beliefs and values on other groups, but every group's demands on society should get some satisfaction. Politics in such a society is an unending appeasement of relatively small but organized groups. No group gets everything it wants, but each group gets enough to keep it willing to play the political game, and so the game goes on forever. As the political commentators say, the system works.

But as Thomas A. Spragens Jr. has pointed out in *The Irony of Liberal Reason,* attributing the stability of the American political system to this "interest-group liberalism" may be an error in judgment. "In fact," he says,

> it may well be that the more fully the American polity approximates the pattern of interest-group liberalism, the more unstable it may become. To the extent that the policies of such a system are increasingly perceived as the product of purely self-interested logrolling, the more that system will be subjected to intellified demands and afflicted by loss of support. The system loses support because it loses its moral legitimacy, and intensified demands are placed on it as each group seeks to compensate for the real or imagined influence of its rivals. For both reasons, the system suffers from an erosion of its authority and, with it, a diminution of its capacity to govern effectively.

There is a lesson in this, I believe, for men of the church as well as of the state. Bishops, religious superiors, and administrators of Catholic institutions dissipate their authority and lessen their ability to govern by trying to keep everybody happy. The temptation to listen patiently and to make concessions to organized and vociferous groups of nuns, priests, academics, homosexuals, or self-appointed "spokesmen for the laity" is understandable. One does not want to break the bruised reed or quench the smoking flax. Above all, one does not want to drive people out of the church. But it must also be understood that the concessions made to them always exact a price in the loss of moral legitimacy.

To illustrate what I mean, the press quoted the feminist theologian, Rosemary Radford Ruether, as saying that "the more we become feminists, the more difficult it is for us to go to church." But of course. Naturally, the more we become feminists, or Marxists, or individualists, or adherents of any other "ism," the more difficult it is for us to go to church.

Conversely, however, the more the Church becomes feminist (or Marxist, or individualist, etc.), the more difficult it is for the rest of us to go to church. More importantly, if the Church's accommodations to the demands of the ideologues are seen as a surrender to pressure-group tactics, it becomes harder for the faithful to believe in the moral authority of ecclesiastical superiors. The more often those who exercise authority in the name of Jesus Christ act like politicians in a pluralistic liberal democracy, the more they engender, not open revolt, but something that in the long run is even worse. That is a chronic, low-grade infection of disillusionment, cynicism, apathy, and loss of interest in the Church and her works.

This is not the kind of phenomenon that makes tomorrow's headlines, and it may take some years to register in the statistics of sociological surveys. But its effect on the Church is nonetheless real; it means that the Church loses the confidence of her people.

This infection among believing Catholics is also fed by the steady exploitation of religious symbols for political purposes. There may be some short-term political gain in having priests and nuns marching and waving placards. But the gain can only be for the short term. Once, perhaps twice, people may be willing to believe that the cause for which the clergy and religious demonstrate must be a serious moral cause, or they would not be leaving their ordinary roles in order to agitate for it. But when people come to see that the Roman collars and the religious habits are taken out of the closet only when activists need them in order to lend the authority of religion to political action, religious authority suffers erosion. People cease to take it seriously.

It is true that the demonstrators, the petition signers, the pressure-group tacticians may sincerely believe that the causes they serve are moral and religious, rather than merely political causes, and that they are in fact only carrying the gospel of Christ into practice. Unfortunately, almost no one else believes it. Many years ago, before Vatican II, the Protestant theologian Reinhold Niebuhr remarked that Roman Catholicism had always been more successful than Protestantism in controlling its crackpots. That is no longer true, and the Catholic people know it.

The people I refer to are ordinary practicing Catholics. They are men and women who believe the Catholic faith, who accept the teaching authority of the Catholic Church, who try with some consistency to live according to her teachings, and who go to Mass on Sundays. Most of them, as is the case in any large group, are not profound thinkers or articulate speakers and writers. They are neither saints, nor heroes, nor prophets. But they are the Church as it exists on earth, and if the Church has any effective authority, it is in their eyes. When the Church loses authority with them, she has lost it, for practical purposes, altogether.

For these people are not pluralists in their religion, whatever they may be in their politics or their daily social relationships. Like other Americans, they live in a pluralistic democratic political system. By and large, they accept it without much question. It might be better for the system if they did ask some searching questions about it. But however that may be, it does not follow that they want to live in a pluralist church that gives the impression of not being sure of what it teaches, or by what moral standards it expects its members to live, or whether it has the right to enforce religious discipline on its clergy.

The Church's authority is from God, but its acceptance depends entirely on the faith and the confidence of the faithful. To sacrifice that to "pluralism" is not only bad theology, it is not even good politics.

Preaching by Silence

February 1984

Someone once asked the late Archbishop Fulton J. Sheen how to become a popular preacher. He replied with an ironic smile, "Talk about the sins they don't commit." Or, to put it another way, don't tell them what they'd rather not hear.

This technique makes for popularity, if that is all the preacher wants. But it is also useful to the sincere and dedicated preacher who has lost his faith in what he is supposed to teach. He does not contradict the doctrine of his church. He just doesn't mention it, and concentrates instead on those themes and causes, usually of a "progressive" nature, which he judges to be true and important.

He thus succeeds in preaching heresy, so to speak, by silence. No one can lay a glove on him, because he has denied no essential doctrine of faith, but the Christianity he preaches lacks several elements of the Apostolic Creed.

If theologians are loath to notice this trait in one another, others who do not claim to be Christians at all have pointed it out. Hans Blumenberg of Kiel University in Germany, for example, in *The Legitimacy of the Modern Age* tells us that as life expectancy has lengthened and old age has become less unpleasant, interest in life after death has waned. "It appears," he says, "that even contemporary Christianity, around the world, scarcely mentions immortality any longer, and thus unintentionally has abandoned a principal element of its historical identity."

It is not clear how Blumenberg knows what contemporary Christianity, around the world, does or does not mention. He probably means that among the enlightened and advanced theologians whom he happens to meet, one does not hear much about immortality and eternal life. Still, there is something in what he says.

A highly intelligent Catholic layman gave a talk not long ago in which he made a telling remark. "Where I go to church," he said, "we never hear anything about hell. In a way, I suppose, that is understandable, but what is really surprising is that we seldom hear anything about heaven either."

As a report from the pews, that is striking. One can scarcely read a page of the New Testament without coming across the words "eternal life." The point and purpose of the life, death, and resurrection of Jesus Christ was to open for us the gates of heaven and to save us from the gates of hell, to make it possible for us to win eternal life and escape eternal exile from that life. But, at least in some parishes, it seems, we don't talk about that anymore. One wonders why.

To explore the reasons for this development, however, would take us off on a tangent. What is immediately of interest is the way in which religion can change, not merely in its accidental and external forms, but in its very substance, simply by ceasing to teach what Blumenberg calls "a principal element of its historical identity." The teachers and the preachers may go on calling it Christianity, but sophisticated outsiders will notice that it is now something else.

So, too, eventually, will the people in the pews — those, that is, who are still in the pews. The others, for whose sake the preachers supposedly made the change, lest crude Christian doctrines — sin, death, judgment, heaven and hell, that sort of thing, you know — drive them away, will no longer be out there facing the pulpit. It takes a little effort to go to church, and when the church is telling you nothing that you could not hear with less effort from a TV commentator, you don't make the effort. The faithful who still come to church do it in the hope of hearing something different from what the enlightened secular world tells them. When they have been disappointed often enough, they will stop coming, too, and will go elsewhere.

The preachers, however, and those who taught them, do not really care what the people in the pews believe, for they see their task as leading the people to a more enlightened religion. As sincere men, they take seriously St. Paul's injunction to preach the word in season and out of season. The word as they understand it, however, is shorn of all premodern, historically conditioned, and mythological elements. One will find in this gospel no virgin birth, or physical resurrection from the dead, or real presence in the Eucharist. Whether we can believe in the incarnation of God the Son or whether there is a Son distinguished from the Father and the Holy Spirit is left vague.

None of these things will be explicitly denied, unless perhaps by a pulpit orator who is both young and foolish and will therefore get himself into trouble. Older and more experienced preachers just won't mention the embarrassing Christian doctrines. If enough preachers refuse to talk about them, they will die of inanition and will fade away. Then we shall have a truly contemporary Christianity. There may be few people left to believe in it, but it will be contemporary.

Heresy-hunting, as we all know, is passé and went out with the Inquisition and the Holy Office. Besides, it is rather pointless in an age that is too sophisticated ever to explicate and teach an heretical doctrine. Today's Catholic, therefore, will not look for heresies that would require a pre-modern clarity of mind to formulate. He will do better in understanding what is going on if he begins to pay close attention, not only to what people say, but to what they don't say.

The Real World

March 1984

Our mother Eve ate the apple and got us all in trouble. We must not judge her harshly, for she had no mother of her own to warn her against talking to snakes. But the consequence of her folly and Adam's fall from grace has been the sad history of our race.

We therefore have good reason to believe, founded in both faith and experience, that things will never work out in this vale of tears quite as we should like them to do. Certain aspirations of the twentieth century, in particular, noble though they may be, are unlikely to be realized. Trying to make them come true, in fact, may make our situation worse instead of better.

We may wish for a world free of crime, war, poverty, ignorance, disease, and death. To reduce these evils is a goal worth working for, but to expect their elimination is to hope for a return to the Garden of Eden. It should not escape our notice that the most massive tyrannies of our century have been established by men who intended to create an earthly paradise.

Even without a crystal ball, one may venture certain predictions. We are not going to have a world peopled by altruists who are concerned as much or more with the welfare of others as with their own. A social, economic, and political order built upon the free and uncoerced cooperation of all citizens will not come into being, and no amount of change of social structures will bring it into being. Private property, however regulated for the common good, will continue to be necessary. So will police forces, courts, and jails.

It may even be that the death penalty, now widely regarded with horror, will again be generally accepted as an appropriate penalty for crime. If this happens, it will not be because bloodthirsty and benighted reactionaries have insisted on it, but because, as social controls break down, criminals will increase the number and atrocity of their violent crimes. Someone once remarked that every generation is faced with a new invasion of barbarians — its own children. In a weak and permissive society, some of the children grow up to be very barbaric indeed.

In its international relations, the world will not become pacifist, and wishing will not make it so, even though we seem to have an unusually high number of wishful thinkers today. The Founding Fathers of our republic knew better. As Alexander Hamilton said in *The Federalist*, No. 6, "The causes of hostility among nations are innumerable. There are some which have a general and almost constant operation upon the collective bodies of society.... Has it not invariably been found that momentary passions, and immediate interests, have a more active and imperious control over human conduct than general or remote considerations of policy, utility, or justice?"

We have weapons today that can destroy whole countries. The weaponry of the eighteenth century had no such awesome power, but there is no evidence that advances in military technology have changed our fallen human nature from what it was when Hamilton wrote in 1787. The instruments of mass destruction make keeping the peace more imperative than ever before. They do not change the fact that the peace must be kept by and among the poor banished children of Eve and that force is ultimately controlled by force.

The unisex society will not arrive either. As the economy changes, the places taken in it by men and women will change, too. But men and women will continue to misunderstand each other because men will still be men and women will still be women, and they will vibrate as before on different emotional wavelengths. It boggles the mind to think of it, but Archie Bunker may have been smarter than Norman Lear.

Men and women, nonetheless, will still find each other as fascinating as they always have. We may agree with the feminists that men are a bad lot entirely and women would be well advised to stay away from them. No experience teaches us, however, that women will take that advice.

We might do better to go back to St. Paul's advice and notice what the feminists always overlook, that his heaviest emphasis was not on "wives, obey your husbands," but on "husbands, love your wives." It is a fairly safe guess that most women prefer having fully grown up, responsible, and loving husbands to enjoying an equality that really means mutual independence. Human nature being what it is, it is an even safer guess that many women will not get such husbands.

They certainly will not get them or deserve them in a society that makes the emancipation of the individual its highest priority. That is another ideal that will not be realized: the individualist utopia in which everyone does his own thing and finds happiness in his own way, while tolerantly respecting everyone else's right to do the same. A society populated by porcupines, each bristling with rights, will not be a happy or a stable one, John Stuart Mill and Hugh Hefner to the contrary notwithstanding.

It would be easy to list other twentieth-century aspirations that will not be achieved, but the point is already clear. There is a real world, and we are really in it, and it really does limit what we can hope to accomplish. One may reject this proposition as being too "conservative," on the ground that it assumes that the world is hopeless, and nothing can be done about it, and therefore there is no use trying to change it. But a sane conservatism knows that, as Edmund Burke put it, "we must all obey the great law of change. It is the most powerful law of nature, and the means perhaps of its conservation." Nor can a Christian, however conservative he be, regard as hopeless the human nature that Christ has redeemed. But he knows that, while grace heals the wounds of nature, it does not transmute nature into the substance of ideological dreams.

The New Sacraments

May 1984

The sacraments of the new law are three: contraception, abortion, and divorce. Progressive theologians are still debating whether premarital sex, homosexual relations, and euthanasia deserve sacramental status. What the remaining sacrament might be that is needed to fill out the traditional number of seven, is a question it is best not to let the mind dwell on, at least for the present.

To put the matter in that way, however, while it may be clever, is not really fair. It assumes that the secular sacraments of our age rest upon a carefully-thought-out theory developed by serious thinkers. On the contrary, what educated public opinion today regards as sacred and absolute depends for the most part on no theory at all but on a set of attitudes.

One could analyze these attitudes, and point out the assumptions behind them, and explain how there is a theory of man and society implicit in them. But it would be a mistake to believe that the multitude of people who hold these attitudes — and that includes most of the spokesmen who publicly propagate them — have thought deeply about them or have any reasoned justification for them that deserves the name of theory.

It is true that a tidal wave of print about contraception, abortion, etc., has rolled off the presses. We could fill a library with books and articles that have appeared on the subject of abortion alone. Some of these publications, on both sides, are the products of hard intellectual work. But they are not the major reason for the remarkable shift in moral standards that has taken place in this and other countries in the past generation.

In the United States, insofar as the change in standards is the result of the dissemination of ideas, Hugh Hefner's *Playboy* and Phil Donahue's television show probably have had more to do with bringing it about than anything published by a university press. Ann Landers and Dear Abby reach more minds than the philosophers and theologians do. At that, even committees of the Catholic Theological Society of America have at times shaped opinion less by the force of their arguments than by their response to people's yearning to be told that what they are going to do anyhow is morally right.

Teaching is, after all, a bilateral process. No opinion maker simply makes opinions inside other people's heads. He must have an audience that is receptive to his teaching or, at least, can be enticed, cajoled, or manipulated into being receptive. There must be something in the student to which the teacher can appeal in order to be able to teach at all.

It could be the love of truth and the desire to know. In teaching at its best, it is that to which the teacher does appeal. But it can also be the natural attitudes of what the French call *l'homme moyen sensuel*, "the average sensual man."

He is no saint, obviously, but neither is he a devil who does evil for the sheer joy of doing evil. He is only human, all too human. He is the embodiment of that natural love of pleasure and dread of pain with which we are all born.

Small children live on little else. Very few human beings ever rise fully above these natural reactions and live their lives completely on their grasp of what is truly good and truly evil; when these few die, we canonize them. Most of us spend our lives in a wavering battle between our passions and our consciences. In the average sensual man, the smart money lays its bets on the passions.

Half a century ago R. R. Palmer caused something of a stir with his *Catholics and Unbelievers in Eighteenth Century France*. The conventional wisdom was — and to a large extent still is — that the eighteenth-century revolt against Christianity, generally called the Enlightenment, was a triumph of reason over faith, intelligence over superstition, light over darkness. Palmer showed that the struggle was by no means so one-sided, and that the Christian spokesmen had as much intelligence and were as good at argument as their unbelieving opponents.

Yet the unbelievers won and shaped the mind of the average modern man. Although they called themselves philosophers, Palmer suggests a somewhat less than philosophical reason for their victory. "Religious writers," he says, "were quite correct in calling the infidels apologists for the passions. To vindicate the emotional life against Christian doctrines of repression and abstinence, to give men the right to enjoy their natural feelings, to represent their appetites as bodily needs and legitimate parts of their personalities, all this was one of the chief aims of the philosophic campaign."

It was also one of the chief reasons for the campaign's success. The appeal of this "new morality" (which in fact is as old as humanity) is obvious. But its consequences were less clear in the eighteenth century than they are today. Voltaire, that epitome of Enlightenment reason, once wrote: "Pleasure is the object, the duty, and the goal of all reasonable beings," but he may not have foreseen where that would lead us. It is only now that we see that it involves sacramentalizing the means of removing every obstacle to that comfortably happy life which is Everyman's desire, and therefore his right, and indeed his duty.

So deeply ingrained is this conviction about the purpose of human life and about the rights and duties that flow from it, that among both the masses and the intellectuals it has ceased to be a consciously held theory. It has settled into being an unreflecting attitude of mind that is never questioned and is furiously defended against all criticism. This mindset explains why the newspaper editorial writer, the television pundit, and even, at times, the theologian reject any morality that goes against the passions of the average sensual man.

They speak nonetheless not only to us, but for us. They appeal to the weaker side of our nature, but they can do so only because it is already there. We, like them, suffer the effects of what a less enlightened but wiser age called original sin. That is why our age has a growing list of new sacraments.

Nearer to the Heart's Desire

June 1984

When I was in high school, I discovered Edward Fitzgerald's *Rubaiyat of Omar Khayyám*. Like many another high school student, I fell in love with it and at one time had most of it memorized. I still remember one quatrain that occurs toward the end of that long poem:

> Ah Love! could you and I with Him conspire
> To grasp this sorry Scheme of Things entire,
> Would not we shatter it to bits — and then
> Re-mould it nearer to the Heart's Desire!

Now, that is heady stuff of the sort that appeals to adolescent sentimentality, and does no great harm if it stops there. It becomes highly dangerous, however, when adults take it seriously. The utopian revolutionary ideologies of our time have shown us how much damage this sentimentality can do, but they are only the political symptoms of a deeper spiritual disease.

Particularly in recent centuries, God has had a bad press for not making a better job of the world that he created. Much of modern atheism is less the result of rigorous intellectual argument than of emotional refusal to believe in the Creator of a world like this one. People cannot forgive him for not creating the best of all possible worlds, when he could have done so.

If we reflect upon the matter, however, it becomes clear that, if there is no God, this *is* the best of all possible worlds, because it is the only possible world. In the absence of a Creator who existed before the world and had it in his power to create a different one, this world, or universe, or multiverse — put it on whatever scale you will — is the only reality there is. Having no cause outside of and above itself, the only reality that exists is the ground of whatever possibility there can be. Apart from it, no world is or ever was possible.

There is, in that case, no one to praise or blame, for no one is responsible for the universe. It just *is,* and it is what it is. As the realization of what that means sinks into men's minds, it engenders a profound sadness in them. The young and foolish may rejoice in the thought that horrified Dostoevsky, that if there is no God, everything is permitted. Fools see only that, if there is no divine judge, there is no one to stop the fun, but older heads understand that fun is not enough.

Fun is for kids and eventually palls on adults. Pagan *joie de vivre* would be easier to believe in if we could only see a little more of it. Most pagans today seem to be engaged in what the late Leo Strauss called the joyless quest for joy. The more intelligent pagans — the educated, urbane skeptics — follow Bertrand Russell's advice to build their lives on the foundation of a firm and unyielding despair. Being intelligent, they see that despair is the necessary response to a godless universe.

There surely is no use in getting angry at it. A mindless universe that evolves blindly in time and space neither knows or cares what we think of it. Indeed, there is little use even in thinking about it. If the universe is ultimately without purpose or meaning, it is simply unintelligible. It is not mysterious, like God, whose intelligibility transcends our minds, but who is fully intelligible in and to himself. The godless universe, on the contrary, is devoid of intelligibility.

Professor Carl Becker, who was the very model of the urbane academic skeptic, explained that modern science has taught us to regard man "as little more than a chance deposit on the surface of the world, carelessly thrown up between two ice ages by the same forces that rust iron and ripen corn, a sentient organism endowed by some happy or unhappy accident with intelligence indeed, but with an intelligence that is conditioned by the very forces that it seeks to understand and control." Becker's view not only leaves human intelligence with no explanation — how did the mindless forces that rust iron and ripen corn produce mind? — but with no object.

A meaningless universe, after all, is just that: without meaning and so, in the final analysis, without intelligibility. When we have fully peeled the onion of the godless universe, we find at its center nothing at all. We cannot understand such a universe, not because it is too big for us to comprehend, but because in and of itself it makes no sense. A universe that is not the product of Intelligence offers human intelligence no object commensurate with itself. In studying such a universe, our minds finally come up against, not the plenitude of mystery, but a total lack of meaning.

To grasp that is to despair. Why despair is so attractive to so many minds today is an intriguing question that is worth pondering. But one answer we should refuse to be taken in by is that thinking men cannot believe in God. Men do not stop believing in God because they have discovered that the world is meaningless. Rather, they conclude that the world is meaningless because they have stopped believing in God. Their reasons for disbelief, no doubt, are many and various. But one of the more powerful ones is a sentimentality that will not accept the world that is as God's world.

We may dream of shattering the world to bits in order to remold it nearer to the heart's desire. But we really cannot do that and, when we try to do it, the results are disastrous. All rational thinking must begin with this world, the one that is.

We have a choice only between this world without God, in which case we despair, or this world with God, in which case life has a purpose, and therefore a meaning and a ground for hope. For the worst thing that can happen to us is not to endure this world's natural catastrophes or even man's inhumanity to man. The ultimate horror is to stare, eyes wide open, into the void.

The Loyal Opposition

September 1984

Dissenting Catholics today like to call themselves the Loyal Opposition. The term implies that they do not cease to be good Catholics merely because they do not accept — or even actively oppose — certain teachings of the pope and the bishops.

In fact, they would say, the idea that one needs to accept those teachings in order to be a member of the Church in good standing springs from an outmoded ecclesiology. The new and improved ecclesiology of the dissenters presents itself as an effort to "update the structure" of the Church's teaching authority. In practice, however, it is hard to distinguish this "updating" from a denial that there is in the Catholic Church a binding teaching authority. In some instances, it in effect denies that the hierarchy of bishops headed by the pope constitutes a teaching body or, to use the Latin term, a magisterium endowed with ultimate authority in matters of faith and morals.

If there is a magisterium at all, it would seem it belongs as much to the theologians as to the hierarchy. It is the theologians who do the Church's real thinking and, in the long run, it is the body of educated Catholics — college-trained and upwardly mobile — who will tell the teachers what they are willing to have taught to them.

This new doctrine is an ecclesiology, that is, a theory of the Church, but it comes disguised as a political theory when its proponents call themselves the Loyal Opposition. The political theory in turn is the result of certain historical developments in the British constitution.

In British parliamentary history it gradually became accepted that the king must govern through ministers, that the ministers must be chosen from a party having the confidence of a majority in the House of Commons, and that members of

Parliament could oppose the policies of the king's ministers without being disloyal to the Crown. The term "His Majesty's Opposition" was first used in the Commons in 1826. It was used in jest, and it got a laugh. But the notion that an organized opposition to the government in power was a normal and necessary part of the political system finally became an accepted principle of the British constitution.

As a political principle, the idea of a loyal opposition is a valuable one, but it comports ill with a church that professes to teach a divine revelation. "Political problems," as Edmund Burke put it, "do not primarily concern truth or falsehood. They relate to good or evil." The issues with which governments deal concern the goodness or soundness of policies. These are matters over which even intelligent men of good will can and do disagree. But a church that teaches what God has revealed, teaches it precisely as true — or it has nothing at all to teach.

The Catholic Church, of course, has policies as well as dogmas, as any institution operating in this world must have, and the policies are open to criticism. But the Church's policies must be judged in strict subordination to the truth that the Church teaches. About that truth and about the magisterium's authority to determine what it is, there can be no opposition entitled to call itself loyal.

Nonetheless, let us for the moment take the Loyal Opposition on its own essentially political terms. In a parliamentary system, when the government in power demands a vote of confidence, or when the opposition makes a motion of no confidence, the political survival of the government is at stake. If it loses in the vote of confidence, it must resign and allow the opposition to take power. A member of Parliament, therefore, must cast a vote that expresses either his confidence in the present government or his confidence in an alternative government that is waiting to take power.

If we insist on talking about the government of the Catholic Church in those terms, to whom do we give our confidence? Do we give it to the pope and the bishops in communion with him? Or do we give it to the assortment of theologians, clerics, academics, journalists, and Church watchers who call themselves the Loyal Opposition?

It will not be enough to say that we think there is some validity in their criticisms or that we agree with some of their ideas. We are asked to express our confidence in their ability to guide and govern the Church with whatever authority they can claim in accordance with their beliefs, whatever they may be. How much confidence one is willing to put in them is a question which everyone will answer for himself. But let us all at least be clear in our own minds what question we are answering. It is who shall have the power to determine what the Church may teach as moral and religious truth.

For the real question that is raised by the Loyal Opposition is not a political one. It is the eminently theological question of who has the last word on faith and morals. It is true that popes and bishops seldom do the "original" thinking in the Church; that is not their function. What properly belongs to them is to speak the final and decisive word on what can be taught, and believed, and acted on as Catholic doctrine.

There is room in the Church for controversy and debate. But discussion in the Church always has for its aim the Church's determination of the truth. That is not arrived at through a political process, as the term "The Loyal Opposition" would lead us to believe.

It is one thing to present new interpretations of doctrine and criticism of old interpretations for consideration and possible acceptance. It is quite another to contest the hierarchy's right to decide whether they are acceptable. Those who do the latter are what we used to call Protestants. If that is what they are, we should not confuse the issue by calling them the Loyal Opposition.

Standing at Armageddon

October 1984

"**W**e stand at Armageddon and we battle for the Lord," thundered Theodore Roosevelt at the Bull Moose Party convention in 1912. That was one of the more memorable lines that have been delivered in American political rhetoric. One might also describe it as archetypal. In our political idiom we stand forever at Armageddon and battle for the Lord. The republic is always in danger, the enemy is always at the gates, if not already within them, and the citadel must always be defended to the last man and (as we must now add) woman. The native style of political speech is hyperbole.

All of this is good clean fun and adds a little excitement to our otherwise dull lives. It does no great harm, either, if we do not take it too seriously, and for the most part we do not. Still, our way of talking about political issues produces a fair amount of regrettable mental confusion.

The confusion lies in this, that at one and the same time we overmoralize political issues and politicize moral issues to the point where we deny that they are moral issues at all. Which issues we moralize and which we politicize depends more on our political objectives than on any reasoned moral philosophy.

There is a sense in which every political issue is, at some outer limit, a moral one. An old saw in the literature of public administration has it that there is no Democratic and no Republican way to pave a street. *A fortiori,* there is no Christian, Jewish, Muslim, or agnostic way to do it. We can say, nonetheless, that the moral way to pave a street is the one that gives the public the best road that can be obtained at the price it is willing to pay, and not the way that best lines the pockets of public officials or of their supporters in the contracting business.

There is therefore a moral principle involved even in decisions about paving streets. The principle, however, tells us nothing about the kind of materials to be used, the structure of roadbeds, or the method of building road drains. Those are engineering questions, and highway engineers can and do differ about them.

Politicians and taxpayers, too, may differ on whether we should spend more to get the best roads that can be built or spend less in order to have more money for other community needs. Those who insist that this is a purely moral issue understand neither morality nor politics, let alone engineering. On the other hand, the engineer who thinks that morality and politics have nothing to do with roadbuilding, since it is simply a question of efficiency, has failed to reflect on the further question: efficient for what? We cannot discuss the efficiency of means without discussing the ends for which they are efficient.

Moral principles, therefore, are necessary for the conduct of politics and government, but they are not enough. They are necessary because, if we pretend to be moral agents, we never can disregard our consciences on the ground that we are engaged in political rather than merely private action. As Edmund Burke once said, "There are some things a good man would not do even to save the commonwealth." We may add that there are some things a good man would not do even to save the world from population growth. But, except at such outer limits, moral principles alone will not furnish us with complete and adequate answers to questions of public policy. Political judgment also is needed.

Now, political judgment is always affected by a measure of uncertainty. We may, for example, take it as a moral given that the tax policies of a nation must be framed for the good of the whole country, not for that of a favored few alone. That does not tell us whether taxes should be cut, or raised, or remain as they are. Nor does it tell us which taxes should be cut or raised. The answers to these questions, even assuming an unrealistically high degree of dispassionate devotion to the common good, depend on a long series of calculations about the future effects of any move we make in tax policy. The truth is that no one really knows what the effects will be. Some judgments about them are shrewder and sounder than others, but no one simply *knows.*

If this is true in such a dollars-and-cents calculation as taxation, it is all the more true in the general range of political issues, both domestic and foreign. These issues require decisions about large and complex matters. They depend for intelligent resolution on long and broad experience, the mastery of vast numbers of present facts, and an ability to discern future consequences. It is therefore unwise to dogmatize about them. Yet it is precisely here that the urge to dogmatize is strongest, because political passion persuades us that we stand at Armageddon and battle for the Lord.

Not many years ago there were people in this country who would tell you that there are no absolute moral principles and that we should not presume to impose our principles on others, but of course the Vietnam War was absolutely immoral. Today we have people who profess not to know whether abortion takes human lives or homosexuality is a perversion. Yet they regard their political agenda as a direct deduction from the Constitution of the United States, or from the ineluctable dictates of moral conscience, or even from the gospel of Jesus Christ.

This is a fault, it must be admitted, that is characteristic of activist lawyers and clerics rather than of professional politicians. For instance, a priest told the National Council for Evangelization in 1984, "Catholics of the future will be more credible if their pro-life stance is complemented by a rejection of sexism, racism, ageism and other prejudices." He thus invited us to move from a stance where we can be sure of our ground into the swamp of a broad, sweeping, and vague egalitarianism as if it were all on the same moral plane. We might in fact be more credible if we confined ourselves to insisting that the politicians stay within certain basic moral limits, and left the rest to sound political judgments.

Tadpoles and Babies

November 1984

Is a tadpole a frog? One answer to this question is another question: Who cares? What difference does it make to us? It is not a bad answer, either, since we care no more for frogs than we do for tadpoles. Whether a tadpole is a frog may be an interesting question to some few people, but to most of us it is certainly not an important one.

It would be important, of course, to a primitive tribe that regarded the frog as a sacred animal. Frogs, to such a tribe, would be untouchable. Yet the tribe might come to feel that too many frogs were too much of a good thing. Murmurs might arise about a Frog Explosion. Something, clearly, would have to be done.

At this point the wise men of the tribe would confront the question whether a tadpole is a frog. Some of them would argue that a tadpole is not a frog because it does not look like a frog. But, they would say, looks are all we have to go by: only that is a frog which looks like a frog. A tadpole, therefore, is not a sacred animal and may be killed at pleasure.

Others among them would point out that tadpoles, if they survive, always come to look like frogs and therefore must already have the nature of frogs. Looks are not all we have to go by. We can recognize the nature of the frog as having been present from the beginning in the tadpole. To kill a tadpole, therefore, is to kill a frog.

The anti-tadpole school would probably carry the day, but not because of their superior philosophical intelligence. They would win the argument on the highly pragmatic ground that the way to get rid of unwanted frogs without feeling guilty about it is to kill tadpoles before they look like frogs.

Besides, primitive peoples tend to go by appearances and to use separate words for ice, hail, snow, rain, mist, fog, and steam because they do not recognize these apparently distinct things as different states of the same substance, water. They often take the same attitude toward embryos, infants, children, women, and men. The idea of a common and universal human nature is too abstract and sophisticated for the primitive mind.

Modern Man (the eponymous hero of our age) is nothing if not sophisticated and has risen above all that. He does not regard frogs as sacred animals. In fact, he does not believe that any animal is sacred, not even himself. From his positivistic and skeptical point of view, to argue about whether a tadpole is a frog or a fetus is a human being is beside the point.

As he sees it, we *feel* differently about the proper way to treat men, dogs, trees, and stones. But the differences are only in our feelings, not in any traits that our minds can recognize in the things themselves. To a truly modern mind, even human beings have only such worth and such rights as other human beings collectively choose to assign them. There is no natural or transcendent standard of judgment to which we can appeal to determine the worth of humanity. We may therefore make such distinctions as we choose to make among the born and the unborn, the deformed and the normal, the mentally healthy and the insane.

Such enlightened clarity of thought, however, is too strong a draught for most of the population to swallow, and so recourse to sophistry is necessary. We must talk much about rape and incest as justifications for abortion even though we know that they are the cause of very few pregnancies. We must go on endlessly about the impossibility of knowing when a fetus becomes a person, because abortion is not murder unless it kills a person. We can then quietly assume, without discussion, that a fetus, being a nonperson, may be aborted for any reason or for no reason other than the mother's will to be rid of it.

One could answer this assumption directly: we do not know that a fetus is *not* a person; therefore, to abort it is to be willing to kill it if it is a person. But even waiving that argument, we may still question the assumption that there is nothing wrong with abortion unless it is murder.

For the very least we can say is that the product of human conception is a living human being. It is a being because one does not abort nothing: something has to be in the womb to have an abortion. It is a living being because it is going through a rapid process of growth and development. This growth is not the random multiplication of cells that characterizes a tumor but a steady, progressive development into the shape and organic structure of humanity. The living thing in a woman's womb is endowed from the beginning with a uniquely human genetic program that directs its future development and constitutes it as a member of the human species. Even before it looks human it has all the biological determinants of humanity.

Whether or not it has achieved what we choose to call "personhood," there is no stage of its development at which it is an acorn striving to become an oak tree or a tadpole on the way to becoming a frog. Its development, from conception on, is simply the process by which a human being grows — as all of us did — from the initial stage of its life into the stage at which it is capable of living outside the womb.

What do we think this living human being in the womb is? That is the key question. If we start with the determination to find reasons that will justify killing it, we shall say that it is not human, or that it is not alive, or even that it is not a being — a mere "nothing" as one enthusiastic abortionist called it. Or, recognizing the weakness of all those assertions, we shall fall back on saying that it is not a person, or that no one can know if it is a person, and so we are justified in killing it when in our judgment killing is necessary, or useful, or desirable. But none of these pronouncements, however stridently made, will get us past the fact that, at bare minimum, the human embryo has a human nature and is a living human being. We wade into deep and dangerous waters when we justify killing that.

The Sermon on the Mount

December 1984

The late John Courtney Murray, S.J., once told me that at a convention he attended, a Protestant theologian said to him in a rather worried tone of voice, "I don't see how we can base a foreign policy on the Sermon on the Mount." Replied Fr. Murray, "I never thought we could." He was right, too. One need only read the following passage from the Sermon on the Mount (Matt. 5:38-42) to see that, whatever it is, it is not a prescription for a foreign policy.

> You have heard that it was said, "An eye for an eye and a tooth for a tooth." But I say to you, Do not resist one who is evil. But if anyone strikes you on the right cheek, turn to him the other also; and if anyone who would sue you and take your coat, let him have your cloak as well; and if anyone forces you to go one mile, go with him two miles. Give to him who begs from you, and do not refuse him who would borrow from you.

Even in matters closer to home than foreign policy, these words of Our Lord do not prescribe a set of rules to be followed to the letter. Anyone who has lived or worked in a parish rectory is acquainted with the stream of panhandlers, grifters, and confidence men who come to the door looking for handouts, and knows that in order to keep funds to help the really needy, it is often necessary not to give to those who beg and to refuse those who want to borrow. We all know that civilization would collapse if we repealed the criminal law and never resisted evil men. Civilization would be in equal peril if we got rid of the civil law and saved people the trouble of suing us by immediately giving them whatever they wanted and more besides. But if we know that much, we may presume that Christ knew it, too.

We shall make more sense of the Sermon on the Mount if we do not think of it as an early edition of the Code of Canon Law or a proposal that we renounce the rule of law altogether in order to live on love alone. It is, after all, what it is usually called, a sermon. As such, it is an exhortation, not a set of rules. What it exhorts us to do is give up certain very natural human attitudes and replace them with opposite and supernatural ones.

If we look at small children — those cute and lovable little kids — we see in them a number of unlovable attitudes which no one has to teach them. They know instinctively the difference between mine and thine, and while this does not stop them from grabbing what is thine, it makes them loudly possessive of what they regard as "mine." The urge to retaliate and to return injury for injury is also inborn and strong in them. If someone calls them a name, they have to call him a nastier one. If someone hits them, they have to hit him back. These childish propensities, if left unchecked by moral and religious training, grow and wax stronger in later life, producing antisocial monsters. Even with the best of training, few of us outgrow them entirely.

It is these selfish, possessive, and revengeful traits of our fallen human nature that the Sermon on the Mount addresses. It speaks deliberately in exaggerated and hyperbolic language because it aims at bringing about a change of mind and heart and not at laying down a fixed code of action. Our Lord does not command us to let people walk over us whenever they want. But we'll be easier to live with and we'll contribute more to civilization if our first impulse is to turn the other cheek rather than to let someone have it between the eyes. We may even say that we'll have a civilization worth defending only if it has people in it who are willing to take the Sermon on the Mount to heart.

Christians, God knows, have often made a travesty of Christian civilization. Our Christian faith carries on an unequal and frequently losing battle with our natural passions. Yet it is well for us that the battle is fought at all.

I recall something I heard from a friend of mine in the Foreign Service when I visited him in the Middle Eastern country in which he was then stationed. It was a remark the Italian ambassador to that country had made to him: "I never realized how much a Christian I am until I came here — these people don't understand mercy."

The great tyrants of our century, who slaughtered human beings by the tens of millions, have been emancipated ex-Christians like Stalin and Hitler, who dismissed the Sermon on the Mount as sentimentalism, or pagans turned atheists, like Mao Tse-tung and Pol Pot, who possibly never heard of it. Their policies, foreign and domestic, would doubtless have been less "realistic" if they had been tempered by any degree of Christian sentiment. But how much of their kind of realism can the world stand?

Before we reject the Sermon on the Mount as hopelessly unrealistic, we ought to ask ourselves whether we should want to live in a place where everyone was of that opinion. I am thinking of a place where people constantly try to beat each other out, where everyone grabs, where no one lets anyone get ahead of him, where no slight or injury is left without retaliation; where the highest wisdom is, don't get mad, get even; where the highest form of wit is the one-liner that leaves its victim helpless and humiliated; where, at least in certain circles and in certain parts of town, the life of a man is, in the familiar phrase, solitary, poor, nasty, brutish, and short.

If you would really like to live in such a place, let me know and I'll send you a bumper sticker that reads, "I Love New York." Or, if that seems too harsh a judgment on my native city and its genial population, let me send you a neatly hand-lettered sign that says simply, "Go to Hell." Hell, you know, is where no one takes the Sermon on the Mount seriously.

The New Skepticism

January 1985

I have two lists. One is of things not to be worried about, the other of things that don't have to be believed in. Put them together and you have a philosophy which I like to call the New Skepticism. It is, I can confidently assure you, the wave of the future.

I don't worry, for instance, about the Moral Majority. I know nothing about it, except what I learn from its critics, and have never once heard the Rev. Jerry Falwell speak on television. But I figure that a movement which alarms the presidents of both Yale and Georgetown universities is already sufficiently worried about, without further help from me.

The press worried, to put it mildly, because the reporters and the TV cameras could not accompany the troops as they invaded Grenada. More generally, the press worries about anything that could have a "chilling effect" on its own activities. But the republic will probably survive even if reporters are not always able to do what will help them get ahead in their profession.

Not much worry is necessary over the need of homosexuals for social acceptance, imposed if necessary by force of law. Capital punishment is another thing that does not seem to require profound emotional concern. There may be convincing rational arguments against it (calling it "barbaric" isn't one) and, if there are, we should be willing to listen to them. But it is hard to get upset at the thought that a rapist, who stabs a young woman to death because she resists him, might lose his own life by execution.

Nor need we lose sleep over "the suppression of dissent" in the Catholic Church. It can be overdone, no doubt, and sometimes has been. But even the dissenters need a Church to dissent from and, if some of them got their way, they wouldn't have one.

One could go on, and you surely will have your own items to add to this list. But let us turn to the things we don't have to believe in.

We may look skeptically, for example, at the notion that maximizing individual freedom is the highest goal of a civilized society. Libertarians believe that, but we are not obliged to. We may even wonder how civilized society would be if it achieved the libertarian goal.

It is also possible to entertain doubts about the unfailing efficacy of the free marketplace of ideas. We have had one for some two centuries now, and its major result appears to be that we are increasingly unable to agree on anything.

Doubt, of course, is a dangerous road to go down and we should be cautious about setting foot on it. Followed far enough, it could lead us to lose our faith in liberalism, egalitarianism, pluralism, feminism, sexual freedom, and the policies advocated by the American Civil Liberties Union. Still, in an age in which we are constantly told that there are no absolutes and all truth is relative, we may be willing to run that risk.

Take feminism for example. Women are real, live human beings, and they are half the human race. Feminism, however, is an ideology about women, not a comprehensive and accurate description of the feminine reality. Like other ideologies, it is an oversimplified version of the facts, designed to fuel a program of action with a powerful charge of anger. It can and has generated an intense emotional faith. It also generates disbelief in those who are not possessed by the emotion.

Consider this line, written by a feminist professor of psychology: "If social equality for women requires psychosexual freedom, the prerequisites for equality are freedom to control our own bodies; freedom in autoeroticism, lesbianism, multiple relations, monogamy, and celibacy; freedom from the energy-draining anxiety about becoming pregnant; and freedom from the 'imperfections' of available contraceptives." If that is the feminist new dawn, the rest of us may ask why we should pray for it to break.

As adherents of the New Skepticism, we do not have to put much faith in any prophets of new dawns. Our century has seen so many of them, and most of them have either failed or have had to resort to a massive use of force to make the dawn come.

The prophets do not deserve much faith even when we find them in the ranks of the clergy and the religious orders. Some of them are social revolutionaries intent on solving the world's problems. Others, of a more pastoral bent, concentrate on solving people's personal problems. If the Church's teachings stand in the way of a solution, they ignore the teachings, confident that the Church will have to change them anyhow. Still others are advanced theological thinkers — some of them even have advanced degrees in theology — who can prove that whatever you thought was Catholic doctrine, really isn't. It is not, however, obligatory to believe any of them.

On the secular plane, we don't have to believe that courts of law are better agencies for framing public policy than legislatures are. Not that the legislatures themselves are in great shape. As Gregg Easterbrook said recently in *The Atlantic Monthly*, because of post-Watergate reforms, "Congress was transformed from an institution in which power was closely held by a few to an institution in which almost everyone had just enough strength to toss a monkey wrench." But that only justifies a certain skepticism about reforms.

Our age abounds in things not to believe in. There was a time when Christianity was the established orthodoxy and the infidels had all the fun. They could be the freethinkers, the scoffers, and wits who made the world laugh by ridiculing the established beliefs. Many of us still don't realize it, but that time is gone. Today, Christians are the people who don't have to believe in anything except Christianity, and therefore not in the orthodoxies of the day. Now it is our turn to laugh. Or, if that is too painful, at least to indulge in the luxury of doubt.

The Hierarchy of Beings

February 1985

In its December 31, 1984, number, *Time* published a lengthy review of David Lean's new film, *A Passage to India.* The review included this line from the novel by E.M. Forster on which the film is based: "Everything exists, nothing has value." It ended with the reviewer's judgment that David Lean's film is "true to its source and . . . true to our sense of the world as it echoes in the common consciousness of our times." That remark raises a fundamental question about our understanding of the nature of the world in which we live.

Let me illustrate the question with two examples. I remember several years ago reading a review of a book about Adolf Eichmann as an administrator. Eichmann, you recall, ran Hitler's extermination program, which put several million human beings to death. That the program was an organized system, and not an indiscriminate mass slaughter, meant that it needed a capable administrator.

He had to organize the roundup of people, by thousands at a time, in such a way that the rest of the population would not be unduly alarmed. He had to get them to railway stations, provide freight trains (in a nation at war, where transportation was in short supply), and ship these people to the death camps. There they had to be sorted out and processed, again in such a way that they would not foresee clearly what was in store for them. Eventually, they had to be herded into the death chambers and killed.

Having described the extermination program at length, the reviewer paused and commented that, of course, to talk about it as an administrative problem was black comedy. So indeed it was — but why? After all, we run a very similar program year in and year out in our own country. We round up herds of living creatures, ship them to slaughterhouses, and systematically kill them—all so that you and I can have hamburgers for lunch and roast beef for dinner. Evidently we see a difference between killing human beings and killing cattle.

We also see differences among orders of beings that are lower than man. I once saw a TV news broadcast which included pictures of wild animals running in terror from a forest fire as flaming trees crashed around them. The broadcast did not—and surely would not—show a picture of a deer trapped under a tree in flames and screaming in agony as it burned alive. But if you did see such a picture, how would you react?

No doubt with intense sympathy ("suffering with," in the original Greek meaning of the word) for the animal's pain. But would you sympathize with the tree? Hardly. You might regret the loss of valuable timber, but it would be difficult to "suffer with" a tree, because trees do not feel pain. We see a difference, not only between men and cattle, but also between animals and plants.

The fundamental question, then, is where do we get our conviction about these differences? It is considered a sign of intellectual sophistication today to maintain that our judgment in favor of human beings over cattle is nothing more than a subjective preference for our own kind. We are human, so we read our preference into reality and assert that humans are better than cattle. In reality, however, cattle are as "good"—if that term has any objective meaning—as human beings.

The obvious differences among the many species of beings are explained as differences in degree of chemical complexity. Humans are more complex organisms than amoebas, but not essentially superior. Thought, sensation, life itself are only more complicated forms of the same chemical reactions that take place in nonliving beings.

Everything exists, nothing has value. Things just "are," and what they are has no value in itself, but only such value as our species or some other species gives it.

The alternative position is that there are real distinctions in the nature of things. "To be human" is "not to be a cow." But "to be a pig" is also "not to be a cow," yet that does not stop us from slaughtering pigs. Therefore, our judgment about the nature of reality is not only that "to be human" is "not to be a cow," but also that "to be human" means "to be superior to a cow, or a pig, or any other species of animal."

We are thus faced with an issue in that branch of philosophy which is called metaphysics. Do all beings exist basically on the same level? We can give either of two answers to that question, and it makes an enormous difference which one we give.

We can hold that all the beings which make up the universe exist on the same level. They simply are, and there is no ground in reality for saying that some of them are on higher levels of being than others. In reality there are no levels of being.

This line of thought, followed all the way through, leads to the conclusion that Adolf Eichmann was not a nice man, but there is no rational ground for believing that what he did was wrong. Strange as it may seem, I have heard men who identified themselves as Jews say just that.

Alternatively, we can hold that the universe we inhabit is a structured one in which there is a hierarchy of beings. They do not merely exist, but exist on higher and lower levels, and have distinct modes of being and action.

God, men, beasts, plants, and rocks have this in common, that they all "are," but they have their being on different levels. God *is*, necessarily, eternally, and perfectly, but our being is finite and contingent. The being of a deer includes the capacity for feeling pain and pleasure; the being of a tree does not.

Attaching more importance to human beings than to beasts, in this view, is not an expression of our feelings but a recognition of the structure of the real world. We may feel that it is revolting to kill baby seals, but we know that it is not the same thing as killing human babies.

Infanticide

April 1985

Sir Alfred Zimmern, despite his German name, was an Englishman and a professor at Oxford University. In 1911 he published what is still an excellent book, *The Greek Commonwealth,* on the culture and civilization of the pagan Greeks of the ancient world. The following lengthy paragraph is taken from pages 330-331 of the fifth edition, published by Oxford University Press:

> It has not been easy for admirers of the Greeks to admit that Greek theory and practice condoned the deliberate exercise of checks upon the growth of the population. Yet the evidence shows us that such was indeed the case. When a child was born it remained, by a custom universal, so far as we know, at least down to the fourth century, within the discretion of the father whether it should be allowed to live. On the fifth day after birth, at earliest, new-born infants were solemnly presented to the household and admitted to its membership. Up to the time of this ceremony the father had complete power of selection, and, what is more, it appears that this was quite frequently exercised, particularly in the case of female infants; for the provision of a dowry for his daughters weighed heavily on a Greek father's mind, and what was easier than to evade it by pleading inability at the outset? When it was decided that the infants were not to be "nourished" they would be packed in a cradle, or more often in a pot, and exposed in a public place, the poor mother, no doubt, hoping against hope, like Creusa in the *Ion,* that some merciful fellow-citizen might yet take pity on its wailing. It is strange and horrible to think that any day on your walks abroad in a Greek city you might come across a "pot-exposed" infant, as the Athenians called them, in a corner of the market-place or by a wrestling ground, at the entrance of a temple or in a consecrated cave, and that you might see a slave girl timidly peeping round to look if the child might yet be saved, or running back to bear the news to the broken-hearted young mother. For though the custom was barbarous, and promoted, if not enforced, by a barbarous necessity, the Greeks who bowed before it still

remained civilized men and women. "I beg and beseech you," writes a husband in a Greek private letter which has lately returned to us from the underworld, "to take care of the little child, and, as soon as we receive wages, I will send them to you. When — good luck to you — you bear offspring, if it is a male, let it live; if it is a female, expose it."

The world has changed, of course, since those distant pagan days. But how much the world has changed — how much have we changed — in the twentieth century! In 1911 Zimmern thought that an educated audience would be shocked at the idea of putting deliberate checks on the growth of population. Seven decades later, schoolchildren are being taught by almost all the social-studies textbooks used in the public schools that they have no higher duty than checking population growth. Zimmern also assumed that modern readers would find it horrible to think that, if they could take a walk around ancient Athens, Corinth, or Thebes, they might come across infants exposed to die of starvation. Today, with more tender sensibilities, we let them starve to death in closed hospital rooms. But the babies end up just as starved and just as dead.

We don't like to talk about that: nonetheless, we are ceasing to be shocked. The mere fact that infanticide is now a controversial issue is significant. In 1911 there would have been no controversy over the proposition that killing infants through the denial of care is simply wrong and not to be done.

A profound shift in attitudes toward human life has taken place in this century, and is still going on. The legalization of abortion was a very important step in this process but, as the current discussion of the obligation to keep infants alive shows, the process is not yet finished. It fact, it has only begun.

A news report that appeared in the *New York Times* a few years ago throws a cold, clear light on our contemporary mentality: "Faced with a growing number of malpractice claims and the rising expectations of patients, a significant number of the nation's doctors have either abandoned the practice of obstetrics or are seriously considering it." In the most revealing remark in the whole report, the *Times* quoted a doctor in North Carolina who explained why he quit the field of obstetrics: "There's an attitude that says, 'We're going to have fewer

41

babies, so we want a perfect baby.'"

Another doctor commented that unfortunately a baby doesn't always turn out perfect. "Twenty years ago it was considered an act of God. Today there are no more acts of God. They expect you should have been able to do something."

We want a perfect baby, and if we don't get one, it must be someone's fault, therefore we sue the doctor. The *Times* naturally did not mention it, but the same attitude often explains the decision to abort or to allow a deformed infant to die. We must admit that from a purely secular point of view, killing infants makes a kind of sense. If there is no God, then there are no acts of God. If this world is the only one there is, and this life is the only one we'll ever live, why should we let our uniquely precious lives be marred by taking care of less than normally healthy children?

It is a grim kind of sense, however, and one that will appeal only to people who hold a certain view of the world and have certain expectations from it. As the less admirable features of ancient paganism re-emerge in our society, we shall indeed be more free to pursue happiness on our own terms, but it will be rough on children and other weaklings who get in our way.

Liberty, Equality, and Order

May 1985

Liberty, equality, fraternity was the slogan of the French Revolution. Liberty and equality were the Revolution's operative goals, and fraternity was brought in as a cement to hold them together. For liberty and equality are not necessarily in harmony and, in fact, are often at war with each other. Keeping the peace between them therefore became the role of fraternity. Alas, fraternity has not been terribly successful at it, as the history of class struggle since the French Revolution has shown.

In the evolution of democratic theory in the past two centuries, two main currents have emerged from the same wellspring of radical individualism: the liberal stream, emphasizing liberty while acknowledging equality of civil rights, and the egalitarian stream, emphasizing equality while preaching the liberty guaranteed by civil rights.

Liberal democracy understands rights as immunities from governmental interference. Their function is to prevent government from unduly restraining any individual's liberty. The egalitarian conception of rights is much broader than the classical liberal one and includes a wide range of positive benefits to be conferred by government. It tends toward an equality of results rather than merely of opportunities. To put it crudely, it means not only that you are free to apply for the job, but that you get it and you keep it.

Liberal democratic thought has as its economic counterpart the ideology of capitalism and a free-market economic system. The egalitarian stream issues in the ideology of socialism and a government dedicated to bringing about substantial economic equality among all citizens.

Liberalism as it exists in the United States today is an effort to have the best of both ideological worlds. It assigns to government the duty of fostering, not complete economic equality, but general prosperity and a more equal share in it for all citizens. At the same time, through an ever-expanding array of civil rights, it seeks to emancipate the individual from religious, moral, and social restraints that are not of his own choosing. The contemporary liberal ideal would be a country in which everyone was employed at high wages in work which he/she found fulfilling, without distinction of race, color, creed, gender, ethnic origin, educational background, or sexual preference, and could live by any "lifestyle" that he/she chose.

Contemporary American conservatism is largely a reaction to this brand of liberalism, and therefore is a mixed bag of views. Among its adherents we find "conservatives" who are really nineteenth-century liberals eager to get government off the back of business. We also find "social-issue" conservatives angered by the liberal dissolution of our public morality. Still others are "libertarians" who want no public morality at all but oppose liberalism because of the large role it gives government. Another group of conservatives are regionalists or "states-righters" who are against, not government as such, but the federal government.

The ideological conflict between and among liberals and conservatives is carried on in terms of liberty and equality. We all agree that all men are created equal and are endowed by their Creator with certain inalienable rights, among which are life, liberty, and the pursuit of happiness. Even if we leave the Creator out of the discussion — because he is "divisive" and so best not talked about in a pluralistic society — we still agree that we are equal and somehow endowed with inalienable rights.

Our political disputes consequently have a way of becoming arguments about rights. We operate in this country on what the late Alexander Bickel called a "liberal contractarian model" of society, which "rests on a vision of individual rights that have a clearly defined, independent existence predating society and are derived from nature and from a natural, if imagined, contract. Society must bend to these rights." All that is left to argue about is what the rights are, in the possession of which we are all equal. Clearly defined though the rights are assumed to be, we do not agree on what is included in them.

To that question there is no answer in terms of liberty and equality alone. Without some ordering principle that specifies the content of liberty and equality, we cannot harmonize the two goals. The ordering principle, to work effectively, must be outside of and above liberty and equality. It cannot be a vague "fraternity" but must be some commonly held judgment on what human beings are and what is truly good for them.

The mere thought of such a common moral principle superior to liberty and equality makes the contemporary liberal mind — and some conservative minds — shudder. We lack such an ordering principle because we are so devoted to liberty and equality as the supreme norms of a democratic society that we will not admit their subordination to any higher norms.

Yet liberty and equality cannot be the highest values of a political system because they relativize and ultimately destroy all other values. When we make them our supreme norms, we have no set of objectively valid human ends that can provide answers to the questions, liberty for what? and equality in what? We therefore cannot have the communal beliefs without which in the long run there is no community.

We have no firm basis on which such societal values as we happen to hold at a particular time can be transmitted from generation to generation. Even the most devout among us are prone to consider their moral convictions as merely private beliefs. Their children become unthinking moral relativists, as many a teacher today can testify.

In short, American society now lacks what Walter Lippmann called the public philosophy. We shall lack it increasingly as the moral and religious capital of our culture, on which liberalism has always traded even as it eroded it, is drained away. We are left with an unending battle between conflicting claims to liberty and equality, and no publicly acknowledged principle with which to resolve the conflict.

The Law Unbound

June 1985

Edward Koch, mayor of New York, and John Cardinal O'Connor, archbishop of New York, have been engaged for some time in a legal battle over hiring homosexuals. As the archbishop quipped in a talk he gave in Mr. Koch's presence last fall, he and the mayor are such good friends that they use the same courtrooms and the same judges.

One of the courts they use recently handed down a decision which raises an issue of national, and not merely local, concern. The question before the court was whether the mayor had the legal authority to issue an executive order barring discrimination against homosexuals in hiring by private agencies that do business with New York City. Three religious agencies which administer social service programs under contracts with the city have contested the mayor's authority to issue the order. They are Agudath Israel, the Catholic Archdiocese of New York, and the Salvation Army. They won their case in the trial court, but last month a New York State appellate court reversed the decision and upheld the mayor.

So far we are talking about a local squabble. The court that upheld the mayor sits in Manhattan, which houses what may be the maddest collection of civil libertarians in the nation, and its decision will certainly be appealed to a higher court. When the final decision in this case is rendered, it may turn on the narrow question whether the mayor exceeded his authority by issuing his executive order in the absence of a city ordinance.

New York's City Council has several times refused to pass an ordinance forbidding job discrimination against homosexuals, and the lone dissenting judge on the appellate court remarked that "the failure of the City Council to act in a matter within its sphere of action has not created a vacuum into which the Mayor may step." But whether a mayor has usurped legislative authority is not a question that need keep law-abiding

Americans awake at night from coast to coast.

They would do well, however, to wake up and take notice of the reason which the appellate court gave for upholding the mayor's executive order:

> The Mayor, as chief executive officer of the City of New York, sworn to uphold the Constitution of the United States and of New York State, had authority to assure that the city did not discriminate against any of its citizens. Not only does he have authority, he is *obligated* to enforce the fundamental constitutional principles.

Now, that is a truly extraordinary statement for a court of law to make. In its implications, it amounts to a constitutional revolution. Yes, I know, the statement was made by an intermediate-level court in one state out of fifty, and it probably will not be adopted by any higher court. Still, as one of our Founding Fathers said, we must take alarm at the first attempt upon our liberties, and what the New York Court said was an attack on the idea of liberty under law.

For the court said that the Constitution of the United States *obligates* the Mayor of New York — and therefore every executive officer in the country — to take affirmative action to bar all forms of discrimination that are not related to job performance in hiring either by governmental agencies or by private agencies that receive public funds for their services. The press reports that I have read do not indicate where in the Constitution the court found this obligation. But it is a safe guess that its source was the clause in section 1 of the Fourteenth Amendment which provides that no state shall "deny to any person within its jurisdiction the equal protection of the laws."

That clause was put into the Constitution in the aftermath of the Civil War to preven Southern states from enacting different codes of law for whites and the newly emancipated blacks. Whatever laws the people of, say, Georgia or Mississippi chose for themselves must apply to all persons within those states without distinction by race. For the rest, it was left to the people of those and all the other states to decide what laws they would or would not adopt.

Now the New York court tells us that the equal protection clause is a blanket mandate to all public executives to stamp

out job discrimination. Not only discrimination against homosexuals, but any discrimination not related to job performance,
is unconstitutional. Any state, county, or city legislative body
which refuses to do its duty and bar discrimination violates
the Constitution, and the executive branch may and must act
without legislative authorization to carry out the constitutional
command.

More significantly yet, such an interpretation of the Constitution makes that document a blanket grant of power to the
courts. They, and they alone, are empowered to determine the
meaning of the equal protection of the laws. They may, as the
New York court has done, turn it into a general commission to
promote equality, and it will mean what the judge says it
means.

If that is so, however, the judges are not under the law;
they are the law. If the Constitution is only a mandate to promote equality (or liberty, or justice, or prosperity), it is not a
law. It is a blank check issued to the courts which they may fill
in with their conceptions of equality, liberty, justice, or sound
economic policy. It is irrelevant whether you or I or anyone
else thinks that there should be law forbidding discrimination
against homosexuals. The question is whether the Constitution empowers judges to make such a law. Liberty under law
means that judges as well as legislatures are bound by the Constitution as the supreme law of the land. But a Constitution
which contains blank checks issued to the courts has ceased to
be a law. Judges unbound by the law can be as guilty of the
arrogance of power as kings ever were.

The Pope's Dutch Treat

July 1985

Pope John Paul's visit to the Netherlands in 1985 is now history. In an age in which nothing is deader than yesterday evening's news broadcast, we could even call it ancient history. Nevertheless, old though it is as news, it still merits reflection and comment.

Before the pope got to the Netherlands, *Time* remarked that the purpose of his trip was "to defend orthodox church teachings before Holland's more than 5.6 million Catholics, whose freethinking clergy have been heavily influenced since Vatican II by Calvinist individualism and Protestant independence." Calvinist individualism usually conjures up a picture of the individual soul standing alone before God, confessing its utter sinfulness and total depravity, and hoping to be saved by an inscrutable divine decree of predestination. That, however, was not quite the picture which the American press presented of Holland's neo-Calvinist Catholic clergy and lay intellectuals.

In preparation for the pope's arrival, dissidents organized public protests against his stands on contraception, abortion, clerical celibacy, and the role of women in the Church. At a demonstration in The Hague, theologian Edward Schillebeeckx proclaimed: "We are gathered here not only to show the other face of our church but to celebrate it." Displays at the dozens of booths which the demonstration's sponsors had set up showed what the other face of the Dutch church is. "Among the positions advocated," according to the *New York Times,* "were the rights of homosexuals to be given the sacraments and to become priests, permission for priests to marry, and equal roles for women in the church."

Press reports during the pope's visit mentioned the same and similar themes of dissent. For example, in the pope's presence, Hedwig Wasser, an official of a Catholic missionary group, asked if Catholicism could be credible "if we exclude rather than make room for unmarried people living together, divorced people, homosexuals, married priests and women." She did not explain, so far as I know, to whom the Church would be credible if it "made room" for such people. The pope listened to her but made it clear in a later talk to Dutch youth that the Church's teachings on "marital love, abortion, sexual relations before or outside of marriage, or homosexual relations remain the standard for the Church for all time."

Except for one mention of "liberation theology," those were the only issues about which Dutch Catholics allegedly influenced by Calvinist individualism and Protestant independence appeared to be concerned when confronting the pope. Their grievances all seem to have centered on the restraints which Catholic moral doctrine puts on the sexual appetite. One is left sadly wondering: Has the Reformation come to this?

You will understand that I am no great admirer of the Reformation. Had I been alive in 1517, I'd have voted against Martin Luther. If I had been alive and young just four hundred years ago in 1585, I'd have become a Jesuit to play my part in the Counter-Reformation. But looking back across four centuries, I have to admit that today's Catholic heirs of Calvinist individualism make the sixteenth-century reformers look awfully good.

Martin Luther, John Calvin, Ulrich Zwingli, John Knox and the rest of them may have been wrong, but at least they were wrong about high and very important theological issues. They disagreed with Catholic doctrine on such questions as sin and its effect on human nature, redemption, grace, the sacraments, the possibility of human merit, predestination, and salvation.

John Morley, the Victorian man of letters, once said that the great crime of the Reformation was that it taught men to argue about theology in the marketplace. But let us give credit where credit is due. The arguments in the marketplace four hundred years ago were on a higher plane than today's complaints about the frustration of sexual needs.

One may protest that this criticism of modern liberal Catholic thought is not only snide but unfair. Sex is not really the issue in such questions as the ordination of women. The real issue is the equality of all members of the Church. But even if we accept this reply, it is striking how rapidly the demand for equality becomes a demand for recognition of the equal worth of all sexual proclivities and desires.

It is no accident that individualism, carried all the way through, flowers in the emancipation of the sexual appetite. For some centuries the consequences of individualism were held in check — as they still are among conservative Protestants — by belief in God's law revealed in the Bible and/or in a natural moral law revealed based on our common human nature. But as faith in divine revelation and belief in reason's ability to discern the moral law dissolved in the acid of individualism, the equality of all individuals became the equality of all individual opinions. This in turn became the equality of all individual desires, because no standard higher than individual preference was left to appeal to.

Sexual desire is one of the strongest human desires, and therefore its demands come powerfully to the fore in claims to equal treatment for all individuals. For that reason the message the pope got in Holland was that the modern, liberal Dutch Catholic (who has learned from Calvinists to think for himself) wants sexual satisfaction without moral restraints and insists that the Church should justify him in throwing off the restraints. If the pope heard some background noise while listening to this message, it may have been the faint, whirring sound of John Calvin spinning in his grave.

Losing the Faith

August 1985

I have a confession to make: I have lost my faith. It did not happen suddenly but gradually over a long period of time. I can understand how a man might wake up one morning and realize that he no longer loves his wife. But, surely, on reflection he would see that he had been ceasing to love her for months and years. Loss of faith, too, is not like a sharp and unexpected blow on the head. Rather, it is like a steady waning of vital energy that ends finally in death.

One does not lightly surrender childhood pieties and give up beliefs that one learned in school, if not at one's mother's knee. It is only with a profound sense of loss that one lets go of a warm feeling of identity with the sentiments and convictions of one's friends and neighbors, and becomes an alien in one's own society. Yet it happens, and it has happened to me.

Painful though it is to admit it, I have ceased to believe in progressive views. Not just this or that view, on this or that subject, but the progressive view on any subject. It has gone so far that I not only suspect that liberal and enlightened opinions are wrong, I doubt whether they are even intelligent.

It was not always so with me. When I was growing up, it was generally understood that certain people were reactionaries and had benighted views. They usually occupied positions of authority in church or state, and were a constant source of embarrassment to the rest of us. You never knew what a bishop was going to say, or a senator from a Midwestern state.

Thank God, there were always intelligent people who would write editorials in the liberal Catholic or secular press and explain what the enlightened way of looking at the matter was. In that remote and simple age I always knew who was reactionary and who was intelligent.

Now I am no longer sure. As progressive ideas have taken over in religion, politics, education, and arts and letters, they have come to appear less and less impressive to me.

There is a sort of reverse Pilgrim's Progress in one's loss of faith in progressive enlightenment. I don't know how many advanced theologians one has to read before one stops putting implicit faith in theologians. It probably varies with individual readers; for some, Daniel Maguire alone might suffice. How many modernist Scripture scholars does one have to read before becoming critical of the historical-critical method? Hard to say, but in any case the end result is disbelief, not in Scripture, but in Scripture scholars.

One begins to wonder if the people of God are quite as eager for vibrant liturgies as the younger and more progressive clergy think they are. The feminist nun, heard too often, palls on one. (*L'éloquence continue ennuie*, as Pascal said.) She achieves a certain shock effect the first time she announces that the pope has had it and is in big, big trouble with the National Council of Dissident Nuns. But the twenty-fifth time a glaze comes over the eyes of her hearers.

I remember reading, years and years ago, an article in a British magazine — *The Spectator*, I think it was — in which the author made a sarcastic reference to the Church of England, "where miniskirted vicars prance trendily about, advocating a cautious reappraisal of sexual morality." Today the Catholic Church, too, has miniskirted clergy and religious who prance trendily about, and they have thrown caution to the winds.

Progressive ideas seem to work little better in politics than in religion. Spain's transition from dictatorship to democracy must be counted as progress, but with it has come what the *New York Times* calls "a virtual revolution in sexual mores." It reported last April 8: "Divorce was legalized in 1980, and the Parliament approved a law permitting abortions in limited cases two years ago. . . . Topless bathing on the nation's crowded beaches is now common. . . . A side product has also been an increase in prostitution, pornography and cabarets featuring transvestites."

Some will say that these changes in mores are the price a country pays for democracy. They may only prove that liberalism is the Achilles' heel of democracy. We have had a democracy in this country for two centuries, but not until recent decades have we become so liberal that "daring" now means dirty and "adult" means sick. That may be progressive, but only liberals believe that it is a necessary adjunct of democracy.

It is progressive to think that Marxist-Leninist guerrillas can solve the problems of Third World countries, but I don't believe that. It was progressive for one of our major political parties to adopt a series of democratic reforms in its own structure since 1968, but I notice that as a result it now seems to be incapable of winning national elections.

Civil rights are a progressive cause, and undeniably we have made some real progress in that field. But a doctrinaire devotion to civil rights has produced a growing number of most uncivil rights. When "rights" are used to undermine the authority of parents over children, to impair the ability of schools to maintain order, let alone teach, and to keep the community from recognizing the difference between homosexuality and heterosexuality, one's ardor for progress understandably begins to cool.

Merely reading the decisions of courts on a subject like "wrongful birth" is enough to shake anyone's faith in progressive views. But the cumulative effect of all of the above is shattering. At least it was for me.

So that is how I lost my faith. I must admit, however, that I have derived one benefit from this experience. Now I can tell all you folks out there who have lost your faith that I understand your feelings and share your pain.

Vive la Différence

September 1985

There are females and there are women, as a clever writer (French, of course) once wrote. To which women could retort that there are male animals and there are men, and the male animals seem to have the men outnumbered. Both the Frenchman and the women would be right: we are all born male or female, but only some of us achieve manhood or womanhood.

Manhood and womanhood are the maturity of the human species. The basic fact is that we are human males or females. Men and women are what we become if we develop our humanity as we should. There are no people who are simply human beings devoid of sex, neither are there persons whose sex is irrelevant to their personality.

Sex is not a characteristic added on to human nature; it is a constituent part of our nature. Just so, our bodies are not additions to our souls. Human souls are the life principles of human bodies and can come into being in no other guise. We are ensouled bodies just as truly as we are embodied souls. Body and soul, together and as one thing, constitute us as human beings. But to be a living human body is to be a member of one sex or the other. Human beings don't exist except as males or females.

Aristotle held that nature always intends the male but produces the female when it falls short of the mark. His view was one way of understanding the insight that sex is a constituent element of nature. If nature is inherently sexual and nature is one, then, he thought, it must intend one sex and produce the other by accident or defect.

Too many still believe that maleness is the perfection of human nature, feminists not least among them, as their rabid resentment of the male shows. Still, it was a strange thing for a man as intelligent as Aristotle to say. It meant that nature can continue to reproduce itself only by falling short of the mark half the time.

It would seem more realistic to recognize that when we say that sex is a constituent element of human nature, we mean that it is of the essence of humanity to be divided into two sexes. Men and women are not two species but the two halves of a single species whose very nature it is to consist of two sexes.

A sexless humanity is a contradiction in terms: our humanity must realize itself in manhood or womanhood. Both are equally human. Both are necessary to the fullness of humanity, but not in the same way. The human race is not a collection of individuals who happen to be men and women but a society (or collection of societies) founded upon a relationship between men and women.

Men and women, no matter how mature and fully human they become, are and remain males and females. As we grow up, we may and we should transcend mere animality. But to outgrow being males and females would be to cease being human.

Now, to be male and female is to be complementary principles of generation or procreation. It is not merely that procreation is what we need males and females for. Procreation is what gives masculinity and femininity their meaning.

The technological mind, which rejects the notion that anything has a natural purpose, can and does aspire to finding a way of producing human beings that will eliminate the necessity of sex altogether. The ultimate technological dream is to produce living beings from inorganic matter in the laboratory. Should the technologists succeed, however, they will have not only eliminated the need for sex but destroyed its intelligibility.

For it is their roles in procreation that constitute men and women as what they are. They are two sexes — and can be human only as distinct sexes — because of their radical, built-in capacity for playing complementary roles in procreation. That is just as true of those of us who have remained celibate as of the mothers and fathers of families.

Nor are those roles only the obvious physical ones: males fertilize, women conceive and give birth. Men are men and women are women in everything they think, say, and do—and, as another and even more clever Frenchman said, vive la différence. There are psychological differences rooted in the physical differences between men and women. They are not in the least deplorable nor should they be considered as defects to be overcome, for they are differences in affectivity rather than intelligence. Men and women never get to the stage where they are simply and merely persons. If they did, they wouldn't be human.

It is a fact of common observation that women are softer, gentler, and more sweet-tempered than men. These are admirable and lovable qualities; they are in fact the reason why men fall in love with women. They are also the qualities that suit women for mothering, as distinct from "parenting" (which is just one more attempt to deny the difference between the sexes).

The feminine qualities, it must be admitted, make it possible for men to exploit women as often as they do, sometimes ruthlessly. The remedy, however, is not to train little girls to grow up as hard as nails. It might be more difficult but in the long run it would be more truly human to train boys to appreciate and esteem womanhood as something more than mere femaleness.

We could make a beginning toward this end by reviving devotion to Mary, the virgin mother of God. Some will object to this proposal as an attempt to put women "back in their place," and so it would be, but it would also help to put the male animal in his place. It is a place in which we may hope that he will someday grow up to be a man whom women can appreciate and esteem.

Liberalism and the Catholic University

October 1985

The other day at lunch I heard someone at the next table say, "The trouble with right-wingers is, they think people who disagree with them are wicked." In contrast, we may point out, moderates (as the press calls liberals these days) regard their opponents as simply stupid.

Of the two attitudes, the moderate one is the more insulting, for a bad will can change, but stupid is forever. *Entre nous,* however, since we are all right-wingers here, let us admit that we do tend to attribute bad motives where mere muddle-headedness or the force of circumstances would suffice for an explanation.

This tendency to blame rather than to try to understand is particularly apparent when accusatory questions are asked about what is happening in Catholic institutions of higher education. The questions often assume a degree of bad will in the administrators of those institutions far greater than they are really guilty of. The situation, I believe, is much more complex.

First, it seems to me, many Catholic colleges and universities allowed themselves to get too big. Often enough they did it at the request of bishops who wanted Catholic educational programs to be available to their people in all fields and at all levels. The result, however, was a massive expansion of teaching staffs: a school can't offer a course without having someone in the classroom to teach it. The religious orders which had founded the schools found themselves outnumbered by lay faculty, many of whom were devoted Catholics, but not all of them, and a growing number were not Catholic at all.

Next, after World War II, there was an increasing emphasis on professional qualifications for university teaching; one had to have a Ph.D. in one's field. In screening applicants for teaching posts, the overriding consideration became their purely professional qualifications. Not how an applicant would fit into the faculty of a Catholic college, not what he would contribute to the college's mission, but did he have a degree from a prestigious university in molecular biology, or seventeenth-century French literature, or public policy formation was the paramount question.

At the same time, faculty power in the colleges increased greatly. The most important power in any institution is the power to hire and fire, for it shapes the institution. This power has to a large extent passed into hands of the faculty as the persons best able to judge the qualifications of new teachers. As the faculty has become less Catholic in its composition, it is less and less concerned with maintaining the Catholic character of the school. Many faculty members would regard a suggestion that they should be concerned about it as an attack on their academic freedom.

Faculty power is by no means absolute, but it is primarily the faculty in each department of a university who decide which junior teachers shall be hired, reappointed, and granted or denied tenure. Expecting college presidents or boards of trustees to "do something about it" is to misunderstand how far the colleges and universities have passed beyond their power to control.

Their power is further diminished by the proliferation of civil rights laws and judicial decisions at the federal, state, and local levels in the past two decades. As long as the American legal establishment remains mad for equality at any price, the ability of any college to choose its own faculty will be significantly limited. As for the price of equality, ask the college of your choice how much money it spent last year in legal fees to defend itself against charges of discriminating against faculty members. The answer, if you can get it, is likely to stagger you.

Where colleges have accepted government funds — and few of them have not — they have subjected themselves to an array of governmental regulations against discrimination. When you take the Queen's shilling, you have joined the Queen's army and must expect to obey orders. But, as the Grove City College case shows, even when a college refuses to take government money, bureaucrats still try to impose their regulations on it on the ground that its students, or some of them, have government loans. Yet a college that cannot exercise discrimination in staffing and governing itself progressively loses its distinctive character as a school.

It would be misleading, nonetheless, to imply that the Catholic colleges and universities have been merely passive victims of an historical flood. The developments mentioned above took place in a period in which upwardly mobile American Catholics felt an enormous yearning to be accepted by the larger society in which they lived and worked. Whether they wanted to join the country club or to be recognized by their academic peers in other universities, they put themselves under pressure to conform.

What Catholic academics conformed to was the secular liberal model of a university. They overlooked the essential distinction between academic excellence and that particular model of a university—a model no older than the Enlightenment. George Bernard Shaw's famous jibe that a Catholic university is a contradiction in terms is valid if—but only if—we build liberalism and the liberal conception of truth into the definition of a university.

Many Catholic academics, both clerical and lay, however, did not pause to ask why we must make liberalism part of the definition of a university. They simply took it for granted and tried to carry Catholic water on one shoulder and liberal water on the other. Naturally, a lot of the water got spilled, especially from the Catholic bucket. But that is a topic which must await further comment in another column.

Liberalism and the Catholic University II

November 1985

Every thinking Catholic has the lifelong task of harmonizing his faith with the findings of human reason that are available in his time. He could shake off the problem, as some do, by renouncing his faith. But we are speaking of a man who wants to keep his faith, who regards it as a boon rather than a burden, and who finds that it helps rather than hinders him in understanding the world in which he lives. Nonetheless, he will have the never-finished task of bringing the teachings of faith and the conclusions of reason into a coherent and harmonious relationship: the Catholic mind is by native instinct a synthesizing mind.

But if establishing a coherent worldview based on both faith and reason is a project for the individual Catholic, then the project can be institutionalized. What one can and must do for himself, he may do in cooperation with others. A Catholic university therefore can be conceived of as an institution designed to enable Catholics collectively to address the intellectual problems which any one of them has to face individually.

Such an institution is built upon a commitment to the truth of the Catholic religion. It does not have to enter into the question whether its religion is true before it can begin its work. The institution exists for persons who have already answered that question on grounds which they find satisfactory; persons who do not find them satisfactory presumably will go to other institutions. This institution is for those who want to move on to the further questions which arise out of what is believed by faith, what is known or speculated about by reason, and the relationship between the two.

It does not follow that a Catholic university is an institution dedicated primarily to studying and teaching revealed religion, or that its purpose is indoctrination. To perform its task, it must study and teach all the subjects that make up the ordinary curriculum of universities in its time and place. It is through the study of these subjects that the members of the university will confront that rationally known reality which they wish to understand in the light of faith and in whose light faith itself must be interpreted. A relation, after all, always has at least two terms. If one wishes to reflect on the relationship between physics and theology, for instance, it is as necessary to know physics as it is to know theology.

A Catholic university, furthermore, cannot do its work properly unless it studies and teaches these subjects objectively — but "objective" is not a synonym for "neutral," "agnostic," or "value-free." It means only that the first intellectual duty of any man, believer or non-believer, is to understand the *real* as it is, to the best of his ability, without distorting it to fit his general view of the world.

There is an unresolvable contradiction between this model of a Catholic university and the liberal model which is commonly considered to be the only one appropriate to a free and pluralistic society. Pluralism, in this view, connotes a wide diversity of beliefs held by individuals, all of whom are equal. But to found a university on a particular belief is to give that belief a privileged position in the university. It is therefore to deny the equality of all individuals, because it denies the equality of their beliefs, and so it is an attack on pluralism.

The proper name for this theory, however, is not pluralism but individualism, which is the reigning ideology of our liberal society. The liberal model of a university is a replica of the liberal society. It can rest upon no agreed body of truth, for that would limit the rights of individuals; its highest commitment can be only to the pursuit of a truth which is never to be attained. A century and a half ago, the great prophet of liberalism, John Stuart Mill, as a young man looked forward to a society which would have "convictions as to what is right or wrong, useful and pernicious, deeply engraven on the feelings by early education and general unanimity of sentiment, and so firmly grounded in reason and in true exigencies of life, that they shall not, like all former and present creeds, religious, ethical and political, require to be periodically thrown off and replaced by others." Today, when skepticism has replaced reason as the foundation of liberty, the man who wrote that line would be regarded as a fanatic intent on imposing an orthodoxy on society.

The liberal university in our day stands only for a process which is never to end in an established truth; it is by definition neutral, agnostic, and value-free. It therefore can insist only on procedural rules of scholarship which prohibit such offenses as plagiarism and falsification of evidence, but not on any substantive truth. It cannot even have a common moral code for its faculty and students. To be sure, even in a liberal university one could invite censure for committing a truly atrocious act, such as allowing oneself to be debriefed by the CIA on returning from a trip abroad, but not for a purely private fault such as leaving one's wife and children in order to cohabit with a graduate student.

In the 1977 volume of the *Journal of Church and State,* Leo Pfeffer announced that "it is only a question of time, and a comparatively short time, before Notre Dame and Fordham will be like unto Yale and Columbia." With Dr. Pfeffer, one suspects, the wish is father to the thought. But those Catholics who have accepted the liberal model of a university as normative will find it difficult to prove him wrong, if indeed they even want to do so.

Rights as the Beginning and End

December 1985

I was paging through the *New York Times Book Review,* as is my wont of a Sunday afternoon, when my eye was caught by a brief, unsigned review of yet another book on abortion. According to the review, the author of the book concludes that, while the fetus has a right to life from the moment of conception, "this right to live does not entitle the fetus to use a woman's body against her will."

The issue, one notices, is posed in terms of rights and entitlements. "May I use your body, madam?" "Yes, dear, of course you may" or "No, you are not entitled to it and anyhow, I don't want you." Such language does not surprise us in a liberal society which thinks habitually in terms of rights. Yet even in a liberal society one must wonder by what tortuous mental process a man comes to discuss the morality of destroying human life as though he were a lawyer arguing a case of trespass on private property.

The fetus is cast as the party of the first part who pleads his right to live, which he cannot sustain without a temporary lease of the woman's body. She is the party of the second part who asserts an absolute property right to her own body. The court must decide which of these rights should prevail. Since the fetus, when all is said and done, is an intruder on someone else's property, he loses. That what he loses is his life may be regrettable, but the superior right has prevailed and so justice has been done.

But how does one come to think of the beginning of human life and the morality of ending it in these terms? The answer, I believe, is that one is an intellectual heir of John Locke and therefore thinks of a human being as essentially an individual proprietor.

In this view, each man is an island, of which he is the sole owner. He owns his body, the actions he performs with it, and the goods he acquires by those actions. In Locke's terminology, he is endowed by nature with original rights to life, liberty, and estate, which collectively form his "property." His only obligation is to respect the equal rights of other persons, all of whom are individual proprietors like himself.

Since disputes over rights inevitably arise, these proprietors enter into a social contract with each other, by which they form a civil society and set up a government with authority to resolve conflicts of rights. The contract into which individuals have freely entered obliges them to accept the government's decision in such cases.

But they remain what they were by nature: individuals distinct and separate from one another, each the owner of his own life, liberty, and estate. The relationship they have formed with one another by joining together in society is artificial, external, and contractual; it is not rooted in their nature as social beings. They formed the relationship so that each one could better protect his individual proprietary rights, and society's government has no function other than to protect those rights.

In the same spirit, the leaders of the French Revolution proclaimed in their Declaration of the Rights of Man and the Citizen that "ignorance, neglect, or contempt of the rights of men are the sole causes of public misfortunes and corruptions of Government." Implicit in this remarkable assertion is the proposition that if we only get our conception of rights straight and implement it in practice, we shall have solved all the problems of society and accomplished all the legitimate purposes of government.

This attitude prevails in influential circles in America today. Philosophers begin their political theories with the individual self and then seek to show how it can be incorporated into society without compromising its selfhood. Novelists depict and sometimes celebrate the war of the self against the restraints of society's culture. Newspapers and magazines, as the discerning reader will notice, often translate issues that affect all of society into struggles between conflicting rights.

Thus, for example, school busing becomes a conflict between the right of black parents to send their children to an integrated school and the right of white parents to send their children to a neighborhood school. Pornography is regarded, not as a social problem, but as a conflict between the right of some people to have access to "adult" material and the right of others not to have the same material thrown in their faces. Even what to do about AIDS turns into a debate about rights.

The question, however, is not whether human beings have rights; they do, and few today will question that. Rather it is what model or picture of society should guide our thinking. In one model, which comes down to us from Aristotle and Aquinas, we think of man as a social being from whose nature flow relations to his family, neighbors, fellow-workers, the community, and the political order. These relations are the foundation of both rights and obligations which are prior to and independent of consent. In the Lockean model we conceive of man as an independent proprietor whose social relations are only those to which he has freely consented.

Individualists understandably prefer the second model, and the American Civil Liberties Union is hopelessly in love with it, but it leads to strange and distorted conclusions about social reality. If we take the principles of liberal individualism as axiomatic, we find it possible to think of the fetus and the woman as the parties of the first and second part arguing over their respective rights. We are then able to blind ourselves to the natural fact that they are related as mother and child and that the child is in the only natural place for him to be, his mother's womb.

The Americanization of Catholics

January 1986

Let us lift up our eyes to the polls, whence cometh our strength. During the Extraordinary Synod of Bishops the results of a New York Times/CBS News poll on the views of American Catholics were released just in time to strengthen us against any possible bad news from Rome. The *Times'* report on the poll laid it out in its opening sentence: "Majorities of American Catholics hold views that differ sharply from teachings of their church on such issues as women's ordination, divorce, birth control, and marriage for priests." On these issues Catholics are markedly more in agreement with their non-Catholic fellow citizens than with the pope.

The pollsters gathered their data through random telephone calls to 927 Americans across the nation, of whom 280 were Catholics. The reader may ask how we can take 280 persons as representing the views of scores of millions of Catholics in the United States, but I have no answer to that question. I took a course on statistics once, but that was decades ago and I am in no position to argue with professionals who assure me that if you know 280 of them, you know them all.

Before making up my mind on the answers given by our 280 representatives, however, I'd like to know more about the questions they were asked. For example, in the summary of poll results published in the *Times*, we are told that 63 percent of all Catholics (and 67 percent of non-Catholics) "favor letting priests marry." But what does "favor" mean?

If the question means, or was taken to mean, do you think priests should have a right to marry if they want to, I don't find an affirmative response surprising. We are Americans and as such believe in rights and little else: everyone should have the right to do what he wants to do (so long as it doesn't hurt anyone else, of course).

Suppose, however, that "favoring" the marriage of priests means that you are willing to pay tithes, i.e., ten percent of your income, in order properly to support the priest and his family along with other church expenses. Is the answer still yes? Does "favor" mean that you would attend Mass more often, confess your sins more frequently, keep the commandments more faithfully if priests were allowed to marry?

Would you expect better sermons (or homilies as we now call them), more friendly relations between priests and the laity, more devoted service by priests to parishioners? If not, then what does "favor" mean, and why are you in favor? One would like to know before coming to a conclusion based on the answer given by 63 percent of the American Catholics who were polled.

One may be even more curious about the views of the 52 percent of Catholic women who "favor women as priests." How many women want themselves to be priests? Not one in a hundred thousand, I should guess. How many women want to be able to point with pride to "my daughter the priest"? How many would attend Mass more often, confess their sins more honestly, keep God's law more earnestly than they now do, if only they could have women priests?

Or are we dealing with nothing more than a standard American reflex? In this Land of the Free, everyone should have the right to be a priest, even though I don't want to be one myself and would not be happy if one of my children did. But everyone should have the right and of course the right must belong to both sexes equally. Anything short of that would be unconstitutional.

I do hope that I don't sound cynical or even reactionary. I must point out that my remarks find some support in a comment on the poll made by David C. Leege, the director of research for a four-year study of Catholic life by the University of Notre Dame, which has arrived at some parallel conclusions. The poll indicated, he said, "that Catholics still remain very loyal to both the faith and to the Church as an institution, but that Catholics are increasingly assimilated to American cultural values." The poll data bear him out inasmuch as 79 percent of the Catholic respondents "think it is possible to disagree with the Pope on birth control, abortion, or divorce and still be a good Catholic."

The 79 percent constitute a new sociological category. Ex-Catholics and lax Catholics we have always known, but now we have semi-Catholics or, as the sociologists call them, communal Catholics. They love the Church, you understand, and wouldn't dream of leaving it, but they do not intend to let the Church tell them how to live. They have assimilated American cultural values which, as Dr. Leege explains, "indicate that no one holds absolute authority and that the individual is a reasonable judge of what is moral and what is conscientious."

These are the cultural values which for more than ten years have given us a birthrate lower than the rate necessary to replace the population; a divorce rate which, as *Time* magazine has phrased it, "hits 1 of every 2 U.S. marriages"; and an abortion rate which terminates one third of all American pregnancies to the number of 1.5 million abortions a year.

Time also reports: "If present trends continue, researchers estimate, fully 40 percent of today's 14-year-old girls will be pregnant at least once before the age of 20." Some 45 percent of them will have abortions and more than half of those who do not abort will have illegitimate children; 78 percent of Americans, according to a *Time* poll, "favor" teaching contraception in the schools as the answer to this situation. It would probably be too much to expect any other response in a culture in which no one has absolute authority and the individual is a reasonable judge of what is moral and conscientious.

I recall a series of articles by Harold E. Fey which appeared in the *Christian Century* 40 years ago under the title, "Can Catholicism Win America?" Mr. Fey feared that it could, but if he is still alive today, the polls should cheer him up. The Catholic Church has not converted America, but America is doing a pretty good job of converting the members of the Church.

Stooping to Folly

March 1986

Two hundred and more years ago, in what must seem to us a vanished Age of Innocence, Oliver Goldsmith wrote:

> When lovely woman stoops to folly,
> And finds too late that men betray,
> What charm can soothe her melancholy?
> What art can wash her guilt away?

No poet could write that verse today, for lovely woman no longer stoops to folly. Or rather, she does, but she doesn't know it's folly and she doesn't know she stoops. A true child of her time, she is simply "sexually active" and unaware of sin, or guilt, or shame. Neither does she see any inherent meaning or significance in what she does. She is an emancipated woman, committed to nothing but the satisfaction of her own needs.

She and her boyfriend have learned to think for themselves, which is no strain on their brains, however, since what they really want is freedom to decide for themselves, and they can do that either with more thought or less. If they are in a hurry, they make do with less.

In the nineteenth century it was still possible for John Stuart Mill to advocate maximum freedom for the individual as the source of society's intellectual and moral progress. Mill recommended "the fullest liberty of professing and discussing, as a matter of ethical conviction, any doctrine, however immoral it may be considered." But he proposed this liberty of discussion in the belief that unlimited discussion would lead society at large to a fuller grasp of the truth. "As mankind improves," he said, "the number of doctrines which are no longer disputed or doubted will constantly be on the increase" and there will be "a consolidation . . . of true opinions" and "a gradual narrowing of the bounds of diversity of opinion."

Similarly, he argued, society needs exceptional and unconventional persons "to commence new practices and set the example of more enlightened conduct and better taste and sense in human life." Shocking as society may at first find these persons' "experiments" in living, if the experiments prove successful, they will elevate society's manners and morals and society will make progress.

I have several times taught a course on Mill's essay, *On Liberty,* from which the above quotations are taken. Toward the end of the course I have asked a question: Now that society has so largely accepted Mill's doctrine and established the freedom of speech and conduct that he advocated, have we achieved the results that he promised? Do we find in our society a growing agreement on truth and a steady elevation of the standards of taste and conduct?

The students' response is to look at me as if I had just come in from outer space and were asking the way to the next galaxy. They cannot imagine why freedom should have any connection with truth or morality. What difference does it make whether our intellectual and moral standards have gone up or down? What indeed can "up" and "down" mean in relation to such highly subjective concepts as truth and moral good? We are free for the sake of being free, not because freedom will make us wiser and better.

When I see the students' puzzled looks, I realize once again how hopelessly out of date both John Stuart Mill and I are (each, of course, in his own very different way). Contemporary society does not believe in a common human nature or in any other objective standard by which we may judge up and down, true or false, better and worse. It believes only in what a writer in *Time* once called "the new secular religion of the self."

Like most things new, this secular religion has roots far in the past. As Hannah Arendt explained in *The Human Condition,* "One of the most persistent trends in modern philosophy since Descartes, and perhaps its most original contribution to philosophy, has been an exclusive concern with the self, as distinguished from the soul or person or man in general, an attempt to reduce all experiences, with the world as well as with other human beings, to experiences between man and himself."

"All men are created equal" thus becomes the proposition that all selves are equal precisely in their quality of being selves. Much of contemporary liberal political theory is based on the primacy of the self. The self, to John Rawls in *A Theory of Justice,* is prior to the ends that it affirms. Human life has no natural or God-given purposes, but only those which the self chooses for itself. Therefore, as Ronald Dworkin says in his essay, *Liberalism,* "government must be neutral on what might be called the question of the good life." The conservative critic, George Will, makes the same point in *Statecraft as Soulcraft:* "The fundamental goal of modern liberalism has been equality, and it has given us government that believes in the moral equality of appetites."

Liberal individualism leads also to what John Zvesper has called "the reduction of education to urbane, enlightened skepticism." If all values are individual and subjective, they are all relative, and all that education can do for us is to show us that. There is a further consequence, which Thomas Spragens points out in *The Irony of Liberal Reason:* "Since all the dogmatic relativist can conceive is individual interests anyway, he would be unable to see or describe a process of cultural disintegration if it unfolded before his very eyes." And that, dear reader, is why lovely woman nowadays stoops to folly without being able to see what she is doing.

How to Kill Freedom of Speech

May 1986

Does the liberal mind have a death wish? It gives every evidence of being driven by such a suicidal urge, but it may only be the victim of its own mistaken judgment. If the latter is the case, the mistake it makes is clear: it has abandoned reason as the foundation of liberty and has substituted skepticism.

The liberal flight from reason is beautifully exemplified in a column by Henry Mitchell which appeared in the *Washington Post* under the title, *"Playboy* and the Realm of Religion." Mr. Mitchell said in his column that he was disturbed, which seems to be the normal emotional condition of liberal journalists. What disturbed him in this particular column was the news that a major drugstore chain had decided to discontinue selling *Playboy.*

Mr. Mitchell hastens to tell us that he himself never bought a copy of *Playboy,* which assures us that he is no sex maniac. But neither are we to take him for a prude: he has counted on seeing a copy of *Playboy* lying on someone's desk or finding it in his barber shop. He thus strikes the balance we expect in a man of the world who enjoys his modicum of sexual stimulation but is not so desperately in need of it that he has to pay for it.

So it was not the news that a drugstore chain would no longer sell a magazine he didn't buy anyhow that got Mr. Mitchell's liberal juices flowing. No, it was the coincidental announcement that the Vatican was asking the Rev. Charles Curran of the Catholic University of America to recant certain of his views on sexual morals. By a natural association of ideas, Mr. Mitchell saw that the drugstore chain had yielded to moral pressure, therefore to religious prejudice.

You see, in the liberal universe which the Mitchell mind inhabits, moral judgments are and must be religious prejudices which have no rational basis. "We all know people," he says, "who would die before eating a cow or a pig or drinking a Coke

73

or a Gibson, because such things offend their religion." Crazy people, obviously, and their religions are all on the same level of insanity whether they forbid eating pork or drinking Coca-Cola.

Also on the same level of irrationality are the "many religious people" who "oppose pornography" and by whom "*Playboy* is considered pornographic." These fanatics go so far as to deny that readers buy *Playboy* for "its articles by the best-known serious writers of the nation" and assert that the only motive for buying it is "its raunchy advice on how to score and its pictures of girls."

Mr. Mitchell's only comment on the pictures is that "some say they are art, some say no." At this point you may begin to wonder if he actually ever has paged through a copy of *Playboy,* even in his barber shop. But you must remember that he is a columnist, not an art critic, and may well think it prudent to abstain from artistic judgment. You must also remember that his real point is that no rational judgment on pictures, or on art and literature generally, is possible.

Reason has nothing to do with such subjects because they are matters of taste and can be nothing more. Therefore certain people's feeling that pornography is offensive is only the way they feel about it and should have no influence on other people's right to buy it.

We cannot even allow any distinctions to be made among levels of taste which would classify some tastes as high, others as low; some as noble, others as base; some as truly human, others as degraded and degrading. There is no standard that reason can recognize by which we can make such distinctions.

The great liberal advocates of freedom of speech and press — Milton, Spinoza, and John Stuart Mill — argued for the liberty to utter our thoughts and to read the thoughts of others on exactly opposite grounds. They saw freedom of speech and press as the necessary condition for pursuing truth, virtue, and the welfare of the community. Their faith in reason may have been exaggerated, but they certainly had it. They believed that freedom to speak and publish would liberate reason to pursue rational and moral goals, not that reason couldn't recognize a moral goal if it saw one.

"Who kills a man kills a reasonable creature, God's image,"

said Milton in *Areopagitica*, "but he who destroys a good book, kills reason itself, kills the image of God, as it were in the eye." He also defended the right of "a discreet and judicious reader" to read "bad books," but only because "he that can apprehend and consider vice with all her baits and seeming pleasures, and yet abstain, and yet distinguish, and yet prefer that which is truly better, he is the true wayfaring Christian." Whatever we may think of that argument, it at least clearly supposes our ability to distinguish vice and virtue.

We need freedom to express our views, Spinoza argues, because "human wits are too blunt to get to the heart of all problems immediately; but they are sharpened by the give and take of discussion and debate, and by exploring every possible course men eventually discover the measures they wish." Mill contended in *On Liberty* that "in an imperfect state of the human mind the interests of truth require a diversity of opinions," because he was sure that the human mind would move toward perfection through rational debate among people of different opinions.

Contemporary liberals deny the classic liberal argument for the freedom of speech and press because they fear that if they ever admitted that truth and virtue have a meaning, it could be used to restrain their freedom to read and view whatever turns them on. But in rejecting the rational and moral ground of freedom they are cutting the ground out from beneath their own feet.

Thirty-odd years ago, in his book *The Public Philosophy*, Walter Lippmann explained how skepticism undermines freedom of speech and press: "Divorced from its original purpose and justification, freedom to think and speak are not self-evident necessities. It is only from the hope and intention of discovering truth that freedom acquires such high public significance." We protect the right to utter silly words only because that is the price we pay for the right to utter true and significant words. "But when the chaff of silliness, baseness, and deception is so voluminous that it submerges the kernels of truth, freedom of speech may produce such frivolity, or such mischief, that it cannot be preserved against the demand for a restoration of order or of decency." When we let matters go that far, "it is difficult to remember why freedom of speech is worth the pain and trouble of defending it." At that point, freedom is really in danger.

Dissolving the Norms

June 1986

Any society with clear and strong moral standards breeds hypocrites. Unwilling or unable to live up to the socially approved norms, they pretend to do so for fear of public opprobrium. Hypocrisy is the tribute vice pays to virtue, but the hypocrites understandably resent having to pay it.

They have two avenues of escape from their uncomfortable situation. One is to change their lives and begin to practice what society preaches. The other and easier course is to undermine society's standards. In a society such as ours, which is losing confidence in its right to make moral judgments, the easy way out has become a broad highway crowded with people seeking relief from all moral rules that are not of their own choosing.

The attack on social moral standards is most obvious at the present time in the demand for "gay rights" laws. The demand succeeds as often as it does because in this country's current egalitarian mood it is hard to mobilize public sentiment against laws which only seem to forbid discrimination. But the thrust of these anti-discrimination laws is toward a deep change in social morality.

A columnist in New York's *Village Voice* has explained that the seemingly moderate campaign for an end to discrimination against homosexuals "has radical potential, because civil rights legislation opens the way to acceptance, and acceptance opens the way to dissolution of the norm." Dissolving the norm in regard to sexual conduct is the real object of the "gay rights" movement. Its purpose is to get society to agree that, in the words of another columnist, homosexuality is just another way of living and AIDS is just another way of dying.

Once society accepts this claim, further questions arise. Why, for instance, are homosexuals not allowed to marry one another? Syndicated columnist Beverly Stephen has raised this question in what may be the opening salvo of a barrage on the civil rights front. The present structure of American marriage law, weakened though it has been in recent decades, is still heavily biased in favor of lifelong union between one man and one woman. The law thus expresses a social judgment in favor of one way of life as against other ways, establishes a legally privileged position for heterosexual monogamy, and discriminates against people who engage in other forms of sexual union. This bias in the law deprives homosexuals of legal rights which they could enjoy if only they could get married.

Ms. Stephen explains: "By law, married heterosexuals have inheritance rights, tax benefits, Social Security benefits, access to a spouse's insurance coverage, and rights to make medical decisions or funeral arrangements." Unmarried couples who live together have none of these rights, but if they are heterosexuals they at least can get married. A homosexual couple cannot, and that's not fair. Ergo, we must dissolve the heterosexual norm of marriage so that everyone may enjoy equal rights.

Now, Beverly Stephen is no more an Important Thinker than you or I, and there is no need to panic merely because she has floated an idea. Still, she has allies in the upper echelons of serious thought. Bruce A. Ackerman, who is a professor of law and philosophy at Columbia University, presumably is an important thinker. At least *The Chronicle of Higher Education* takes him as one in a recent article on the revival of political philosophy. What Professor Ackerman thinks is that "our fundamental right is the right to go to hell in our own way."

Society, for Ackerman and other highly regarded academics, exists in order to protect that right: society therefore may not impose norms that impair it. Here we see the real issue that faces American society. Beneath the surface phenomena of struggles over civil rights laws, affirmative action programs, and equal protection litigation, beneath the shouting about discrimination, censorship, and "imposing values" is the question whether society can and should maintain any moral norms at all.

There are those who want to dissolve the norms in the name of liberty and equality in a pluralistic society. It becomes steadily more clear, however, that the basic premise of their argument is what George Will has aptly called the moral equality of appetites. The original American proposition was that all men are created equal and are endowed by their Creator with certain unalienable rights. Now the proposition is that all persons are equally entitled to the satisfaction of their several preferences, urges, and drives. Because the persons are equal, their appetites are equally worthy of society's moral respect and the law's protection.

Some like chocolate, some like vanilla. Some like Mozart, others prefer heavy metal. Some like girls, some like boys. Some love God, others hate him. It is all the same because man is a bundle of desires and each man strives to satisfy the desires that he has. Society's only task is to preside over the striving with impartial neutrality so that we can all live together in peace.

As society's moral standards dissolve in the acid of this attitude, we may not succeed in keeping our domestic or international peace. I am reminded of a billboard which I often saw during World War II. It bore the picture of a particularly stupid-looking G.I., with his fatigue cap on backwards, who proclaimed, "I'm fighting for my right to boo the Dodgers." But no one fights for his right to boo the Dodgers. If you fight, you might get hurt or even killed, and in your right mind you will not risk life and limb for the sake of booing a baseball team. Nor, we may suspect, will many fight to defend an idea of liberty that dissolves every social norm worth living by or dying for.

Slogans for All Seasons

There is the explanation and there is the thing explained. The difference between them is a vital one, because the thing explained is real but the explanation is only our effort to render it intelligible to ourselves and other people. Explanations are necessary if we are to make sense of the world, but they are not identical with the world which they explain. That is why we have different philosophies or theories about the world and its constituent parts.

Not all theories are equally valid, however, because theory is controlled by reality. Despite what Karl Marx said, the ultimate purpose of our thinking is not to change the world but to understand it. The test of a sound theory is its correspondence to a reality which we did not create and which we can change only within limits. Theory can degenerate into ideology and often does in the modern world. Ideology is not an honest effort to understand but a program of action disguised as a philosophy. We imagine some ideal state of affairs and take it as our goal. We then work up a "philosophy" of the nature of the world, of man, and of society which makes the goal both necessary and attainable.

Our ideal may be a socialist state in which everyone gets the same income, or a participatory democracy in which everyone takes part in decisions which affect his interests, or a liberal paradise in which everyone pursues his own lifestyle, or a secularist heaven on earth in which no one takes religion seriously. Or it may be all of the above at once. In any case, the ideal to be achieved dictates a theory about the world in which the ideal can and must be realized. If reality persists in getting in the way of the ideal, so much the worse for reality: we must change it.

Ideologies in turn spawn slogans. The slogans may refer to

something valid and useful, like "the separation of church and state," but even then they are at best oversimplifications of reality. Most of the time they are distortions of reality designed to serve ideological ends. Sometimes they don't mean anything at all but only sound good.

The word "progressive," for example. "It will never be known," said Charles Peguy, "what acts of cowardice have been motivated by the fear of not looking sufficiently progressive." Yet the word is meaningless until we add meaning to it. It suggests movement in the right direction, but we have no idea what direction that is until we learn what goal we are progressing towards and why we should move toward it. Progressives seldom say; they just assume that everyone knows.

"Peace," "freedom," and "equality" all stand for desirable states of affairs, but they are not particularly useful terms while they remain abstractions which can mean whatever anyone wants them to mean. All men want peace but, as St. Augustine remarked, they want it on their own terms; hence the prevalence of wars. It is doubtful if anyone ever brought about peace simply by being for it or prevented war by being against war as such. On the contrary, turning "peace" into a political slogan may help to bring on a war.

Freedom is another word that signifies something of which we must all approve. For that very reason it is subject to vast abuse. Since the Civil War, no one in this country cares to admit that he is against freedom and for slavery. Sophists trade constantly on this devotion to freedom. Killing babies becomes "freedom of choice," peddling pornography becomes freedom of the press, ideologizing students becomes academic freedom, and a babble of lies, special pleading, and outright nonsense becomes the free market of ideas.

Any suggestion that what is offered in that marketplace should at least be an idea rather than a raw appeal to passion is met with cries of "Censorship!" Those who cry the most loudly, however, are not always concerned to preserve freedom of discussion. More often, discussion is what they want to prevent, and they have discovered that reciting the ritual word "censorship" is an effective way to do it.

"Chilling effect" is another good discussion stopper. So is

"imposing your beliefs on others." If they don't work, the sophist will try "due process of law." If all else fails, he will tell people who disagree with him that they are wedded to beliefs which modern scholarship has shown to be "historically conditioned." That usually shuts them up and once again saves the freedom of the mind from the rednecks and the obscurantists.

Equality, too, is a subject on which it is easy to prevent any real discussion. All it takes is mouthing slogans about racism and the poor. If slogans do not come readily to mind, invective will do. This country has a sad history of real and sometimes brutal racial oppression, the effects of which last to this day. But shouting "racist" at anyone who raises questions about poverty programs is no help in addressing the real problems of America's ghettos and slums.

The poor we have always with us, and we have it from the Lord himself that whatever we have done or failed to do for them, his least brothers, we have done or failed to do it to him. That, he tells us, is the test by which he will judge us. But not everyone who says "The poor! the poor!" will enter the kingdom of heaven or deserve to be elected to public office in this world. Neither, of course, will everyone who preaches the virtues of self-reliance and free enterprise.

Slogans are useful for rallying us to a cause, but they are no substitute for thought. Sophists use them to keep us from thinking. But we can beat the sophists by insisting on being told what the slogans mean and why we should believe them.

Intrinsically Evil Acts

October 1986

Western culture, nourished on the Bible, once believed in God's foresight and providential care of man. Today, while many of us still live on trust in God, our prevailing culture does not. Whatever bows we may make in God's direction, in our public discourse we talk as if man were alone in the world and had no providence to rely on but his own.

Granted, there was never a Golden Age of Faith in which everyone surrendered the direction of his life to God's will. The Bible itself makes clear that the sons of Adam and the daughters of Eve have been more distinguished for their unfaithfulness to God than for their humble compliance with his will. Yet in reading the personal correspondence of people in earlier centuries, one cannot but be struck by the sincere and ingenuous faith in God's providence which they so often expressed.

To take a particularly striking example, when Sir Thomas More was in prison awaiting Henry VIII's decision about his fate, he wrote to his daughter Margaret: "And therefore, my own good daughter, do not let your mind be troubled over anything that shall happen to me in this world. Nothing can come but what God wills. And I am very sure that whatever that be, however bad it may seem, it shall indeed be the best."

Modern man no longer talks that way. (Who is this guy "modern man," you ask? Well, you know: he lives on your block, he went to college, he reads *Newsweek,* and he listens to talk shows on TV.) Even if he has not become an atheist—and usually he hasn't—he has effectively stopped believing in a personal God who created and governs the world.

Now, God's providence has long been recognized as mysterious; the Bible's Book of Job tells us that. So much happens in this world that to us seems senseless, purposeless, and downright cruel. Yet our pious ancestors were willing to believe that it made sense to God and fitted into his plan for our ultimate good. Our reluctance to express that kind of faith reveals a profound change in the modern mentality.

In *Natural Right and History* the late Leo Strauss explains what happened:

> The theological tradition recognized the mysterious character of Providence especially by the fact that God uses or permits evil for his good ends. It asserted, therefore, that man cannot take his bearings by God's providence but only by God's law, which simply forbids man to do evil. In proportion as the providential order came to be regarded as intelligible to man, and evil came to be regarded as evidently necessary or useful, the prohibition against doing evil lost its evidence. Hence various ways of action which were previously condemned as evil could now be regarded as good.

According to the theological tradition, man must accept what happens in history as God's will but he cannot take his bearings by it. We do not understand the mysterious ways in which God guides history to his ends, and so we cannot justify evil actions on the ground that they advance his plans. Our duty is simply to obey his moral will and leave the ultimate results of history to him.

It was the German philosopher Hegel, above all, who taught the West that philosophy can discern the divine plan in history. Consequently, he said, those who on moral grounds have resisted the working out of that plan may "stand higher in moral worth than those whose crimes have been turned into the means of realizing the purposes" that God intends, but their moral worth is only "a formal rectitude deserted by the living Spirit and by God." Alexander the Great, Julius Caesar, and Napoleon committed crimes on the grand scale, but they were justified because, albeit unwittingly, they furthered God's plans.

Karl Marx denied the existence of God but, taught by Hegel, he thought he knew the laws by which history necessarily operates. He therefore thought he knew the goal toward which history is inexorably moving: the classless society. He concluded that no actions are good or bad in themselves but are good or evil insofar as they hasten or impede the coming of the class-less society.

The skeptical West, unlike the Marxist East, is no longer confident that we know the laws of history, but it has clung to the notion that no action is right or wrong, good or bad in itself. Now the West feels that, not only do we not understand nor can we trust God's providential will for us, we do not know and therefore cannot obey his moral will either. We are here as on a darkling plain and must find our way through this world by our own light.

This post-Hegelian and post-Marxist skepticism has lately dawned on certain Catholic intellectuals as a new revelation. A typical example of their thinking is a letter to *Time* from Jerome A. Welch, publisher of *Catholicism Today,* in which he defends the Rev. Charles Curran's "valid objections to traditional Roman Catholic positions, including those on natural law and intrinsically evil acts, contraception, sterilization, homosexuality, masturbation, abortion and divorce." In opposition to this view, Pope John Paul II insists that "there exist acts which are always and everywhere in themselves illicit," and derives this proposition from "the metaphysics of creation which is at the center of all Christian thinking." In these conflicting statements on whether actions can be intrinsically and by their nature evil we see the fundamental issue in moral theology today, and we know how it got to be an issue.

The Logic of Contraception

November 1986

When the encyclical *Humanae Vitae* was published in 1968, it met with a storm of protest among theologians. Two years later, in the March-April 1970 issue of *The Critic*, John Giles Milhaven remarked:

> The dissent, which was motivated by the practical needs of married people, was justified ethically by the principle that deliberately willed sexual activity need not always be open to procreation. The principle is a direct contradiction of the classic natural law principle that not only excluded any use of contraception in marriage but was also the key principle prohibiting any deliberate sex outside of marriage. So far as I know, the theologians who rejected the natural law principle in order to permit contraception have found no convincing one to replace it to prohibit all extramarital sexual behavior.

Dr. Milhaven not long afterwards left the priesthood, married a wife, and took upon himself the burdens of married people. It cannot be said, therefore, that he was unsympathetic to their practical needs. The point he made in 1970, however, remains a valid one. So far as he knew, no one then and, so far as I know, very few now have even tried to find an argument that allows contraception in marriage but prohibits all sexual activity outside of marriage. It is doubtful if those who have tried have been convincing.

Certainly they have not convinced most of the dissenters from *Humanae Vitae*. The drift of liberal theological opinion has been toward permitting premarital and even extramarital sex. Granted, as the Rev. Charles Curran has carefully explained, it must be engaged in "responsibly," for sound reasons, and only in certain circumstances. Nonetheless, the position of the theological liberals is that what makes the sexual act outside of marriage wrong is not the nature of the act, because the act has no natural and morally obliging structure and purpose. It is only the intention with which and the circumstances in which the act is performed that can make it morally impermissible. Since liberal moral theology does not base its sexual morality on the nature of the act, it does not stop with allowing sexual intercourse, modified by contraception, both inside and outside of marriage. It also sees that the logic of contraception calls into question the idea that any particular kind of sexual act is the uniquely normal and permissible one.

Now, here is a question which is seldom confronted by pious liberals (they are the worst kind, because they piously refuse to admit unwelcome facts or to face what they regard as shocking and alarmist questions). The question is why, if it is permissible to sterilize the sexual act while performing it, it is nonetheless necessary to perform it with the organs of procreation, and with them alone. It is really no help to say that that is the only sexual act that decent Christian married couples want to perform. True enough, no doubt, but it does not tell us why other and more exotic kinds of sexual activity are wrong even for those who want to indulge in them and say that they find them helpful in cementing the bonds of love.

This is not a merely speculative academic question which may be discussed in courses on ethics and moral theology but is of no interest outside the classroom. It is, in fact, the issue that forces itself on our attention in debates on "gay rights," the transmission of AIDS, and the status of homosexuals in our society. The issue is whether homosexual relations are wrong in themselves and deserving of no protection by society or are merely the object of popular but irrational disgust.

Hardnosed liberals say flatly that there is nothing wrong with homosexual relations *per se* because no sexual relations of any kind are or can be wrong in themselves. Pious liberals confine themselves to deploring homosexual promiscuity while pleading for understanding for homosexuals. As between the two of them, we must prefer the hardnosed liberals, because they at least know what they mean and say it.

From their point of view, there is also no compelling reason why any other person at all, either of the opposite or one's own sex, need be brought into sexual activity. One may seek relief behind closed doors, with or without the help of *Playboy* and *Penthouse,* and one should not feel guilty about it. Whether it is a morally good thing to do depends entirely on one's intention and the circumstances, not on the nature of the act. So far has liberal moral theology gone, and it was only to have been expected. In the debate on contraception that took place in the Church of England in the 1920s, prior to the Lambeth Conference of 1930, conservative Anglicans predicted that all of the above consequences would follow from the acceptance of contraception; liberal Anglicans piously denied them. The evolution of sexual mores in the last sixty years has verified the conservatives' predictions, and the reason is not hard to see. To accept contraception as legitimate, even within marriage and for serious reasons, is to pull out the linchpin that holds the whole structure of Christian sexual morality together.

In *Humanae Vitae* Pope Paul VI restated the age-old teaching of the Church in carefully chosen words: "Each and every marriage act must remain open to the transmission of life." Whether transmission of life takes place or not — most often it does not — the openness remains the linchpin. Take it out and the structure of Christian sexual morality falls apart. In their own way, the dissenting theologians confirm that conclusion by what they are willing to accept as permissible today.

Argument Stoppers

January 1987

Freedom of speech and press, academic freedom, the pursuit of truth, pluralism, ecclesiology, and other interesting topics are much talked about these days, but they are seldom discussed in any meaningful way. In practice, their major use is not to furnish matter for discussion but to put an end to it. They are argument stoppers — words and phrases which have only to be recited and the argument is immediately over.

For, clearly, any adversary who is accused of violating academic freedom, or not appreciating pluralism, or holding an outdated ecclesiology, should put his tail between his legs and skulk off the field. If he does not leave but insists on staying around to debate, there is no point in continuing to argue with him because he has revealed a closed mind that is impervious to argument.

Academic freedom, for example, is supposed to guarantee the freedom to discuss any and all subjects. But academic freedom is not itself a subject of discussion among academics. They readily man the ramparts to defend their freedom. But they usually defend it as a given that needs no justification rather than with reasoned arguments which define the limits as well as the substance of the freedom.

Yet academic freedom could be discussed. It is a set of rights which has been established to serve certain intelligible purposes. One may therefore ask what those purposes are, what means serve them, and to what extent the purposes are in fact achieved, and what claims to academic freedom should be dismissed as spurious. We may also ask whether academic freedom is a univocal idea with a fixed, necessary, and unchangeable content that has the same meaning in every context, or whether its meaning depends on the kind of university to which the freedom is applied.

How do we know that the only permissible meaning of academic freedom is the one that prevails in secular liberal universities in the United States in the latter half of the twentieth century? Could it have a meaning adapted to the nature and self-chosen function of universities devoted to developing particular philosophies or theologies? If not, why not? These questions could be discussed, but they are not discussed because to raise questions about academic freedom is taken as an attack on it. Academic freedom, as the term is most frequently used, is an argument stopper.

So is the pursuit of truth which is alleged to be the end that academic freedom serves. One cannot help being a little amused when what goes on in universities is described baldly as the pursuit of truth. It is not that we do not know scholars of great integrity who dedicate their lives to seeking the truth in their particular disciplines. The conception of truth may be and often is narrow — truth is what is found in a test tube or comes out of a computer — but their devotion to it is genuine. But in large areas of thought, and those the most important ones for human life, academics seem to feel that commitment to truth would be incompatible with their professional integrity.

In theology, philosophy, literature, and moral, social, and political theory, ideas may be considered interesting, creative, even exciting, but only an obscurantist would make an issue of their truth. A steady stream of articles and books proposing fresh approaches and revisionist theories flows into the marketplace, stimulated in part by the need to "publish or perish" (for what is more publishable than a new revisionist view of something or other?). A stronger impetus is supplied by the primacy which a liberal society gives to freedom over truth.

Leading liberal theorists, in ethics and in politics, base their defense of liberty on skepticism. They insist that no alleged truth can be allowed to limit the individual's freedom to choose his own goals and fashion his own version of the good life. In the disciplines which most directly influence how people think, feel, and act, the liberal academy may ask, What is truth? But like jesting Pilate, it will not stay for an answer. As with academic freedom, the pursuit of truth is chiefly useful as an argument stopper; even those who don't believe truth is attainable can use its pursuit to shut up importunate questioners.

In Catholic circles it is now customary to put down critics by accusing them of nostalgia for the past, a pre-Vatican II mentality, a neo-Scholastic mode of thought, and insensitivity to "pluralism." Whatever ideas the critics rely upon as the premises of their arguments are easily disposed of as culturally conditioned, time-bound, and lacking in historical consciousness. (These are phrases, dear reader, that one learns in graduate school, and if you had gone to graduate school, you'd know them too.) One may reply that nothing is more culturally conditioned and time-bound than the secular enlightenment of our day — but the reply will not be heard because the argument is already over and the audience has gone home.

Does it follow that academic freedom, the pursuit of truth, the sociology of knowledge, pluralism, ecclesiology, and the Second Vatican Council are not to be taken seriously? No, they are serious subjects and should be seriously discussed. All that follows is that we should refuse to be buffaloed by question-begging putdowns and argument stoppers. The point we must insist on is simply that reciting certain phrases as ritual incantations does not foreclose discussion. If that point is established, we may be able to get on with intelligent argument about the important subjects behind the phrases.

A Divorce Culture

February 1987

In June 1986 the people of the Irish Republic, in a referendum, rejected a proposed constitutional amendment which would have permitted legal divorce. The London *Daily Telegraph* opined that the "massive vote against the introduction of divorce" manifested that "obsession of the Irish people with the past rather than the future" which is "both their national curse and a substantial part of their national charm." Des Hanafin, a member of the Irish Senate who led the campaign against the divorce amendment, had a briefer and more perceptive explanation: "The people did not want a divorce culture."

The key term in Senator Hanafin's comment is "culture." A culture is the set of customs, conventions, attitudes, and beliefs that shapes both the way in which people understand themselves and their society and the way in which they expect one another to act. A divorce culture not only allows divorce but affects a whole people's understanding of marriage—and their expectations of its permanence.

The liberal individualist mind, focused on the individual hard case, sees divorce only as a necessary escape hatch from a failed marriage. Such a mind does not, perhaps cannot, see the extent to which the solution to the hard case becomes the social norm, as it has become in this country, not only with divorce, but with contraception and abortion and may yet become with social acceptance of homosexuality and euthanasia.

The significant issue, however, is not whether a case can be made for some divorce, some abortion, or some euthanasia. It is whether we can maintain a society whose culture is increasingly permeated by the assumptions of liberal individualism. "For liberal individualism," Alasdair MacIntyre explains in *After Virtue,* "a community is simply an arena in which individuals pursue their own self-chosen conception of the good life, and political institutions exist to provide that degree of order which makes such self-determined activity possible." This individualism is the root from which spring our changing attitudes on the particular issues listed above.

The freedom of the individual, however, can come at a high price for other individuals and can reshape our culture with less than happy results. Feminism, for example, is a late-blooming variety of liberal individualism, but even the feminist columnist Joan Beck has expressed some misgivings over the consequences of recent advances in sexual freedom for men and women alike.

"Women have been big losers in the changes in sexual mores in the last two decades," says Ms. Beck. "No-fault divorce laws, adopted in almost all states since 1970, have turned out to be enormously unfair to women and children. They have pushed millions of mothers and young children into poverty. . . . The big increase in single, female heads of households is a major reason the poverty rate remains so high."

It is a commonplace in the press today that almost one marriage in every two will end in divorce, with the consequences Ms. Beck noticed, not to mention the psychological damage done to children. In this situation it seems silly to talk as if all there were at issue was the right of autonomous individuals to escape from unhappy marriages. One could more realistically argue that the American divorce culture does not allow young people to marry in the sense of making a binding, lifelong commitment to each other, does not support them in the facsimile of marriage into which they do enter, and encourages them to break it up when the going gets tough. The culture deprives millions of young Americans of a real choice to marry.

After a while, we may expect, they will cease to care whether they marry or not. That has already happened to a large extent in Sweden, according to David Popenoe, a professor of sociology at Rutgers, the State University of New Jersey, who has been a visiting professor at the University of Stockholm. In an article distributed by the Swedish Information Service in New York, he says: "The Swedish marriage rate is now the lowest in the industrial world, and the non-marital cohabitation rate is the highest." But whether Swedish couples marry or just live together, they very often don't stay together, for "the rate of family dissolution in Sweden may also have become the highest in the industrial world."

"Many Swedes (especially younger Swedes)," says Prof. Popenoe, "see little if any significance" in "the decline in marriage and the rise of non-marital cohabitation." Some Swedish experts, he reports, attribute this indifference toward marriage to "government policy since the change in divorce laws of the early 1970s," as a result of which government is "officially 'neutral' between the two forms of living together."

Sweden's divorce rate "falls just behind that of the Western world's acknowledged divorce leader, the United States." But then, divorce assumes that a couple has been married, and in Sweden, about one quarter of all couples don't marry, and the rate of "family dissolution" is higher among non-married than married couples, so Sweden may outstrip the United States after all.

"One could think of many such non-marital unions as 'trial marriages,'" says Popenoe, "in which the step of formal marriage is taken only after the union has matured and the couple desires to signify a certain permanence to the relationship," but in fact, "the marriage rate continues to drop while the divorce rate continues to climb."

All of which suggests that the Irish voted the way they did, not because they were obsessed with the past, but because they had looked at the present in America and the future in Sweden and decided they didn't want it.

The Methodology Is the Message

March 1987

At a political science convention which I attended some years ago, one of the speakers mentioned toward the end of his talk that the education code of every state in the Union gives the public schools a mandate to form moral character. In the discussion period that followed a young woman with a marked Southern accent protested: "Ah am shocked by what Ah just heard — it goes against everything Ah learned in graduate school!"

She had studied political science in a graduate school and had been taught a methodology based on the philosophy known as positivism. This philosophy makes a radical distinction between "facts," which can be established by the rational methods of science, and "values," i.e., judgments about good and evil, which are beyond the competence of science to establish. Since positivism recognizes only science as an exercise of reason, it regards judgments of value as expressions of feeling or emotion: to say, "this is good," means nothing more than "I approve of this," which is to say, "I like it." Political science therefore must look upon judgments about moral character as unscientific, beyond the scope of reason, and out of place in public schools.

That young lady was a good example of the kind of person who should be strongly discouraged from going to graduate school — bright enough to master a methodology but not intelligent enough to criticize it. For such people a methodology easily becomes identified with reason itself and is taken as the sole and only road to truth.

Lewis S. Feuer explains in *Spinoza and the Rise of Liberalism:*

> Whenever a new "method" has been proposed in the history of thought, its converts and proponents have seen it as the promise of a new age. Bacon with his inductive method, Descartes with his

geometrical method, Hegel's dialectical method, Spencer's evolutionary method, Russell's mathematical logic, the logical empiricists with their semantical analysis all have been regarded as prophets whose insight when extended to social and human issues would bring the final solutions. Every method has had its methodological madness.

That passage came to mind as I read "Jesus Among the Historians," an article by the Rev. John P. Meier, professor of New Testament at the Catholic University of America and general editor of the *Catholic Biblical Quarterly*, which appeared in the *New York Times Book Review* on December 21, 1986. Fr. Meier went to a graduate school and learned the historical method. The purpose of his article is to explain what this method can tell us about the "historical Jesus."

He is aware, however, of the method's limitations. The "historical Jesus" is not to be identified with the Jesus who existed in time and space but is only "my fragmentary hypothetical reconstruction of Jesus through historical research," and on this reconstruction, he says, "my faith in Christ does not rise or fall." He can and does believe many things about Jesus as Christ, and believes them as true. He does not think, however, that these beliefs can be established by the scientific method of history.

One may agree with him that this recognition of the limits of science is "paradoxically liberating." It must come as a relief to realize that I am free to believe in truths that lie beyond what science can prove, precisely because the scientific method as we now understand it is so limited in what it can accomplish.

On the other hand, it is not entirely clear whether Fr. Meier fully appreciates the limits of science. The Catholic approach to the historical study of the earthly life of Jesus, he says, has one advantage over a conservative Protestant approach — "the clear distinction between what is known through historical research and reason and what is affirmed in faith. The historical Jesus belongs solely to the former realm."

One should not press a man's words too hard and make him mean what he did not intend to say. Still one may point out that Fr. Meier's words seem to identify reason with historical research, therefore with a particular conception of both reason and scientific method. This conception has its roots in the triumphs of early modern physical science in the seventeenth century and has saddled us ever since with a particularly narrow and truncated idea of what human reason is and what it can do.

The very distinction between the Christ of faith and the Jesus of history is not of Catholic origin and did not spring from a Catholic understanding of the relationship between faith and reason. Catholic thought has always recognized the difference between what can be known by reason and what can only be accepted by faith in God's revelation. But, like the distinction between facts and values, the distinction between the Christ of faith and the Jesus of history is not one that fits easily into a Catholic mode of thought.

It was, in fact, the result of an attempt by nineteenth-century German liberal Protestants to save faith in Christ from the corrosive effects of Enlightenment rationalism. Yes, they said to the rationalists, we will give you the Jesus of history as the only one who can be rationally known, but we will keep the Christ of faith because we have never allowed reason to play a role in faith anyhow. The distinction between the Christ of faith and the Jesus of history is harmless enough if we keep clearly in mind that the Jesus of history is only the hypothetical reconstruction that can be arrived at by a certain limited methodology. But the general reader can hardly be blamed if he sees in it an invitation to choose between a Christ who cannot rationally be believed in and a Jesus who is not worth believing in. We may doubt whether that is what the New Testament has in mind.

Order in the Soul

March 1987

In Europe during the Middle Ages, the cure of souls was public, the cure of bodies private," says Michael Walzer in *Spheres of Justice.* "Among medieval Christians," he explains, "eternity was a socially recognized need, and every effort was made to see . . . that every Christian had an equal chance at salvation and eternal life: hence, a church in every parish, regular services, catechism for the young, compulsory communion, and so on."

One could correct Walzer by pointing out that, while medieval knowledge of medicine was primitive, the same Church which cared for souls also cared for bodies by providing for teaching and applying such medical knowledge as there was. The universities which the Church founded had Faculties of Medicine and, although medieval hospitals could do little more than keep patients warm, dry, and nourished, it was the Church that ran the hospitals. Nevertheless Walzer is right in saying that for the Middle Ages the immortal soul was more important than the mortal body.

The situation, as he also says, has been reversed as "we have lost confidence in the cure of souls, and we have come increasingly to believe, even to be obsessed with, the cure of bodies." There has been a major shift of attitude in our Western culture, with the result that "as eternity receded in the popular consciousness, longevity moved to the fore." If, after death, there is no eternal life in the next world, it becomes of supreme importance to remain alive as long as possible in this one.

But we must immediately modify that statement because our concern for longevity has not reduced the suicide rate nor will it check the growing campaign for legalized euthanasia. Modern men want, not mere life, but life in health. The health, moreover, must not only be physical but psychological. Life, to be worth living, must not only be long and healthy but also enjoyable, as the current discussion of AIDS reveals.

Our contemporary culture, officially at least, does not care what kind of sexual activity you engage in so long as you don't smoke cigarettes while doing it. Smoking, you see, is dangerous to your health. So is promiscuous sexual intercourse because it is the chief means of transmitting AIDS. The way to avoid getting AIDS would therefore seem to be "no sex" but our society instead promotes "safe sex," which supposedly allows the promiscuous to eat their cake and have it too.

We may infer from this that health is not modern society's *summum bonum* or highest good to which all other goods must be subordinated. Greatly though our society values health and however much money we are willing to spend on it, health is desirable less for its own sake than as the necessary condition for that subjective state of satisfaction that is our true end in life. The highest human good, then, is pleasure.

Yet we may doubt this proposition, too, on the ground that there is no *summum bonum,* no highest good which can serve as the organizing goal for the life of man individually and collectively. The only goal of life is a negative one: the flight from pain.

Jean le Rond d'Alembert expressed this belief at the high tide of the Enlightenment in his introduction to the famous *Encyclopédie* of Diderot, which was published in Paris in 1751. "Such is the misfortune of the human condition," he wrote, "that pain is our most lively sentiment." Instead of wasting time trying to define the highest good and supreme end of human life, he concluded, philosophers "would have known our nature better if they had been content to limit their definition of the sovereign good of the present life to exemption from pain." Progress, on this view of life, becomes a movement away from pain and from those things that cause pain, chief among which are poverty and disease. It does not consist in pursuing the good.

The movement away from known evils rather than toward a knowable and objective good has been characteristic of the modern idea of progress. We can agree on what we are trying to get away from — starvation, polio, cancer, AIDS, etc. — but we find it impossible to agree on where we are trying to go.

If we add to poverty and disease such psychological states as boredom, frustration, and resentment as causes of pain, we begin to understand why alcoholism, drug abuse, and compulsive sex are increasing rather than fading out in the progressive societies. Those who become enslaved to these addictions are indeed pursuing pleasure, but they pursue it so avidly in order to fill an inner emptiness that has become too painful to live with. In a more subtle way the same may be, and often is, true of those major sources of disorder in society, the craving for wealth and the drive for power.

If one reads the "social encyclicals" of the modern popes, beginning with Leo XIII's *Rerum Novarum* in 1891, one is struck by their repeated insistence that there will be no cure for the disorders of society unless men return to belief in God as their supreme goal and final end. The popes, of course, have been voices crying in the wilderness, easily dismissed by both Left and Right as unrealistic. Yet we must ask if they are not right in this: there is no order either in the individual soul or in society without an ordering principle, and that can only be a valid purpose in life. The only adequate purpose is attaining a true and supreme spiritual good; all other purposes fail and produce disorder if they are taken as ultimate. The care of souls really is more important than the care of bodies.

Going to Hell

April 1987

On the Last Day, when the living and the dead are judged, they will not be judged by me. You find that a consoling thought, I'm sure. So do I, because I don't feel up to passing the final judgment on anyone, let alone the whole human race.

Nevertheless, the human race will be judged. Each of us must hear from the lips of him who can pronounce them the words, "Come, you blessed of my Father, inherit the kingdom prepared for you from the foundation of the world," or "Depart from me, you cursed, into the eternal fire prepared for the devil and his angels." We have it from the Lord himself that the latter "will go away into eternal punishment, but the righteous into eternal life."

Now, however, we have it from Professor Martin E. Marty, a church historian at the University of Chicago, that the idea of eternal punishment in hell is not "culturally available." That is to say, we can no longer appeal to the fear of hell to get people to do anything or to abstain from anything, because almost no one really believes in hell anymore.

There is no denying that what Professor Marty says is true of an indeterminate but surely large number of people today. But it is curious that it should be true in a society in which most people profess to be theists and even Christians.

It is not strange, of course, that those who do not believe in God do not believe in hell, either. (There are others who do believe in God but not in the immortality of the soul or the resurrection of the body. Life in this world, they hold, is God's gift but it is his only gift, and when it ends, we cease totally to be.) What is strange is that those who hope, however vaguely, for eternal life with God would take it as a given with no alternative.

Human beings are good enough at creating hells on earth

that it should occur to them as a distinct possibility that they may be headed for something similar in life after death. Lenin, Stalin, Mao, Fidel Castro, and Pol Pot may sincerely have intended to bring about heaven on earth, but in fact they produced the opposite. The small-scale but brutal criminals about whom we read every day in the newspapers have not turned New York, Chicago, or Los Angeles into the earthly paradise. Others — active alcoholics, drug addicts, men and women enslaved to compulsive sex drives — may be more to be pitied than censured, but they make life a hell for themselves and others while they are here.

Nothing in our experience in this world assures us that all stories must have happy endings. No empirical evidence gives us ground for believing that, if there is life after death, we are bound to live it in heaven. The evidence that meets our eyes suggests the contrary.

We have an understandable resistance to the idea of an eternity in hell, but our repugnance for it is sentimental rather than intellectual. "To understand everything is to forgive everything" is a famous phrase but, as George Bernard Shaw commented, it is the devil's sentimentality. Human wickedness is real, God knows — and we know it too.

But, we feel, nothing that a human being can do is so wicked as to merit punishment forever, and a good God would not inflict it. This objection, however, assumes that we are born saved and do not need to achieve salvation. But we are not born saved; the Bible tells us that we are born in sin. Leaving aside the doctrine of original sin, it is clear that we are born immature. Small children are enormously appealing but they are also enormously demanding and self-centered. If they do not develop past that stage as they grow up, they turn out to be monsters. Even in purely this-worldly terms, we all need salvation from our innate selfishness, and it is not guaranteed in advance. It is a mistake to think that God could have created us in heaven, with salvation already achieved, and that it was hardhearted of him to make us pass a test to get what he could have given us gratis in the first place. It is a child's view of life to look upon all standards of performance as imposed on us from without by Mommy, Daddy, teacher, the parish priest, the cop on the corner and, behind them all, that Super-cop, God. The standards of performance are given to us from within by our nature as human beings.

We are indeed creatures who have nothing that God did not give us. But we are free creatures endowed with intelligence and the power of choice. President John F. Kennedy was fond of the French aphorism, *gouverner, c'est choisir* — to govern is to choose. More generally, to live a human life is to choose. God's grace gives us the inspiration and the power to choose the good, but God cannot choose for us. He only makes the final and infallible judgment on what we have freely made of ourselves.

"We must picture Hell," says C. S. Lewis in *The Screwtape Letters,* "as a state . . . where everyone has a grievance, and where everyone lives the deadly serious passions of envy, self importance, and resentment." Such persons are in hell because they have made themselves incapable of heaven. As a seventeenth-century archbishop of Canterbury explained, "The pleasures of Heaven itself could signify no good or happiness to that man who is not so disposed as to take pleasure in them."

Culturally available or not, the thought that we determine our eternal destiny for good or ill is worth reflecting on in this Easter season. We shall rejoice the more in the resurrection as the pledge of our salvation if we understand clearly what we are saved from and how much we need a Savior from it.

Ladies in Writing

May 1987

A year or so from now we shall find ourselves listening to an updated set of New Testament readings at Mass. If we listen carefully, we'll notice that these readings avoid using the word "man" in any context where it refers to both the human sexes. No longer shall we hear that man does not live by bread alone; it will have become "One does not live by bread alone."

To say that man does not live by bread alone, you see, implies that woman does, because the word "man" is "exclusive." It never includes women as well as men, even though you and I and just about everyone else always thought it did.

How did this piece of ideological feminism get into our liturgy? It was put there by a committee of scholars whom the American Catholic bishops commissioned to revise the flat and pedestrian translation of the New Testament that we have been using for liturgical readings since 1970. According to press reports, the committee has devised a more dignified and less banal translation, but it seems also to have fallen into the feminist trap.

Perhaps it would be accurate to say that it jumped in. The committee's secretary, the Rev. Stephen J. Hartdegen, says that one of the most difficult issues the committee faced was how to translate texts that were seen as "discriminating against women." To avoid this invidious discrimination, the committee resolved to use the noun "man" and the pronoun "he" only when referring to persons of the male sex. In so deciding, they accepted the feminist definition of "man."

It is fixed in the feminist mind that "man" means and can only mean "male." The trouble with that idea is not only that it is false. Even worse, it makes it impossible to speak English coherently. The effort to speak English as feminists would have us do leads to Henry Higgins' cry of rage in *My Fair Lady:* "By rights she should be taken out and hung for the cold-blooded murder of the English tongue!"

The original and root meaning of the syllable "man" in all the Teutonic languages was "human being," and so it remains to this day. English is exceptional only in that precisely the same set of letters, m-a-n, denotes both the human species and the male sex of the species. (German, for example, uses two words from the same root, *Mensch*, human being, and *Mann*, male human being.) In English, "woman" is "man" with a prefix meaning "female." Only a feminist can believe that a woman is a female male; the rest of us know that she is a female man, i.e., human being.

Fr. Hartdegen knows this, too. "The generic sense of 'man' is traditional in English," he admits, but "many today reject it." Many? Some nuns, lawyers, academics, and other female yuppies reject it, that is true. But they are a relatively small class of professional people who identify themselves with their careers and have convinced themselves that allowing "man" to be used in the generic sense blocks their progress in their careers. The overwhelming majority of English speakers of both sexes couldn't care less about "exclusive" language and will not take the trouble to speak the new "inclusive" language.

For to use feminist Newspeak consistently is a lot of trouble. We must practice an awkward, cumbersome, and ultimately silly way of speaking English in order to refer to the human species without ever using the only name we have for it: man. It is like the children's game whose point is to answer questions without using a certain word. "Green," let us say, is the forbidden word. Q.: What color is grass? A.: A shade between yellow and blue.

This is fun if we are playing a game. But it is a tiresome nuisance if we are forced, day in and day out, to resort to such barbarisms as chairperson, policeperson, fireperson, and even (God deliver us) clergyperson, or to say "he or she" every time we use the third person singular pronoun with a general reference. Yet if we are to satisfy the feminists, we must speak this clumsy and stilted language. Either that, or we must resort to endless circumlocution like the Faculty Statutes of my own university, which avoid personal pronouns by repeating the noun, "the individual," every time a pronoun would be called for.

Needless to say, the statutes read like a document drawn up by a committee of pixilated schoolteachers.

Feminists may succeed in compelling bureaucrats—who don't speak English anyhow—to use "non-sexist" language. But why are our bishops giving in to them? The mushy-headed cleric who is all heart and no brain is a familiar figure, but he usually does not become a bishop. From bishops we may reasonably expect the intelligence to recognize nonsense when they see it and the courage to stand up to it.

The temptation of the busy administrator, however, is to placate a clamorous and persistent pressure group by making what he regards as a mere token concession to it. The row, after all, is only about a word, and the word is not worth fighting about, so let them have their word. From now on we shall not say, "Man does not live by bread alone," but "One does not live by bread alone," and that should shut these irksome ladies up.

But whether going along with them when they are making fools of themselves is really doing them a favor, and whether in fact it will shut them up, are questions whose answer only the future will reveal. In the meantime, let me suggest one more change in the liturgy: the response to the readings at Mass should be, "Speak English yet!"

Lost in the Cosmos

June 1987

If you want to know what is wrong with the Catholic Church, you read the *National Catholic Reporter.* You need go no farther. In fact, you really don't have to go that far. Almost any metropolitan daily or weekly newsmagazine has a number of disaffected Catholics on its staff who seldom miss a chance to point out the Church's deficiencies and defects.

One of them, not long ago, reporting on the exodus of young people from Ireland, remarked that it was not only the country's depressed economy that made them leave, but its repressive atmosphere. He quoted one young lady as saying that when the predominantly Catholic Irish people rejected a constitutional amendment to legalize divorce last year, she realized that she had had it with her native land. Not yet married, she could not abide the thought of not being able to get divorced. So brightly does the love of liberty burn in certain youthful hearts.

That the Church opposes liberty is the ordinary burden of the complaint against her. The liberty of which she unjustly deprives her suffering children usually turns out to be sexual freedom. The reason for the Church's harsh attitude, we are told, is a fear and hatred of sex that dates back to St. Augustine (or is it to St. Paul?), and prevents her from understanding modern men and women's healthy and guilt-free acceptance of their own sexuality.

But more interesting than what ex-Catholics reject is what the post-Christian world they have joined has to offer. Freedom to choose a lifestyle, yes, but beyond that, what? Well, success and money, of course; also devotion to approved progressive causes, and an interest in the arts. (Man does not live on sex alone.) But not much in the way of truth to believe in, or hope to live for, and none but human love to live on.

Post-Christianity is mostly a negation.

It is intriguing to speculate on what makes negation so attractive to the modern mind. We must not underestimate the allurements of the world, the flesh, and the devil: they explain more than intellectual difficulties do. But there is a deeper reason, I believe, for contemporary loss of faith.

Part of it is a hatred of all authority, a hatred rooted in the modern ideal of the autonomous self. Modern man, formed by the liberal tradition, can see nothing in the exercise of authority but the imposition of one will on another.

John H. Hallowell, in *The Decline of Liberalism as an Ideology,* says that liberalism in its original seventeenth-century form combined two elements: "first, the belief that society is composed of atomic, autonomous individuals; and, second, the belief that there are certain eternal truths transcending individuals and independent of either individual will or desire." Because they were confident that reason could recognize these transcendent truths, liberal societies were able to regard moral judgments and civil laws as exercises of reason and not merely as the imposition of the will of some people on others. But as liberal faith in reason's ability to rise above will and appetite waned, the liberal conception of society became that of a collection of individual wills guided at best by enlightened self-interest. Hence the hatred of authority, particularly ecclesiastical, but even of the authority of the democratic state.

Liberal societies today grant reason the ability to determine facts, discern patterns of causal relationship among facts, and figure out the most efficient means of achieving desired ends. Beyond that reason cannot go. Because it is saddled with this truncated conception of the scope of reason, the modern mind has an inborn dullness toward the very idea of transcendent truth. The notion of a truth beyond what meets the eye or is discovered by the scientific method is simply opaque to the typical mind of our age. Such a mind does not give a different answer from the Christian one to the question of the meaning and purpose of life; it does not even ask the question.

A number of sociologists have seen the roots of modern secularism in the industrialization of society, which applied to human work the purely instrumental conception of reason described above. Industrialism mechanizes work and "rationalizes" it by relentlessly pursuing the most efficient means of maximizing production while minimizing costs. The workers themselves become role-players in a mechanized process. Society as a whole is governed by bureaucracies which perform specified functions in accordance with impersonal rules. As Bryan R.Wilson puts it in *Religion in Sociological Perspective:*

> A modern social system is increasingly conceived as operating without virtues; it becomes a neutral, detached, objective, rational co-ordination of role performances. The system induces those who actually man the roles — that is, human beings — to behave as if they had neither virtues nor vices. The pressure is towards the neutralization of human personality so that roles might be performed with ever greater calculability.

We live, the sociologists tell us, in a world whose consciousness has been formed by these conceptions of man and his work. It is little wonder that the staple concerns of religion — good and evil, virtue and vice, the meaning and purpose of life come to seem irrelevant in such a world — or that the human self now feels itself to be, as Walker Percy says, lost in the cosmos.

"Imposing" Moral Beliefs

July 1987

New York's archbishop, John Cardinal O'Connor, once wrote a pointed and pungent criticism of an unnamed public official for taking the waffling stand on the abortion issue which is now customary among certain Catholic politicians. This politician professed to have his own "deep reservations about abortion," but said, "I will not impose my own moral beliefs on others," apparently in the belief that abortion is a matter of purely private morality. The cardinal commented that this was George Orwell's Newspeak, a species of doubletalk "deliberately constructed for political purposes."

As the cardinal pointed out, this public official (like many another) "seems not to hesitate at all in 'imposing' his moral beliefs on others in regard to other highly contested public policy issues." It is only in regard to abortion (and certain other delicate subjects) that he develops scruples. Yet abortion raises the question of the worth of human life, and if that is not an issue of public policy, what is?

It does not cease to be a public issue because it is a moral issue. As another Catholic politician once remarked, "Of course you can legislate morality; there really isn't anything else to legislate." No one believes that more devoutly, most of the time, than the politicians who "refuse to impose their moral beliefs on others." Listen to their rhetoric and notice how often it is couched in terms of respect for rights, justice, charity, mercy, compassion, and other moral virtues.

Yet they use this moralistic language to justify public policy proposals which some people object to in equally moralistic terms as unjust and violative of *their* rights. There is no getting away from it: if justice is to be done at all, the morality of the larger and, we may hope, sounder part of the community will necessarily be imposed on some people who disagree with it.

No culture can last if it concedes a veto power to every group in its midst that rejects the culture's norms.

Our American political culture, however, is in a fair way of granting that veto power in what are now called "social issues." This trend is particularly evident in the Democratic Party. So, at any rate, political scientist Jo Freeman suggests in an article in the *Political Science Quarterly* (No. 3, 1986), in which she maintains that the Democratic and Republican parties have distinct political cultures.

The Republicans, she says, "have a unitary party in which great deference is paid to the leadership, activists are expected to be 'good soldiers,' and competing loyalties are frowned upon." Consequently, they conceive of representation on the model of "a trustee who pursues the long-range best interests of the represented."

To the Democrats, on the other hand, "representation does not mean the articulation of a single coherent program for the betterment of the nation but the inclusion of all relevant groups and viewpoints. Their concept of representation is delegatory, in which accurate reflection of the parts is necessary to the welfare of the whole." For this reason, she adds, "the party is very responsive to any groups, including such pariahs as gays and lesbians, that claim to be left out." I will add that this responsiveness gives homosexuals, feminists, pro-abortionists, and assorted minorities a veto on Democratic nominations. That veto power has more to do with the squeamishness of politicians about imposing their beliefs on others than with any qualms of conscience.

The Democratic Party historically has performed a necessary role, being the avenue through which groups ignored or rejected by the Republicans could make their way into the nation's public life. But the present structure of the party leaves the Democrats paralyzed by political dread where certain moral issues are involved. Dominated by their liberal wing, they are unable to admit that any standards are available for judging what makes for the moral health of the nation. To admit such standards, liberals allege, would deny the equality of all moral beliefs and would impose the beliefs of some on others.

But by rejecting the idea of moral truth and refusing to

pass judgment on the validity of moral beliefs, liberals undermine democracy itself. What is the meaning of such basic democratic concepts as human rights or of such ringing phrases as the dignity of the human person, if we cannot allow ourselves to determine their content lest we impose the moral beliefs of some on others? More concretely, can we sustain the culture on which democracy depends if we refuse to decide such issues as the sanctity of life, elementary sexual morality, and the value of the stable monogamous family as the foundation of society?

Ideally, the democratic process is a serious and intelligent public debate on matters of public policy. (Yes, Virginia, we all know what it usually is in practice.) These are matters which inevitably involve issues of public morality. Because the process is democratic, all individuals and groups may take part in it. But because it concerns the *res publica,* the people's welfare, it arrives at public conclusions which at least in part are moral conclusions. The public cannot forever duck them on the ground that it does not want to impose its moral beliefs.

Selective Listening

October 1987

"**I** may attribute all the changes of religion in the world to one and the same cause, and that is, unpleasing priests." I read that line when I was a seminarian, in Thomas Hobbes's *Leviathan,* which was first published in 1651, and I took it to heart. My function as a priest would not be to drive people away from the Church by my selfishness, greed, arrogance, and insensitivity (though no doubt I have often done just that). This resolve was constantly reinforced by seminary professors, spiritual directors, and retreat masters who urged us not to break the bruised reed or quench the smoking flax but always to be understanding and as kind as possible.

When, therefore, in later life I heard lapsed or ex-Catholics tell how they had been driven away from their religion by harsh parents, tyrannical priests, sadistic brothers, and nutty nuns, I was both outraged at the oppressors and sympathetic with the victims. Today, however, having listened to hundreds of these stories, I find them harder and harder to take seriously.

There have been, and still are, parents, priests, and teachers who make religion consist mainly in the threat of punishment. But I doubt if they are the whole explanation, or any large part of the explanation, of lapses from Catholic faith and practice. Such "explanations" leave out at least half of the story, and the more important half at that.

There is the broadcasting station and there is the receiving set. Distorted messages can result from either of the two. When the receiving set is our television and the picture becomes wavy, or when it is our radio and the sound is marred by static, we do not jump to the conclusion that the broadcasting station must be sending out a defective signal. We are more likely to blame the defect on our TV or radio and to conclude that something is wrong with the receiving mechanism.

It is only when we ourselves are the receiving set that we instinctively blame all defective and distorted signals on the broadcasting station. It does not occur to us that we are getting a bad signal because that is all we are capable of picking up.

Imagine (or remember) a stubborn, self-willed but fearful child who wants what he wants when he wants it but lives in a world of overawing adult power. Out of the whole message that well-intentioned parents, priests, and teachers try to give him, what part will he actually hear? Too often, only the words "no" and "punishment." There is more to the message, much more, but he doesn't get it — and may never get it.

If he never listens to the complete message, he will remain an embittered ex-Catholic. If he happens to have talent, he will write novels about the horrors of a Catholic childhood, which will get favorable mention in the book review section of the Sunday newspapers. But he will never understand the religion he has rejected.

There are other Catholics who do not hate the Church and do not leave it, but who listen to it with highly selective hearing. The American press, prepping us against the pope's exhortations, assures us that these people are now the majority of American Catholics and that they love the Church while feeling free to disagree with it.

They love the Church when it gives them a warm feeling of community, but when it makes them feel uncomfortable, they stop listening. If they can't ignore the message entirely, they blame it on the broadcasting station. It does not occur to them that there might be something wrong with their receiving sets.

This confidence in one's own judgment, journalists tell us, is highest among college-educated Catholics who have learned to think for themselves. One gets the impression, however, that when these highly intelligent college graduates think, they think about sex. The sex-related subjects of contraception, divorce, the celibacy of the clergy, and the ordination of women are the most frequently reported topics of "dissent." But it may be that these are merely the subjects on which journalists are most eager to report the views of Catholics. Besides, some enlightened Catholics do have wider interests: when they aren't thinking about sex, they think about Nicaragua.

In any case, it is always the broadcasting station that is wrong. Despite their college education — or because of it — these freethinking Catholics seem unaware that the way they think is very much the product of contemporary American culture. "The American," said the French writer Raymond Aron, "believes that when there's a problem, there's always a solution." Contraception, remarriage after divorce, marriage for the clergy, and the ordination of women solve what have been defined as problems. The American mind, being utilitarian, screens out opposition to these solutions, just as it is beginning to screen out criticism of surrogate motherhood, genetic engineering, infanticide, and euthanasia, which also solve problems.

If you think I exaggerate, try asking a Catholic college class what they think of the Chinese government's policy of allowing only one child to a family. Notice how many of the answers are based on the utilitarian argument that China cannot afford more than one child per family. Then ask yourself what chance a broadcasting station has against receiving sets like that.

Why Anything Goes

November 1987

One can say — if only for the sake of starting an argument — that liberal democracy in a pluralistic society is an endless but fruitless search for the lowest common denominator that can serve as society's moral bond. The more pluralistic the society, however, the more difficult it is to find a common denominator.

Let us try to explain the problem crudely and over-simply, but not entirely inaccurately. We did away with state churches in this country so that all Protestants could feel at home in it. We de-Protestantized the country so that Catholics, too, could feel at home in it. We have de-christianized the country to make Jews feel welcome, then de-religionized it so that atheists and agnostics may feel equally welcome. Now we are de-moralizing the country so that deviants from accepted moral norms will not feel excluded. The lowest common denominator, we have discovered, is like the horizon, always approached but never reached.

As our consensus on basic principles of belief and morals evanesces, we fall back on shared material welfare as the sole social bond that it is both possible and necessary to maintain. We are a national community because we guarantee that no member of society will lack the minimal resources for living, but we leave the goals of life to individual judgment and choice. Freedom of choice in all matters that do not directly and seriously affect society's material welfare becomes society's highest ideal. As Justice Harry A. Blackmun put it in his dissenting opinion in the 1986 Georgia sodomy law case, "depriving individuals of their right to choose for themselves how to conduct their intimate relationships poses a far greater threat to the values most deeply rooted in our Nation's history than tolerance of nonconformity could ever do."

Contemporary liberalism thus manages to be at once both

115

individualistic and statist. This ambivalence explains the otherwise puzzling spectacle of liberals who are simultaneously furiously indignant at anyone who is judged suspect of imposing his moral beliefs on others and grimly determined to use the agencies of the state to impose their vision of welfare on all the institutions of society. Their vision is of a religiously, spiritually, and morally neutral welfare state which confers its benefits equally on all the members of society without distinction of race, creed, age, sex, or sexual preference, and which prevents private institutions from making such distinctions either. Liberals will compel us to be free and equal — on their terms, not ours.

In criticizing this liberal conception of the welfare state, however, I do not reject the welfare state as such. I happen to think that George Will was right when he wrote in *Statecraft as Soulcraft* that conservatism needs "an affirmative doctrine of the welfare state." The issue today is not whether we should have a welfare state, but what kind of welfare state, aiming at what goals and operating on what principles. The disease of contemporary liberal democracy is not its concern with the welfare of its citizens but the shallowness of its understanding of welfare.

Theodore J. Lowi, writing in the *Political Science Quarterly* (1986, no. 2), discusses this problem. "Liberalism," he says, "tries its best to take no position on the morality of conduct," and as a liberal himself he agrees that this is "the most reasonable approach to government in a pluralistic society." But he also argues that liberalism tends to make the ethic of the welfare state unworkable.

The older, pre-welfare-state American ethic, he explains, had emphasized personal responsibility. The person who was primarily responsible for an injury (it could be either the injured but negligent employee or his negligent employer) was expected to bear the cost of the injury. If a person became dependent on the help of others, the question whether he himself had brought about his condition of dependency was considered highly relevant. The new welfare ethic replaced personal responsibility with a different principle: "All injuries and dependencies became part of the social system, and all costs related thereto became *social costs,"* to be borne by society at large through a variety of insurance and entitlement programs. Liberal refusal to make moral judgments, combined with the new welfare ethic, says Lowi, has put liberal government in a bind: "Once the new social ethic removed blame and replaced it with socialized responsibility, everything became good to do, because all injuries and dependencies, regardless of source or cause, became 'social costs.'" Liberal government, he tells us, "has already become obliged to respond to any and every argument putting forward a case that a connection can be established between a particular conduct and some injurious consequence. This is why modern liberal government became a gigantic magnet of open-ended commitments without priorities."

Lowi urges liberals to face the problem they have created in the welfare state, because others are eager to do it for them by liquidating the welfare state. The solutions he suggests, however, remain purely technical and legal. They do not address the real problem, which is that the neutral state in a pluralistic society, having no moral priorities, can hardly avoid becoming "a gigantic magnet of open-ended commitments without priorities."

Sunset of the Enlightenment

December 1987

One way of describing the present state of Western culture is to say that we are living through the fag end of the Enlightenment. The late Crane Brinton, writing in *The American Historical Review* more than 25 years ago, depicted the beginning of that epoch in our culture in these terms: "The basic structure of Christian beliefs survived, not without heresies and schisms, until, roughly, the late seventeenth century when there arose in our society what seems to me clearly to be a new religion, certainly related to, descended from, and by many reconciled with, Christianity. I shall call this religion," said Brinton, "simply Enlightenment, with a capital *E*."

The Enlightenment was indeed descended from Christianity in several respects, its humanitarianism for example, yet it was nonetheless an all-out revolt against Christianity. Peter Gay, an avowed partisan of the Enlightenment, states in *The Enlightenment: An Interpretation:* "The most militant battle cry of the Enlightenment, *écrasez l'infâme*, was directed against Christianity itself, against Christian dogma in all its forms, Christian institutions, Christian ethics, and the Christian view of the world." It was not just a Christian heresy.

The Enlightenment, in fact, attacked not only Christianity but all revealed religions, Judaism in particular, and sought to replace them with a new and worldly religion of reason. The French scholar, Paul Hazard, summarized the enlightened attitude toward revealed religion wittily but well in *The Crisis of the European Mind, 1680-1715:*

> No more priests, no more pastors, no more rabbis, all alike claiming to wield authority. No more sacraments, no more rites and ceremonies, no more fasting and mortifying the flesh, no more feeling that you are obliged, willy-nilly, to go to church, chapel, synagogue, or whatever it may be. . . . The present age will have no more of

divine wrath, divine vengeance; nor, for the matter of that, will it tolerate any divine interference in human affairs. Vague, indefinite, remote, God did not look like causing very much embarrassment. The consciousness of sin, the need for grace, the uncertainty of salvation, which for so many centuries had been a weight on so many hearts, would trouble the sons of men no more.

The Enlightenment not only repudiated Christian doctrine but overturned Christian morals. R. R. Palmer, in *Catholics and Unbelievers in Eighteenth-Century France,* says that Enlightenment thinkers "observed that men sought pleasure and shrank from pain, that they enjoyed the goods of this world, that they were restive under an authority that crossed their wishes, that they lived in society and could suffer or profit from their forms of government. With these facts of human nature they hoped to build an ethical system." This new ethic would combine seeking one's own pleasure with an appropriate concern for other people, and so would lead men to happiness in this world. The religious critics of the new ethic, in Palmer's opinion, "were quite correct in calling the infidels apologists for the passions."

Does all this sound like the famous "spirit of Vatican II"? Well, as Crane Brinton said, many people reconciled the Enlightenment with Christianity in a blend which we have come to call liberal Christianity, and they are still doing it. The "spirit of Vatican II" was in fact a renewal of a three-centuries-old effort to accommodate Christianity to the Enlightenment, not something new.

Nor is it new that Enlightenment should take hold among the clergy. E. E. Y. Hales, in *Revolution and Papacy, 1769-1846,* describes a mentality that existed "quite widely amongst the clergy" two hundred years ago on the eve of the French Revolution. Many of the clergy, he says, "had absorbed, at the universities, the fashionable philosophy of the times — so much more compelling than the definitions of the schoolmen — and with it ideas which sometimes leant towards a Rousseauistic sentimentality, sometimes rather towards rationalism, but always away from a literal acceptance of traditional Christian beliefs."

The "chief difficulty" of these liberal clerics, according to Hales, "came with the Second Person of the Trinity. His incarnation, crucifixion, resurrection, and ascension were apt to offend them. These fundamental beliefs of the Church seemed to them too concrete, literal, anthropomorphic." The liberal clergy were repelled by "the 'Jesuitical' approach to religion, with its emphasis on the personal and particular, on the Rosary, on the human personality of Our Lord or of His mother."

Christmas is the Catholic people's answer to this liberal and enlightened Christianity. The whole Church year is a celebration of the earthly life, death, resurrection, and ascension of the Incarnate God. But no feast in the Church's calendar more vividly impresses the Catholic imagination as personal and particular and as a cause for rejoicing than Christmas, when the infant who was God was born of a virgin in Bethlehem. We celebrate an event that happened at a particular time and place in history, the birth of a Person whose life gives meaning and purpose to our lives and to the world in which we live.

Robert Anchor has told us in *The Enlightenment Tradition* that the "legacy of the Enlightenment" is "a meaningless universe" in which "men must bear the responsibility for giving value to what they create and add to a world which they did not make and which will outlive them." On Christmas Day, as the sunset of the Enlightenment fades around us in the meaningless modern world, we may find comfort and joy in the faith that for us it is the dawn.

Meaning in a Meaningless World

January 1988

I know a man who has been living for years with a woman to whom he is not married. He is a decent, good-humored sort, but when asked, "Why don't you marry her?" he answers: "What difference would it make? Marriage is only a piece of paper."

He thinks of himself as a realist but, because he has never had formal training in philosophy, he does not know that he is an empiricist. Reality to him is what is empirically observable, what meets the eye, is heard by the ears, can be touched and felt; all else is simply imagination and emotion.

The empirically observable reality of marriage is a man and a woman living together, sharing the same bed and board, and they can do that with or without the "piece of paper" that is marriage. The imaginary bond of marriage may be emotionally satisfying, particularly to the woman, but from an empiricist point of view it adds nothing to the only reality there is, namely, what we can observe through our senses.

This kind of realism has a strong appeal to men who pride themselves on being hard-nosed and tough-minded. Determined to live with reality as they see it, they leave the hearts-and-flowers stuff to the opposite and weaker sex who, poor creatures, need to feel that life's most important relationships have meaning as well as factual content. Meaning, however, implies structure, order, and purpose, and these do not fall under the observation of the senses. The empiricist mind, therefore, cannot grasp them and regards them as unreal.

Because the empiricist view of the world lacks any objectively valid principle of order and coherence, an empiricist finds himself unable to talk about reality in consistent language. A striking example of this is the difficulty which sophisticated moderns have in talking about human life before birth.

We are all supposed to know that what is in the womb before birth is not a human being. In *Roe v. Wade,* seven justices of the U.S. Supreme Court could not bring themselves even to admit that it was actually alive, and so they referred to it as a "potential life." We, for our part, must never call it an unborn child, but rather a fetus, an embryo, a product of conception, or a blob of tissue. The only thing of which we are allowed to be sure is that killing it is not murder.

But at times the tongue slips, as happened in *Time*'s review of the film *Fatal Attraction.* I gather from the review that in the film happily married Dan has a weekend fling with a businesswoman named Alex. When it is over, he expects to return to his normal life with his wife and young daughter. But Alex, pregnant by Dan, won't let him go. The film ends in Dan's house, with Dan's wife, Beth, killing Alex.

"There is just one little problem," comments the *Time* reviewer. "In killing Alex, Beth also kills the child — Dan's child — inside her. The first wife saves her family by destroying the potential family of the woman who wanted to be Dan's second wife. One woman movie executive, who is disgusted by *Fatal Attraction*'s message, offers this bitter coda: 'Dan and Beth should be put on trial for the murder of Alex's unborn child.'"

What the woman executive would have said if Alex had wanted to abort the child, we do not know, and it would be unfair to guess. But you see the problem. The blob of tissue is sometimes an unborn child. Which it is depends on whether the mother wants to give birth to it. The empiricist mind must leave it up to her because, limited as it is at best to scientific observation, it cannot decide the question or talk coherently about life in the womb.

This incoherence appears even more plainly in a series of cases reported in the *New York Times.* "There have been at least 21 cases since 1981," according to the *Times,* "in which hospitals have sought court orders to override the wishes of a pregnant woman — by performing a Caesarean, detaining her against her will, or treating the fetus inside the womb." The courts granted the order in all but three cases. In one of them, in issuing an order for a Caesarean operation to save the baby from a possibly fatal infection, the judge explained: "It is one thing for an adult to gamble with nature regarding his or her own life; it is quite another when the gamble involves the life or death of an unborn infant."

It is true that such cases typically involved viable infants who could live outside the womb, and that the Supreme Court had declared in *Roe v. Wade* that the state could proscribe abortion after viability "except when it is necessary to preserve the life or health of the mother." But in the companion case to *Roe v. Wade* the Court laid down a very broad definition of the "health" that would justify a physician in performing an abortion: his "judgment may be exercised in the light of all factors — physical, emotional, psychological, familial, and the woman's age — relevant to the well being of the patient." So we have a situation in which a woman who does not want to abort may be ordered by a court to undergo surgery or other treatment for the sake of her unborn child, but if she wants to abort even a viable child and can find a physician willing to declare that her broadly defined health requires it, the courts are powerless to defend the child.

There is clearly an incoherence in the law that permits this situation. But it is one which the law could remove by making a woman's power over an unborn child absolute in all cases. Doing that, however, would not change the deeper incoherence of the empiricist mind for which, in a world of sheer facticity, no fact, not even a human life, has intrinsic worth or any meaning save that which we choose to give it.

Equal — and Separate

February 1988

The dominant passion of a democratic society is the love of equality, said Alexis de Tocqueville in his classic *Democracy in America*, 150 years ago. In Leo Strauss and Joseph Cropsey's *History of Political Philosophy*, Marvin Zetterbaum paraphrases Tocqueville in these words: "The characteristic feature of democratic society is its atomism. . . . Men confront each other as equals, each independent, each impotent. Individuals comprising such a society have, as citizens, no natural ties to one another; each being the equal of every other, no one is obliged to do the bidding of another." Equality means mutual independence limited only by contractual ties freely consented to.

Today, as the implications of this atomistic conception of equality relentlessly work themselves out, we must add that men and women confront each other as equals, each independent and bound by no natural ties. They are no longer the naturally complementary halves of the human race, but nearly identical and interchangeable units, united only by choice and for so long as the choice lasts.

As one might expect, those implications reveal themselves most clearly in that land of the future, Sweden. In an article distributed by the Swedish Information Service, an American sociologist, Linda Haas, describes Sweden's promotion of "equal parenthood." As the Swedish government reported to the United Nations, its sex-role policy was that "men were to be equally responsible for housework and childcare, while women were to be held equally accountable for the economic support of families." The premise of the policy is that men and women are equal in being identical in their roles in work and childcare.

In pursuit of this social goal, Swedish law provides for one year off from work, with pay, for either parent (or for both on an alternating part-time basis), to stay home and care for a newborn child. But men are not taking advantage of this opportunity in significant numbers, and most Swedish women do not want them to do so. According to a recent government report, says Haas, "only 27 per cent of all fathers whose wives were in the labor market before childbirth took even one day of parental leave for children born in 1982. Those who took leave took an average of only 49 days."

Among the reasons for this reluctance of men to take parental leave, Haas feels that "the most important may be attitudes toward the man as breadwinner. As long as men and women see men (rather than men *and* women) as responsible for the family's economic support, men's energies and interest will be directed toward occupational pursuits outside the home and away from childcare." Not only that, "women would have to be willing to give up their current freedom to choose whether or not to be employed outside the home." In fact, however, "women are still most comfortable with a situation where they are the ones primarily responsible for childcare" and they have "discouraged their partners from taking very much leave."

Changing such "deep-set" attitudes, Haas admits, "probably takes generations to accomplish." Nothing short of "a monumental resocialization effort" will suffice to reverse "traditional sex-role stereotyping." She seems to favor the effort, but she does not go on to consider the strong possibility that, should the effort succeed, it would increase the mutual independence of men and women, and further loosen the already weak ties that bind them together in Sweden.

Others, however, are willing to face the consequences of independence unflinchingly, to the point of renouncing marriage or even cohabitation altogether. One of them is Karen DeCrow, a former President of the National Organization for Women. She recently celebrated her 50th birthday by publishing a column in the *New York Times,* in which she said a number of sensible things about accepting one's age without trying to look younger than one really is. Then, determinedly unmarried though she is, she announced: "At 50, we learn that lust is underrated" and "leaves all other joys in the backfield."

That lust is underrated in this last quarter of the twentieth century came as a surprise to me. But DeCrow speaks from experience, and I do not, so I can't argue with her. I can't help wondering, however, if she fully appreciates the significance of her own remark, "At 50, time is on fast-forward."

At 50, one would think, a woman finds it harder to attract desirable sex partners than she did at 25. At 55, it will be harder still, and at 60, still harder again. A woman who wants to keep up an active sex life through her fifties and sixties may discover that she needs one steady, reliable, and devoted partner; in short, a husband. But Ms. DeCrow will have none of that.

"Perfect love," she says, is possible, but only "if one does not give up one's name or personal finances or place to live." Perfect love, it appears, asks only: Your place or mine? Nor need it ask any other question if one identifies love with the joy that leaves all others in the backfield. Evidently DeCrow agrees with Eliza Doolittle's father in *My Fair Lady:* "You can 'ave it all and not get 'ooked!"

Or, as Fred Astaire sang in one of his films, "It's nice work if you can get it." But can you get it just by trying hard enough? For the definitive answer to that question, we may have to await another report from Karen DeCrow when she turns 60.

Not Tea for Two

March 1988

"**S**ex for one is an erotic concept whose time has come," and universal acceptance of what an earlier age called self-abuse "is the next step in civilization's sexual evolution." You didn't know that, did you? Neither did I, but now we have it on the word of no less an authority than the noted sexpert and feminist, Betty Dodson, in her new book, *Sex for One*.

But why call attention to so obviously trashy a book as this one? Who will take it seriously? Well, the audience at a Phil Donahue show might. Mr. Donahue is quoted in an advertisement for the book as saying, "In the age of AIDS, more and more people are having sex with themselves. It's certainly a lot safer! . . . It is a quite natural experience." And who, looking at a Donahue show on TV, will venture to say that his audience doesn't take him seriously and would not do the same for Ms. Dodson?

Besides, a book like this provides an answer to a question we have all asked ourselves: How far can "civilization's sexual evolution" go? At what point will the Sons and Daughters of the Sexual Revolution sit with Alexander the Great on the banks of the Oxus, weeping because there are no worlds left to conquer? The publication of *Sex for One* suggests that they are already there, because there is no farther they can go in separating sex from natural function and freeing the self from natural norms.

If this be so, we may hail the book as signalizing the final triumph of liberal individualism, a climax in which the self communes with itself alone. Or, conversely, we may see it as the reduction to absurdity of the modern conception of the individual.

This last point, the meaning of individuality, is worth reflecting upon. A Jewish friend of mine, a man of eminently sound principles and conservative views, recently reminded me that Christianity has contributed significantly to individualism. He was right, and he could have reached farther back, into his own tradition, and pointed to the contribution of the Hebrew prophets. The Old Testament presents man as created in the image and likeness of God, and for that reason as free and responsible for his actions. As a creature, man is capable of both sin and repentance, and can merit both reward and punishment. The story of the Bible, it is true, is the story of the relations between God and his often backsliding but beloved people, Israel. Yet, as the prophets made clear, in the eyes of God it is the individual who is found worthy of praise or blame, life or death.

The prophet Ezekiel, for example, proclaimed the standard of divine judgment in these terms: "I will judge you, O house of Israel, every one according to his ways, says the Lord God. . . . The son shall not suffer for the iniquity of the father, nor the father for the iniquity of the son; the righteousness of the righteous shall be upon himself, and the wickedness of the wicked shall be upon himself. . . . When a righteous man turns away from his righteousness and commits iniquity, he shall die for it. . . . Again, when a wicked man turns away from the wickedness he has committed and does what is lawful and right, he shall save his life."

That surely is a kind of individualism, but it is the individualism of a creature, not of an autonomous self-creator. In the biblical worldview, the individual human being is supremely important because he is responsible to God more than to any earthly power. Christianity carries this individualism even farther, with its doctrine of eternal life with God or eternal separation from him as the final destiny of every human being: "It is appointed for men to die once, and after that comes judgment" (Heb. 9:27). Distasteful as the notion that man stands under God's judgment is to the modern mind, it is the source of man's worth and dignity. The individual human being can stand against the state or any other human institution because "it is necessary to obey God rather than men" (Acts 5:29). At the Last Judgment, the Lord will say to individuals, not institutions, "Come to me, you blessed" or "Depart from me, you cursed."

In this sense, we can say that the Old and New Testaments founded individualism. Yet Alasdair MacIntyre is also correct when he says in *After Virtue* that by the end of the seventeenth century, we had "that newly invented social institution, the individual." It has taken three centuries for the full implications of this new conception of the individual to work themselves out in practice, but now they are before our eyes.

There is always a time lag between the first introduction of a new idea and the full appreciation of its consequences. The newly invented individual of early modern liberal thought emerged in a culture which was still largely shaped by belief in divine revelation and natural moral law. For several generations these beliefs held in check the disintegrating effects of the new belief in individual autonomy.

But as the autonomous individual of liberal theory lost his faith in divine revelation and in the ability of reason to perceive a natural moral order, he became an independent self, a subject of rights rather than of obligations, and a sovereign will bound by no law to which he himself had not consented. In the end, he became a bundle of appetites, because his will, lacking any anchorage in a divinely created moral order, was submerged in and identified with his desires. That, too, is a kind of individualism, but a different kind from the freedom of the sons of God, and it explains why some individuals now prefer books like Betty Dodson's to the Bible.

The Severed Link

April 1988

You can't stop progress, can you? As the poet says, the great world spins forever down the ringing grooves of change, and only fools will try to stand in its way.

Inspired by this thought, Dr. Jack Dominian, a British Catholic psychiatrist, has written in *The Tablet* of London that the Pill has brought about "a change which is here to stay: . . . the age-old link between sexual intercourse and procreation [has been] severed for good." For this reason, he says, we need a wholly new basis for our sexual morality.

He is undeniably right in this, that the Pill will not be uninvented. But neither shall we uninvent the hydrogen bomb, chemical weapons, bacteriological warfare, electronic instruments of torture, mind-destroying drugs, modern techniques of abortion, using tissue from aborted fetuses to cure adult diseases, or advanced methods of reshaping the image of God in man through genetic engineering. All these things, too, not to mention other blessings of progress, are here to stay.

Given the fallen state of our human nature, if new technological devices exist and can be used to satisfy people's desires, people will use them. We can use technology either for good or for ill, of course. If I am alive and well and able to write this column, I owe it to modern medicine, which has preserved both my life and my eyesight. Whether that is for good or for ill, the reader may decide, but I at least am in no position to knock modern medical techniques merely because they are techniques and modern.

The problem is that, as the late John Courtney Murray, S.J., once put it, the only canon of technology is possibility. The sole question that technology answers is whether something *can* be done. Assuring us that a device is here to stay and that people will use it tells us nothing about how they should use it or

130

whether they should use it at all. The answers to those questions must come from sources outside technology.

We live, however, in a country and an age which is reluctant to admit any external control on the use of technology because so many of us refuse to accept any moral authority superior to our own will. For example, the morality of using nuclear weapons is a serious and seriously debated issue. But for many of our contemporaries, the issue is simply one of survival. Their reason for wanting to ban nuclear arms is not that they think that using them is in itself immoral (they have got beyond regarding anything as intrinsically immoral), but that nuclear war would end civilization as they enjoy it.

Now that technology has severed forever the link between sexual intercourse and procreation, as Dr. Dominian would have it, we must accept people's right not to have children they don't want. More recently, technology has founded a new right, people's right to have children they do want but have not been able to have through normal sexual intercourse. Their desire to have children, we hear, makes it right for them to use such techniques as artificial insemination, extra-uterine conception, and surrogate motherhood. The end justifies the means, and no further questions need or may be asked.

Mankind has never been very good at controlling technological development by either religious or purely rational norms. I recall once seeing a cartoon in which one caveman shows another a bow and arrow, and explains: "This is a weapon that will end all wars." The cartoon was fictional, but it is historical fact that the Second Lateran Council in 1139 condemned the crossbow as too inhuman to use, at least against Christians. Much good that did; Christians kept on killing Christians with crossbows, and since then the development of weaponry has roared on to the point where we can now wipe out whole cities with a single blast.

Yet there is something peculiarly modern in our conviction that intense desires suffice to justify the technological means of satisfying them. Our attitude stems from what Peter Gay has called "Bacon's and Descartes' grandiose vision of man controlling nature for his own profit and delight." Knowledge is power, said Francis Bacon in the seventeenth century, and its purpose is to master nature for "the relief of man's estate." According to his younger contemporary, Rene Descartes, knowledge is "to be desired not only for the invention of an infinite number of devices that would enable us to enjoy without any labor the fruits of the earth and all its comforts, but above all for the preservation of health, which is doubtless the first of all goods and the foundation of all other goods of life."

Far be it from me to disparage either health or labor-saving devices; I enjoy them both. But we must recognize in Bacon and Descartes the beginning of a cultural shift by which the goods of the body came to be esteemed more highly than the goods of the soul. As a result, our culture is morally ill-equipped to deal with our rapidly developing technology. But let us at least grasp firmly the idea that no technique and no device is either good or bad, and no use of it right or wrong, merely because the thing has been invented and is here to stay.

Christian Freedom

June 1988

Christians though we claim to be, today we dislike the notion of sin, with its connotation of personal responsibility and guilt. If we speak of sin at all, it is not personal sin but social sin, the kind we can wash away by changing institutions without changing ourselves.

Granted, there are unjust social structures which people cling to because of their personal pride and greed, not to mention envy and sloth. As the popes have insisted with increasing frequency in the last hundred years, these structures will not be changed for the better unless multitudes of individuals are willing to reshape their personal attitudes and habits. But blaming the system rather than ourselves remains a tempting cop-out, and many there are who resort to it. Modern men are appalled at the idea that God holds them responsible for what they do and might actually punish them for it. Some of them, including nominal Christians, refuse to believe in a God who could treat them in that way.

Yet if we mean to be Christians, we must recognize that the New Testament takes sin very seriously. The mission of Christ was one of redemption, but of redemption precisely from sin. Jesus, as the New Testament presents him, came to save us from the consequences of our sins, both original and personal, and his life and death make no sense except in that light. If sin means nothing, neither does salvation; we do not need to be saved from a ship that isn't sinking.

According to the New Testament, however, the ship is sinking: "Unless you repent, you will all likewise perish" (Luke 13:3). "Repent, for the kingdom of heaven is at hand," cried John the Baptist (Matt. 3:2). When John was arrested and imprisoned, Jesus took up the same theme and "began to preach, saying, 'Repent, for the kingdom of heaven is at hand'" (Matt. 4:17).

Jesus passed a severe judgment on those whom his preaching and miracles did not lead to repentance: "The men of Nineveh will arise at the judgment with this generation and condemn it, for they repented at the preaching of Jonah, and behold, something greater than Jonah is here" (Luke 11:32). "It shall be more tolerable on the day of judgment for Tyre and Sidon, and for the land of Sodom, than for you" (Matt. 11:22, 24).

For there will be a day of judgment. At the end of this world, Jesus will come to judge us all. To the saved he will say: "Come, O blessed of my Father, inherit the kingdom prepared for you from the foundation of the world." To the damned he will say: "Depart from me, you cursed, into the eternal fire prepared for the devil and his angels. . . . And they will go away into eternal punishment, but the righteous into eternal life" (Matt. 25:34, 41, 46). "And this," says St. John, "is the judgment, that the light has come into the world, and men loved darkness rather than light, because their deeds were evil" (John 3:19).

Sin, therefore, is to be dreaded above every other evil: "If your hand causes you to sin, cut it off. . . . And if your foot causes you to sin, cut it off. . . . And if your eye causes you to sin, pluck it out; it is better for you to enter the kingdom of God with one eye than with two eyes to be thrown into hell, where the worm does not die, and the fire is not quenched" (Mark 9:43, 45, 47).

This is tough talk: hard and utterly uncompromising. It is not the only talk we hear from the lips of Jesus; the parable of the Prodigal Son is as much a part of the New Testament as is the Last Judgment. But there is no denying that the tough talk is there and is basic to the message that the New Testament conveys to us, which is that God became man to save us from our sins, not from our weaknesses and mistakes.

Frightening though we may find the idea of inescapable divine judgment to be, we ought to admit that God really pays us a compliment by treating us as sinners who can repent rather than as automatons which cannot help what they do, or as immature children who are not responsible for what they do, or as victims of our passions who are more to be pitied than censured. Any or all of the above may at times be true of us because we are creatures and are not endowed with complete and divine mastery over ourselves (a fact of which God surely is at least as well aware as we are). But it is the glory of our nature that we are free creatures, made in the image and likeness of God inasmuch as we are endowed with intelligence and the power of free and rational choice. It is as such that Our Lord takes us.

One of the most striking features of the New Testament is that Jesus speaks to very ordinary, undistinguished human beings as to responsible adults who are accountable for their own actions. He honors the humblest of them by respecting their humanity and acknowledging that, much as we all need and depend on God's help (without which, he tells us, we can do nothing), their ultimate and eternal destiny is in their own hands. God's judgment on us registers what we have chosen to make of ourselves.

Four and a half centuries ago, St. Angela Merici, the foundress of the Ursuline nuns, beautifully expressed this Christian appreciation of human freedom. In her spiritual testament, she urged her nuns to treat the girls they taught with firm but loving kindness, so that the instructions they gave them should not seem to be imposed by force. "For God," she said, "has given everyone liberty, and therefore He compels no one, but only points the way, calls, and persuades." God has more respect for our freedom than we often have ourselves.

Those Who Care, Govern

July 1988

Those who don't care are governed by those who do care. Theoretically, in a democracy the majority governs, or at least chooses the officials who govern, and in this way the majority shapes public policy. In practice, however, the moving and shaping forces of politics frequently are activist minorities.

It is probably inherent in the nature of a mass democracy that this should be so. If we want democracy, we want the key posts in government to be filled by election. Therefore, we want public officials who aspire to be elected or re-elected. In order to get elected, they must calculate how many votes they stand to win or lose by what they do. That calculation will often enough lead them to act in ways that have little to do with the public good or the wishes of a majority.

For example, I recall the time when I first heard it proposed to lower the voting age to 18. There was no massive demand for this change but, as I wrote at the time, it was a proposal that could not fail to be adopted. No politician who opposed it would win votes, but he could and would lose some votes. The great majority (including the young) that had no strong feelings about the matter would not thank him for being against lowering the voting age, but the minority that wanted the change would remember at the next election and punish him.

So the proposal to lower the voting age to 18 went through and became the Twenty-sixth Amendment to the Constitution. There is little reason to believe that the republic is better governed as a result or that its supposed beneficiaries are particularly pleased with the benefit conferred on them. The 18-21 age group is even more apathetic than the rest of the electorate in exercising the right to vote.

This example illustrates a more general truth which Robert

A. Dahl enunciated in *A Preface to Democratic Theory:* "The making of governmental decisions is not a majestic march of great majorities united upon certain matters of basic policy. It is the steady appeasement of relatively small groups." That is a pretty accurate description of the way in which our pluralistic mass democratic system actually works, and it throws light on some otherwise strange results that the system produces.

The Civil Rights Restoration Act of 1988, for instance. This act of Congress had its origin in a case involving Grove City College, a small liberal-arts institution in Pennsylvania. The college on principle had accepted no federal funds because it did not want to be subject to federal regulations. Nonetheless, because some of its students had federally backed loans, stipends, or grants, it "became entangled," in the words of the *New York Times*, "in a legal battle with the Government when it separated boys and girls in the school's intramural sports program and refused to file a statement of compliance with Title IX of the 1972 Education Act, which bars discrimination on the basis of sex."

The case was carried up to the U.S. Supreme Court, which held in 1984 that the college was indeed bound by Title IX, but only in that part of its operations which was affected by the student loans and grants, namely, its admissions office. This decision enraged the civil-rights activists but seemingly made little impression on the rest of the population.

After four years of lobbying by civil-rights groups, Congress passed the Civil Rights Restoration Act. It subjects to federal regulation every aspect of the operations, not only of schools, but of all private institutions that directly or indirectly receive federal funds. President Reagan vetoed this act, but Congress repassed it over his veto, and it is now the law of the land.

Why did Congress do this? *Time* explained that, despite last-minute efforts by conservative Protestant groups to persuade Congress not to override the President's veto, "even most Republicans seemed less impressed by the evangelical broadsides than by the dangers of voting against anything called a civil-rights act in an election year." As for the Democratic Party, it is gripped in a stranglehold by the "rainbow coalition" to which Garry Wills has ascribed the defeat of Robert Bork's appointment to the Supreme Court: "minorities, women's groups, civil liberties activists." One cannot imagine the Democrats drawing the wrath of these groups down upon themselves in an election year or any other year.

There is a similar explanation for what the *New York Times* headlined as "A Gay Rights Victory at Georgetown." In an action brought under the District of Columbia's Human Rights Act, the District's Court of Appeals forced Georgetown University to give homosexual students the same privileges as other student groups, despite the university's argument that it would violate the school's Catholic principles and deprive it of its religious freedom. The only concession the homosexual students had to make was an agreement to print on their literature a notice that their views "are not endorsed by Georgetown University."

Georgetown's president has understandably tried to put the best face he can on his defeat by pointing out that the university was not obliged to give the homosexuals "official recognition." But, as he says himself, "the holding of the court is clear: The District of Columbia has a compelling interest in eradicating discrimination against homosexuals, and that overrides the First Amendment protection of Georgetown's religious objections to subsidizing homosexual organizations."

Where does the District of Columbia get this "compelling interest"? Surely not from the "majestic march of great majorities," but from "the steady appeasement of relatively small groups." That's democracy: those who care govern those who don't.

A Disintegrating Culture

August 1988

The American Catholic scene at the present time is populated by Catholics, semi-Catholics, semi-demi-Catholics, communal Catholics and, of course, ex-Catholics. There are also, we have lately been informed, core Catholics, said to be the heart and soul of the American Church, who follow Church teaching when they agree with it and reject it when they do not. It is highly dubious whether a church that accommodates itself to that scene has a future.

The percentages of Catholics, semi-Catholics, etc., may not be accurately reported by the sociologists, pollsters, and journalists, but that is not the question of primary importance. Even if there are more Catholics of the orthodox persuasion than these reporters would have us believe, there is no denying that hosts of American Catholics, both clerical and lay, are more or less typical products of the culture in which they live, and to that extent are semi-Catholics at best.

That is simply a fact which any teacher in a Catholic school encounters almost daily. To cite but one example out of my own experience, not long ago I asked a young woman in one of my classes what she thought of laws which New Jersey and Alabama had passed denying welfare benefits to unmarried but cohabiting parents of children, and which the U.S. Supreme Court had declared unconstitutional as denying the equal protection of the laws to the illegitimate children. She began her reply by saying, "Well, of course, raised as I have been raised, I wouldn't consider having a child out of wedlock, but other people have been raised differently, and for them it might not be wrong." It was, alas, an all too typical student response.

I have no doubts about this young lady's virtue, for she is very much a lady. But her unwillingness to say that something was wrong in itself and not merely for her personally showed that she was, as Mr. Springsteen puts it, born in the U.S.A., a product of our liberal and disintegrating culture.

That culture, insofar as it is shaped by liberalism, is a blend of libertarianism and egalitarianism. As libertarian, it proclaims every individual's right to choose his own "values" and standards of belief and conduct. It thereby weakens people's moral convictions by teaching them that their beliefs have no objective validity and are only statements of personal choice. At the same time it bolsters their faith in their right to do whatever seems best to them. On the other hand, as egalitarian, it calls in the power of the state to impose libertarianism on all the institutions of society, private as well as public.

One of the more extreme examples of this coercive egalitarianism is the District of Columbia's Human Rights Act, under which Georgetown University has been obliged to grant to homosexual student organizations the same access to university facilities and funds as other student organizations. This Act forbids any educational institution in the District to discriminate in affording access to its facilities and services on grounds of "race, color, religion, national origin, sex, age, marital status, personal appearance, sexual orientation, family responsibilities, political affiliation, source of income, or physical handicap."

The statute reads like a list of the only offenses that the modern mind regards as sins: racism, sexism, ageism, the various "isms" of religious and ethnic prejudice, "homophobia," bias against extramarital cohabitation, and what, for want of a better word, I will call anti-slobbism. But since it is a statute and as such has the force of law, it uses the power of government, in the name of equality, to deprive private institutions of the freedom to define their own standards in religion, morals, or even manners.

This is not a matter of merely local interest in the District of Columbia. In February 1988, Jeff Levi, Executive Director of the National Gay and Lesbian Task Force, sent out an "action alert" in which he announced that a homosexual civil rights bill was pending in Congress and that "every Democratic candidate for the presidency has pledged to sign that bill into law" (the Republicans prudently refused to answer him). Should such a bill become law, its legal effect would be that once again equality would override the freedom of private institutions. Its more significant cultural effect would be to impress it more deeply on the public mind that all sexual preferences are only that—preferences and, as such, equal. The flattening-out of our culture and its reduction to an ever-sinking lowest common denominator would reach a new depth.

The important question facing the Catholic Church in this country, its hierarchy in particular, is whether the Church can survive by adapting its teaching to this culture. It is not whether the Church can survive in a democracy; it has long since proved that it can not only survive but flourish. The issue rather is whether the Church can keep itself alive by accommodating itself to the opinions and desires of a membership increasingly infected by a soft, relativistic egalitarianism.

One understands the pastoral urge of bishops, priests, and theologians to "speak to all our people" and to drive no one out of the Church. But the consequences of making that urge the basis of pastoral policy and of trying to satisfy unending complaints about discrimination are likely to be ruinous. One need only look at the experience of the liberal Protestant denominations to see what trying to keep up with the times leads to.

Ordered Liberty

September 1988

I once read somewhere that the trouble with liberals is that they have not yet noticed the twentieth century. That is still true of by far the greater number of them. But as our century staggers to its close, some of them are beginning to take note of it.

The *New Republic,* for instance, which is certifiably liberal, remarked in an editorial on February 8, 1988, on liberal blindness to "cultural decline." Liberals, it said, do not want to see this unpleasant reality because it "challenges their own attachment to the endlessness of personal freedoms. . . . Contemporary liberalism is so intellectually and psychologically invested in the doctrine of ever-expanding rights — the rights of privacy, the rights of children, the rights of criminals, the rights of pornographers, the rights of everyone to everything — that any suggestion of the baleful consequences of that doctrine appears to them as a threat to the liberal idea itself."

Whether it is a threat depends on what one thinks is "the liberal idea itself." Liberalism as a theory of ethics and politics lasted as long as it did and worked as well as it did because it assumed that rational and decent people would see the difference between moral right and wrong and would for the most part respect it. Liberalism, however, was able to do this because it incorporated into its idea of personal freedom moral norms which it did not create but inherited from the classical and Christian past.

As liberals have used up this moral capital, they have come to regard these or any other transcendent moral norms as threats to the liberal idea itself. They may well be right, too, because the core of liberalism has always been the autonomy of the individual and his right to decide for himself which norms he will obey.

Those who think that today's liberals are wrong — as the

New Republic does when it proposes "the subtle truth that it really is wise restraints that make us genuinely free" — will have to revise the liberal idea of freedom. Above all, they will have to remove from the core of liberalism the belief that liberty consists in the sovereignty of the individual and his indefeasible right to decide for himself. More than two hundred years ago Edmund Burke put the key question: "Even in matters which are, as it were, just within our reach, what would become of the world, if the practice of all moral duties, and the foundations of society, rested upon having their reasons made clear and demonstrative to every individual?"

A sounder idea of freedom is contained in the phrase ordered liberty, of which the U.S. Supreme Court has become fond. Despite the bizarre implications the court has found in it (abortion on demand, for example), the phrase in itself is a good one and, properly used, could provide an antidote to the corrosive acid of individualism.

To quote Burke once again (he was speaking of the British constitution, but his words will apply to our own as well): "The distinguishing part of our constitution is its liberty . . . But the liberty, the only liberty I mean, is a liberty connected with order; that not only exists along with order and virtue, but which cannot exist at all without them."

The order without which liberty cannot exist has several levels. It is a legal and political order, a social order, and a cultural order constituted by commonly held conventions, codes of manners, moral principles, and beliefs about the nature of man and his place in the world. At its deepest level, it rests on belief in divine revelation, or on the conviction that the order of creation is open and accessible to human reason, or on both together. Ordered liberty depends upon an ordered universe.

It cannot be produced by a merely fabricating reason which tries to construct its own order out of its desires. Ordered liberty must be based on principles outside of and higher than our wishes, as Burke explained: "Men are qualified for civil liberty in exact proportion to their disposition to put moral chains upon their own appetites. . . . Society cannot exist unless a controlling power upon will and appetite be placed somewhere, and the less of it there is within, the more there must be without. It is ordained in the eternal constitution of things that men of intemperate mind cannot be free. Their passions forge their fetters."

It is the nature of our freedom that, if we abuse it, we lose it. This result is obvious in the case of persons who become enslaved to alcohol, drugs, gambling, or other addictions. But the pride, greed, lust, anger, envy, gluttony, and sloth with which we are all infected also forge fetters which are no less fetters for being called rights. Hence our need for "wise restraints that genuinely make us free," and the further need to recognize an overarching moral order from which we may learn what restraints are truly wise.

This idea will not sit well with liberals who believe in "the rights of everyone to everything." As Burke said of their French revolutionary forebears, "The little catechism of the rights of men is soon learned, and the inferences are in the passions." But if neither reason nor revelation is permitted to furnish us with standards by which to distinguish spurious from valid claims to rights, all such claims must be mere assertions of the individual's passionate desires.

This conclusion, however, leads to the attempt, characteristic of contemporary liberalism, to found the order of law and politics on equal respect for the passions of all individuals. George Sabine, an historian of political thought, has described what lies at the end of that road: "The absolutely sovereign and omnicompetent state is the logical correlate of a society which consists of atomic individuals." Such a state need not be a brutal dictatorship. It could be a soft bureaucratic despotism operating on the principles of the American Civil Liberties Union.

The Feminine Touch

October 1988

I recently made a spiritual retreat, during which I read the gospel accounts of the passion and death of Jesus Christ. I had done that many times in previous retreats, but this time something struck me to which I had not adverted before. It was that in this sad, sorry story, in which so many ignoble parts were played, none of them were played by women.

The traitor who betrayed Christ, the deserters who fled from him, the coward who denied that he knew him, the vindictive chief priests who accused him, the time-serving Roman governor who handed him over to be crucified, the brutal soldiery that tortured and executed him, the mob that derided him on the cross — all were men. In contrast, the women present appeared as ministering angels.

The only exception, and that a small one, was the servant girls of the high priest who pressed Peter to admit he was one of Christ's disciples, and so led him to deny his Master. But theirs was a minor fault and a minor part in the drama of the passion. All the other feminine parts were sympathetic or even admirable ones.

When Jesus was hauled before Pontius Pilate by the chief priests who demanded his execution, Pilate got a message from his wife: "Have nothing to do with that righteous man, for I have suffered much over him today in a dream." When Jesus walked the Via Dolorosa to Calvary, "there followed him a great multitude of the people, and of women who bewailed and lamented him. But Jesus turning to them said, "Daughters of Jerusalem, do not weep for me, but weep for yourselves and for your children." As he hung on the cross, "the women who had followed him from Galilee stood at a distance," and watched with him to the end. Other women were at his side: "Standing by the cross of Jesus were his mother, and his mother's sister, Mary the wife of Cleophas, and Mary Magdalene." When his dead body was taken down from the cross, the women left to prepare spices and ointments to anoint it, and came at dawn on Easter morning to carry out that last work of devotion. They were therefore the first witnesses to his resurrection.

All of this, however, took place long ago, at a time when women may have played sympathetic roles because they were not allowed to play important ones. If a Betty Friedan had arisen in the ancient world, two thousand years before her time, women might well have taken a more prominent part in the events of Good Friday.

It might then have been a woman who betrayed Jesus with a kiss, and another woman who denied three times that she knew him. It would perhaps have been a chief priestess who pointed a finger at Jesus and shouted: "You have heard his blasphemy. What further need have we of witnesses?" The Gospels might tell us that Pontia Pilata, Rome's first woman governor of Judea, washed her hands before the crowd and said, "I am innocent of this person's blood," then abandoned him to his executioners.

It could have been a woman's hands that pressed down the crown of thorns on the head of Christ, and women soldiers who held down his arms and legs while the nails that fastened him to the cross were hammered in. Soprano voices might have jeered at him on the cross, and have cried: "Let God deliver him now, if She wants him!"

All of these are things that might have been in a better and more enlightened age. But in fact, in a world that knew not the meaning of equality, all the dirty work was done by men.

But perhaps I am unfair in assuming that liberated and empowered women would have behaved like men. Given their due, women might have tamed power and rendered it gentle, loving, and kind. The governor of Judea might have been, not Pontia Pilata, but Shakespeare's Portia, who would have delivered a Solomonic judgment that set Jesus free and silenced his accusers.

Possibly so; there is some reason to believe it, since women are gentler and kinder than men. But there is also reason to believe that, while women may feminize power, it is more likely to masculinize *them*. Elizabeth I of England, Catherine de' Medici, Queen of France, Catherine the Great, Empress of Russia, and other great ladies who sat in high places and wielded real power may win our admiration for their Machiavellian toughness, but it would be hard to love them for their femininity.

In our own century we have had Jiang Qing, the consort of Mao Tse-tung and later the leader of China's "Gang of Four." In an interview with a Western journalist who asked about her personal life with Mao, she said: "Sex is engaging in the first rounds. What sustains interest in the long run is power." Sex is all right for the young, but the mature woman seeks more lasting joys. She does not always find and keep them — Jiang Qing lost out in the power struggle after Mao's death — but she knows what they are and, like Lady Macbeth, will unsex herself to get them.

That is the point at issue, isn't it? Is it meaningful to speak of a woman "unsexing" herself in the drive for place and power, or is that just sexist rhetoric designed to blind women to their potentialities and keep them in their place? Is the difference between the sexes rooted in nature or produced by nurture? Are good women the same as good men, or is there a goodness appropriate to each sex? Did women behave so admirably during the passion of Christ because they were powerless, or because they were women, doing what good women naturally do?

I am inclined to believe the latter. Feminine sensibility is different from and finer than masculine sensibility, and it showed itself at its best when Jesus Christ suffered and died.

Plastic People

November 1988

Dustin Hoffman first achieved fame as an actor with the role of Benjamin in *The Graduate.* You may recall that the film opens with a party given in honor of Benjamin's graduation from college. One of the men present puts his arm around him and says: "Benjamin, I have only one word to say to you: plastics." That scene has remained in my memory ever since as a perfect parable for our times and a paradigm of the modern mind.

Plastics are artificial substances made by breaking down natural substances into their component elements, and then reconstituting them in forms not produced by natural processes. All that nature contributes to the final product is its constituent elements; the product's form and structure are the work of man. Plastics, therefore, are another stride forward in man's conquest of nature, by which he bends it to his will. Modern man is the analyzer and synthesizer who breaks the world into bits and reshapes it to serve his purposes.

Plastics, moreover, are not just the stuff of which we make shopping bags and guns that can be smuggled past metal detectors into airports. We are increasingly able to treat living organic material as plastic, capable of being remolded to suit our designs. Much has already been done in that direction with brute animals. The new frontier is the manipulation of human genetic material.

Prof. Lee M. Silver of Princeton University presented a statement to a subcommittee of Congress on July 14, 1988, in which he described some of the things we shall be able to do with human genetic material when the technology we now use on other animals has been sufficiently improved to be used on human beings. He saw four areas in which "advances in human reproductive technology could occur."

The first was a "drastic" increase in the success rate of in vitro fertilization and embryo freezing. As we all know, some "test-tube" babies have already been born who were conceived in vitro, i.e., in glass, outside the womb and later implanted in their mothers' bodies. But the survival rate of such transferred embryos is low. With further research, however, in vitro fertilization might become "a routine medical procedure accessible to the general population."

If embryo freezing (freezing an embryo conceived in glass for further use) should also become a routine procedure, a woman could freeze now, get pregnant later. Or she could have a batch of her ova fertilized, then frozen to thaw out and use if her first attempts at transferring embryos conceived in glass to her womb should fail. What would be done with the embryos she didn't need, Prof. Silver does not say.

Another emerging technology is embryo biopsy. It is already possible to scrape a few cells off an early embryo, analyze particular genes to see if they are defective (e.g., if they carry an hereditary disease), and then decide whether "to transfer this embryo back into the womb of a gestational mother." Or, if a couple is known to be at risk of passing on an hereditary disease, they could have a pool of embryos conceived in vitro. Their physician could then select one of the embryos found to be free of the disease and implant it in the womb; the rest of the embryos presumably would be junked.

A third area in which rapid advance is forseeable is genetic engineering, i.e., injecting a gene from some other source into an embryo. "The most obvious use of this technology in human beings," Prof. Silver remarks, "would be to cure particular diseases through the injection of normal genes into deficient human embryos." But he warns that "genetic engineering is a two-edged sword with a great potential for use and a great potential for abuse," e.g., for producing children with non-human traits.

We must wonder, however, about his norm for deciding what is non-human when we read his speculation on the final technological development, by which human males could become pregnant and carry a child to term. At present, of course, this cannot be done, but there are reasons for thinking it could someday be done: "First, the endocrinology of reproduction is well understood and could be simulated in men. Second, there is no absolute requirement for a uterus to carry out gestation." But why would a man want to undergo "the drastic physiological changes" necessary to bear a child? Well, he might be a partner in a homosexual union. Or he might be the husband of a woman who is physically unable to sustain a pregnancy, and a surrogate mother might not be available. In that case, the husband might be willing to take his wife's place. "One should be cautious," says Prof. Silver, "not to underestimate the lengths to which infertile couples will go to have a baby."

Which is to say that, if people want something badly enough, we should not deny them the means of getting it. Despite his warnings that some of the things that may be technologically possible would nonetheless be "abuses," or even "outlandish," Prof. Silver offers only a crude utilitarianism as the norm for deciding what would be an abuse. He has destroyed the notion of human nature as the norm, because for him nature is only a manipulable collection of cells.

As C. S. Lewis explained more than forty years ago in *The Abolition of Man*, man's conquest of nature turns out to be the conquest of some men (particularly of those not yet conceived or born) by other men who have lost any idea of a human nature of their own. They have only one word to say to us: plastics.

All of This for Me

I stopped the other day at a traffic light in the Bronx and read the bumper sticker on the car in front of me. "Life is tough," it proclaimed, "then you die."

It was a view of life, I am sure, as fully entitled to expression as any other in this land of liberty. Considering the circumstances in which many people in the Borough of the Bronx live, it was even an understandable one. Yet it is strangely popular among people who are neither poor nor denizens of the Bronx.

Take for example Samuel Beckett's *Waiting for Godot,* the message of which is that, if we wait for God to come to us, we'll wait forever. It was recently revived for a limited run in New York. Liz Smith of the *New York Daily News* commented that years ago, when Bert Lahr starred in the play, "people all went around saying they didn't understand it." But "nowadays Beckett's play doesn't seem a bit strange or difficult. The world has grown into his existentialist, nihilistic viewpoint." Liz Smith is not a trained sociologist, but a gossip columnist. Yet her naively sophisticated remark is probably accurate. The world in which she moves has "grown into" acceptance of Beckett's bleak message.

Or, at least, that part of her world that understands the message accepts it. There are surely those who go to see Beckett's play merely because it is a current sensation. Such questions as whether the universe was created by a loving God, or has existed by and of itself from all eternity seem to them to be irrelevant to the practical concerns of real life. After all, if you are running a business, you don't ask your employees or your customers what they think of the universe.

Yet our view of the universe has a real influence on how we live our lives. If there is no God, or if God is indifferent to us and our fate, then we are alone in the universe, simply and totally on our own.

The desire to be on our own has been one of the great driving forces of modern thought. Millions of our fellow human beings have yielded to it, and more are joining them every year. I read recently that a poll taken in Europe purports to reveal that, while the vast majority of Europeans still profess to believe in God, a diminishing proportion of them see him as "personal." Life seems to them to be easier and less ridden by anxiety and guilt if they don't have to worry about what God thinks of them, and an impersonal God doesn't think, certainly not about individual human beings and their sins.

We can take life on those terms, I suppose, so long as we are healthy, prosperous, and able to do as we please. That may account for the popularity of Beckett's view of the world among those who can afford to buy theater tickets in New York.

Yet even they may at times be troubled by the thought that life is ultimately meaningless. If one is sufficiently young and not overly bright, of course, one can screen out that thought. But as we come against the disappointments, failures, miseries, and tragedies that are an inescapable fact of life, we are forced to ask ourselves whether we can handle our lives completely on our own, and we may begin to wonder whether a life that is lost in a meaningless cosmos is worth living.

The answer that the Christian faith gives to those questions at Christmas is a startling one. In his *Spiritual Exercises,* St. Ignatius Loyola has a meditation on the birth of Christ in Bethlehem. At the end of the meditation, he asks us to reflect that Jesus was born there "in dire poverty, so that after many labors, hunger and thirst, heat and cold, injuries and insults, he might die on the cross, and all of this for me."

And all of this for me. Now, there is a radically different view of life: God loves me, individually and personally, and was even willing to become man and die for me. He not only loves all of us collectively, as the Creator of the human race, he loves each one of us individually. Most strange of all, he loves *me.* That is hard to believe, but it is precisely that which the feast of Christmas asks us to believe.

This belief, in one respect, does not change the world at all.

Life is still tough, or at least it can and will be tough in one way or another, and we all sooner or later die. But the belief that God loves us makes an enormous difference in how we take life. For what we believe changes the world as we see and understand it.

What some see only as the inexorable grinding on of an indifferent universe, we see as the mysterious providence of God guiding us onward to himself. A created world is a vastly different place from an uncreated one, and a redeemed world is more different still. A personal God who knows, loves, and cares for us is a different God from an impersonal force in the universe. Life in the created and redeemed world may be hard, and often is, but it is not meaningless and hopeless, we are not alone and helpless, and death is not simply the end.

Those are the tidings of comfort and joy that the Christmas carols celebrate, the reason why they greet us with "God rest you merry, gentlemen, let nothing you dismay." If we can find nothing in the carols but beautiful traditional music, we may send Season's Greetings cards to our friends and present them as gifts with the collected works of Friedrich Nietzsche or, if we can get them, tickets to *Waiting for Godot*. But if we accept, and understand, and feel within ourselves the reality of Christ's birth as God's entrance into our human world, we can truly rejoice. For that birth means, to each one of us, that God loves me.

Dying for Mama

January 1989

$\mathbf{A}$ lady with whom I have long been acquainted told me that at a recent dinner party, an old family friend came up to her and announced: "I think every woman has a right to an abortion if she wants one." She replied, "I think abortion is murder," and walked away. Just as well, too, for he was only looking for an argument and, since he is not one of the brighter lights that gleams amid the encircling gloom, it was not going to be a good one.

But, I thought to myself afterwards, the conversation might have gone like this:

He: I think every woman has a right to an abortion if she wants one.

She: How fortunate for you that your mother didn't exercise that right and abort you.

He: But I was not unwanted. She *wanted* me.

She: Suppose you had been unwanted and she had aborted you at, say, three months, or three weeks, or three days after conception, who would be dead today?

He: I don't get you.

She: Wouldn't the life she ended by abortion have been your life, and wouldn't it be you who were dead today?

He: I suppose so.

She: Have you ever thanked your mother for not aborting you?

He: That would have been indecent. Besides, I can't thank her now; she died some years ago.

She: But you would agree with her having aborted you, if that is what she had decided to do, because you believe she had the right to do it?

He: Absolutely. Every woman has that right.

She: You must have loved your mother very much.

He: How so?

She: Greater love than this no man hath, that he lay down his life for a friend. But it seems to me an even greater love if a son is willing to have laid down his life for his mother's right to abort him.

He: What does love have to do with it? We're talking about rights.

That conversation never took place, of course, and I doubt if it ever would take place in real life. As Plato knew, the advantage of composing a Platonic dialogue is that Plato writes all the lines and can make them come out as he wants them to. Real dialogues seldom come out as either participant planned. Nonetheless, the above dialogue, contrived though it is, does make a valid point.

If you insist on a universal right to abortion, the life that was aborted could have been your own, and the mother who bore you could have been the mother who killed you. Granted, she would have had her reasons (for she was not a capriciously evil woman), but would you have been willing to die for them?

Abortion, after all, involves killing and dying. Technically, it is true, every premature expulsion of a child from the womb is an abortion, and would be an abortion even if removing the child from the womb managed to save its life as well as the mother's. But such an abortion is rare, if it happens at all. It is not the reality we are talking about when we discuss abortion in the contemporary United States.

According to the figure that is now routinely reported in the secular press, there are about one and a half million abortions performed every year in this country, and they terminate from a quarter to a third of all pregnancies. The point of virtually all of them is to kill the baby or, if you insist, to kill the living being in the womb before it becomes a baby. Either way, a human life is deliberately and intentionally ended; if your mother had aborted you before you became a baby, you'd be just as dead. The right to abort is the right to kill, and in abortion as it is actually practiced, a living human being always dies.

The ultimate pro-abortion answer to that proposition is, So what? Take Katha Pollitt, who is identified as "a poet and writer who lives in New York." In a column in the *New York Times Magazine* for November 20, 1988, she argues the pro-abortion case in terms that make it clear that she does not care who or what dies in an abortion.

Let us stop talking, she suggests, only about the hard cases of "pregnant schoolgirls, rape and incest victims," etc., and meet the real issue head-on: "All over the industrialized West, women want education and jobs, couples want small, planned families, and people—men and women, married and unmarried—want sexual intimacy." These "imperatives" are the premises from which all moral reasoning in this area of life must begin, the absolutes to which all other considerations must yield.

We need not pretend that "abortion isn't or shouldn't be a method of birth control." Let us face it, "that's just what abortion is—a bloody, clumsy method of birth control." It is fully justified because the women who resort to it are confronted with "disaster," not "inconvenience": "Women do what they need to do to lead reasonable lives, and they always have. Nowadays, a reasonable life does not include shotgun weddings, or dropping out of school, or embracing the minimum wage for life. Still less does it include bearing a baby for strangers to adopt, as George Bush blithely suggests." In the face of such disasters, "when your back is against the wall of unwanted pregnancy, it doesn't matter whether or not you think the fetus is a person."

That seems clear enough, does it not? Person or not, you kill it when it gets in the way of a reasonable life. But would you still agree with that if the reasonable life were your mother's, and the life she ended were your own?

The Problem of Evil

February 1989

Cardinal Ratzinger has remarked that the problem of evil has exercised the minds of men at least since the Book of Job. That book, however, has not succeeded in putting everyone's mind at rest on the question of why God permits evil to afflict the just as well as the unjust. I remember a lunch-table conversation some years ago in which a young priest said that he had never found God's answer to Job satisfactory. I understood how he felt, but I suspect that it is the only answer we shall ever get, because it is the only answer we can get.

You will recall that after Job's long lament about his afflictions and his friends' efforts to be helpful by assuring him that his sufferings must be the penalty for his sins, God scolds the friends for their presumption, then directs a lengthy speech to Job. Briefly and colloquially put, God's answer to Job comes down to this: "Were you there when I made the world? You weren't? Then shut up!"

And rightly. It would be impossible for the Lord who brought the universe into being out of nothing to get finite minds to see the situation as it was, so to speak, on the day before the creation, when all the options were open. Nor could he enable us to understand why he chose to create this world rather than another and possible one. *Omnia exeunt in mysterium:* at the end of every line of inquiry, the human mind encounters mystery.

We must therefore accept what we cannot possibly comprehend. We must also admit that we have no standards by which we can find God or his universe wanting, because we could get such standards only from the universe that God made. To what are we appealing when we declare the heavens unjust? Beyond the universe as it is, there is only God, and beyond God there is nothing. There is no standard above him by which we can pass judgment on him or his works.

One thought, however, occurs to me, not as solving the problem of evil, but as perhaps throwing some light on it. It is that most of the evil in the world is the result of God's having decided to create free creatures. When we think of evil, we think too readily of the loss of life, the suffering, and the damage caused by earthquakes, hurricanes, plagues, and other natural disasters — what insurance companies call acts of God. But the worst horrors of our world, from the crimes of Hitler, Stalin, Mao, Pol Pot, and Idi Amin to the daily diet of tales of cruelty, exploitation, and degradation served up in each morning's newspaper, are not natural disasters or "acts of God." Directly or indirectly, they are due to human beings choosing evil.

We could, and some of us do, blame God for having made us free, but that is tantamount to blaming him for having made us at all. It is our nature to be free, and without our freedom, we would not be human. Our freedom makes our crimes and sins possible, but it is also what makes us, as the Bible says, the image and likeness of God, capable of freely serving him, capable also of sharing in his divine life forever.

To live as a human being is to choose. Life is choice, a destiny from which we cannot escape by refusing to choose, and the necessity of choice entails the possibility of choosing evil as well as good. From this possibility God will not save us by depriving us of our freedom, for in so doing he would dehumanize us. We are his creatures, but his free creatures, and he will not save us against our wills.

The consequences of the human abuse of freedom are horrendous, and they explain most of the evils from which mankind suffers. We could cope with a world in which the only disasters were natural ones. It is pride, greed, lust, anger, envy, gluttony, and sloth that cause the evils which we inflict on one another and so often make human life a hell.

The consequences of sin fall upon the innocent as well as the guilty, often from generation to generation. Among these consequences is a genuine lessening and diminution of freedom, not all of it due to our personal sins. None of us today enjoys a godlike freedom which easily and without struggle resists temptation. We have inherited a nature which is free indeed, but weakened and blinded by the sins of our ancestors, right back to the first ones, and which is therefore prone to repeat and multiply the sins of the past.

It is this fallen and sinful world into which Christ came to save us. He does not do it by taking us out of this world; our salvation is accomplished here, in the world as it is. Nor does he restore the lost paradise or promise a future one to be built by reforming social institutions. Above all, he does not save us by taking away the freedom that makes sin possible, or by abolishing sin's dreadful consequences. His salvation takes place within each of us individually, through the grace that heals our wounded wills and enables us to grow into a life lived without sin and in harmony with God's will.

I do not mean to imply that social institutions do not need to be reformed — how could the institutions of proud, greedy, and lustful men not need reform? — or that reforming them would do no good. But, as every papal encyclical on social questions insists, no reform will work without a profound conversion of our wills from evil to good. The "problem of evil" lies mainly in our freedom and what we have done with it. The mystery remains: why God in his infinite wisdom chose to create and then redeem the likes of us.

The Rot in Liberal Politics

March 1989

Even liberals are beginning to notice what is wrong with liberalism. In a perceptive article which appeared in, of all places, the liberal Catholic journal *Commonweal* (January 13, 1989), Fred Siegel put his finger on contemporary liberalism's Achilles heel. "Liberalism," he says, "has a proud history of defending individual rights. . . . But liberalism, wrapped as it is in the defense of personal autonomy, is unable to speak to the social breakdown which increasingly plagues us. It is mute before abuses of liberty."

"The law," he explains, "once the cornerstone of ordered liberty, has been trivialized, turned into a game for lawyers." There has been "a decisive break between New Deal liberalism, whose mild economic egalitarianism was based on a sense of shared values, and the moral relativism of post-New Deal liberalism which is grounded in individually held rights. Those assertions of rights which serve to trump the claims of a common morality make it difficult and often impossible for cultural liberals to pass judgment on even the most obviously destructive behavior."

There, he says, we may find a major reason for the Democratic Party's defeat in the last presidential election. Since 1968 the party has been preoccupied with procedural rules designed to guarantee proportional representation to all of its constituent groups, however out of harmony with the general electorate they may be. But this preoccupation with procedures is "a means of avoiding a consensus on at least a core of substantive issues. In that sense the Democratic Party's proceduralism is a faithful reflection of contemporary liberalism's unwillingness to pass judgment on what is or isn't good."

Mr. Siegel's purpose in that article was to warn liberals that they are killing the Democratic Party's chances in national elections. But the rot now so apparent in liberal politics was planted in liberal social and political theory at its beginning, more than three centuries ago. Liberalism in its classical form was, and remains today, a radically individualistic philosophy. Even when it veers toward the welfare state or democratic socialism, it does so in order to equalize everyone's chance to live the lifestyle of his choice. It has no theory of what is a good life for human beings as such.

Liberal thought takes as its starting point the discrete individual who is sovereign over himself and a subject of rights prior to all obligations. The problem which liberal political theory thus sets for itself is to explain how and why such an individual entered an organized civil society and subjected himself to government.

He must have acted on motives of self-interest because, as an absolute individual, he had no other motives to act on. His relationships to other individuals and to society must therefore be contractual: his only obligations to them are those to which he has consented, and his motive for consenting must be his belief that he will thereby further his own interests. On these premises, freedom is the right to do one's own will, limited only by the equal right of other individuals to do their will, and the purpose of government is nothing more than to protect these rights.

I read somewhere, not long ago, that liberalism's great accomplishments were to break the power of absolute monarchs, thus bringing governments under law, and to establish religious freedom. One could point out that constitutionalism, the doctrine that government is limited by law, is far older than the rise of liberalism in the seventeenth century. It was in the thirteenth century that Bracton wrote, "The king is under no man, but under God and the law," and that idea was already old when he wrote. But it is true historically that modern conceptions of limited, constitutional government and of religious liberty triumphed in the modern world under the aegis of liberalism.

But much as we may applaud the historical achievements of liberalism, we must also recognize that one of its consequences has been the steady relativization of the ideas of truth and moral good, and that this was a consequence implicit in liberal individualism from the beginning. For multitudes today, truth is only what the individual thinks is true, good is only what the individual personally prefers, and justice is his right to act on his preferences, so long as they are compatible with the equal right of others to do the same.

That is currently the liberal model of society, and it is falling apart. Constitutional democracy clearly needs a better theoretical foundation than liberal individualism.

It is not that a sounder theory of democracy has yet to be written. We may find powerful essays towards it in John Hallowell's *Moral Foundation of Democracy,* Yves Simon's *Philosophy of Democratic Government,* Jacques Maritain's *Man and the State,* and a host of other books. The major task remaining to us is to persuade the rest of the population — particularly academics, journalists, and lawyers — to stop taking liberalism with its individualism, its relativism, and its assertion of rights that trump the claims of a common morality, as the necessary foundation of democracy. Liberalism, which we may credit with beginning its career as the political philosophy of freedom, has blossomed into mere permissiveness, and is now a menace rather than a support of constitutional democracy.

Good Old Edmund Burke

April 1989

In the 1750s, Edmund Burke began (but never completed) a history of England. In it he made this remark on the esteem in which monks were held in tenth-century England: "The secular clergy were at this time for the most part married, and were therefore too near the common modes of mankind to draw a great deal of their respect; their character was supported by a very small portion of learning, and their lives were not such as people wish to see in the clergy. But the monks were unmarried; austere in their lives; regular in their duties; possessed of the learning of the times; [and] well united, under a proper subordination."

Burke again commented on the Catholic clergy in 1782, when Lord Kenmare, the leading Catholic layman in Burke's native Ireland, wrote to ask his opinion of a proposal to relieve the Irish Catholics of some of the burdens of the penal laws under which they suffered. Although Burke was raised a Protestant and always remained one, he had a Catholic mother and many Catholic relatives, and was sympathetic with their plight. In his reply he advised Lord Kenmare against accepting the terms on which a very limited emancipation was being offered to Catholics.

One of them was to provide some scholarships for the education of Catholic clerics in Trinity College, the seat of Protestant learning in Ireland (and Burke's alma mater). "When we provide for the education of any body of men," said Burke, "we ought seriously to consider the particular functions they are to perform in life. A Roman Catholic clergyman is the minister of a very ritual religion [Burke might better have said, "a *sacramental* religion," whence the emphasis on ritual]; and by his profession subject to many restraints." He went on:

> His life is a life full of strict observances, and his duties of a laborious nature towards himself, and of the highest possible trust

towards others. The duty of confession alone is sufficient to set in the strongest light the necessity of having an appropriate mode of education. The theological opinions and the peculiar rites of one religion never can be properly taught in universities founded for the purposes, and on the principles, of another, which in many points is directly opposite. If a Roman Catholic priest, intended for celibacy, and the function of confession, is not strictly bred in a seminary where these things are respected, inculcated, and enforced as sacred, and not made the subject of derision and obloquy, he will be ill fitted for the former, and the latter will be indeed, in his hands, a terrible instrument.

"The Council of Trent," Burke continued, "has wisely introduced the discipline of seminaries, by which priests are not trusted for a clerical institution even to the severe discipline of their own colleges; but after they pass through them, are frequently, if not for the greater part, obliged to pass through peculiar methods, having their particular ritual function in view."

It was due to their seminary training on the continent of Europe, Burke thought, that the Irish Catholic clergy, living in poverty among their miserably poor flocks, "have been hindered from becoming an intolerable nuisance to the country, instead of being, as, I conceive, they generally are, of very great service to it."

Burke then explained why the ministers of the Church of England and the Church of Ireland could and should get their clerical formation in universities: they "require a different mode of education, more liberal, and more fit for the ordinary intercourse of life." Since their religion gives them "little hold on the minds of the people by external ceremonies, extraordinary observances, or separate habits of living" (i.e., celibacy), they acquire moral authority among the people "by cultivating their minds by all kinds of ornamental learning" of the sort imparted in universities and continued in later life because of "the liberal provision made in England and Ireland for the Parochial clergy, and the comparative lightness of parochial duties." This learning, said Burke, together with the social situation enjoyed by the clergy of the Established Church, "forms a sufficient security for their morals, and their sustaining their clerical character with dignity. It is not necessary to observe," he added, "that all these things are, however, collateral to their function; and that except in preaching, which may be and is supplied, and often best supplied, out of printed books, little else is necessary to a Protestant minister than to be able to read the English language."

Another of the terms of the proposed relaxation of the penal laws was that the appointment of Catholic bishops should be vested in the British Crown. Burke thought it would be insane for Catholics to accept this because, in choosing bishops, the Crown would have to rely on local officials who

> will pick out the worst and most obnoxious they can find among the clergy, to set over the rest. Whoever is a complainant against his brethren will always be considered as persecuted; whoever is censured by his superiors will be looked upon as oppressed; whoever is careless in his opinions and loose in his morals — will be called a liberal man, and will be supposed to have incurred hatred because he was not a bigot. Informers, talebearers, perverse and obstinate men, flatterers, who turn their back upon their flock, and court the Protestant gentlemen of the country — will be the object of preferment. And then I run no risk in foretelling that whatever order, quiet, and morality you have in the country will be lost.

In other writings, Burke advocated a much greater liberty for Catholics than they then enjoyed in Ireland. Here his argument was that the country needed an obedient Catholic clergy under good bishops. For, he said, if priests "are educated without any idea of discipline and obedience, and then put under bishops who do not owe their station to their good opinion, and whom they cannot respect, that nation will see disorders of which, bad as things are, it has yet no idea."

Burke wrote long ago, of course, and in another country, and his words no doubt have little relevance to the present situation of Catholics in America. But the reader may find in them some food for thought as he surveys the contemporary American Catholic scene.

How to Read a Newspaper

May 1989

When reading the *New York Times,* one must ask oneself certain questions: Why is the *Times* telling me this? Why does it tell it to me up front instead of back on page 30? What does the *Times* want me to believe today?

These questions spring to one's mind when reading a news story like the following, which appeared some time ago but is typical of many another. On Sunday, February 5, 1989, on page three of its National Edition, the *Times* carried a report written by one Seth Mydans about Pagsanjan, a town 40 miles southeast of Manila in the Philippines. According to Mr. Mydans, the town flourishes on prostituting boys to homosexuals, many of them visiting or resident foreigners. This trade in young male flesh, he says, is staunchly defended by the town government and the parents of the boys. As a resident who requested anonymity put it, "The moral attitude of the town is pro-prostitution. The attitude is, everyone's doing it, you're not going to get pregnant, and you get the money."

What is going on in Pagsanjan, Mydans reports, can be thoroughly documented by a woman who lives in the town and "will spread on her table hundreds of pictures of local boys performing sexual acts with foreign men, as well as neatly typed index cards with the names of the boys and their customers."

This is interesting and, if true (which I do not question), it is shocking, but is it simply a report on something taking place in an obscure town in a country halfway around the globe, or is something more being conveyed to us? One begins to suspect the latter when one reads the following sentences in the report: "The powerful Roman Catholic Church has had little to say on the subject of prostitution or the exploitation of women and children, in marked contrast to its aggressive stand against artificial birth control. President Corazon C. Aquino, a devout Catholic, also has not made an issue of prostitution, while at the same time avoiding the urgent but controversial problem of population control."

Ah yes, population control through artificial birth control. It would cure the poverty of the Philippines (and of any other Third World country) and no doubt raise the level of its sexual morals to that of the United States. But it is blocked by a Church that is callously indifferent to the plight of the poor, and by a devout but misguided woman who believes what the Church tells her. Members of the U.S. Congress will please note and remember when voting on foreign aid programs.

So will members of state legislatures, city and county councils, and local school boards. Foreign aid does not fall within their jurisdiction, but public health and sex-education programs do, and Planned Parenthood stands ready to help them, if not checked by a certain sinister institution. The scandalous behavior in Pagsanjan, the Philippines, you see, is relevant after all to our American concerns. The sophisticated reader of the *Times* will recognize the message, and the unsophisticated one will get it without realizing that it is a message.

Lest it be thought, however, that editorializing in the news columns is confined to the East Coast, let us mention a story which appeared in California, on page two of the *San Jose Mercury News*. It was hardly a hot-off-the-press story; it began by reporting police raids on an abortion clinic and some doctors' offices in Mexico City on March 16, 1989, but the *Mercury News* did not print it until Tuesday, April 11.

But no matter. The real point of the story, written from Mexico City by Katherine Ellison, was this: "Mexico's abortion law broadly resembles limits advocated in the United States by President George Bush. Under the law, abortions are allowed if the pregnancy could kill the mother or if it has resulted from rape." But Mexican experience shows that George Bush is wrong.

In a section of her story, subheadlined "Illegal abortion horror tales," Ms. Ellison recounts the same sort of statistics and anecdotes about Mexico with which we were deluged about our own country in the years before *Roe v. Wade*. If you were of adult age in the 1960s, you remember them well, and I need not detail them here.

The most important statistic that she alleges is that "every year at least half a million Mexican women deliberately abort their pregnancies. Every year, also, at least 100 of these women die. . . . The actual toll is much higher, perhaps in the thousands, insist doctors and others who have fought since the 1970s for legal abortions." Near the end of the article we learn that "reports in Mexico continue to state that up to 200,000 women each year die from complications, a number foreign experts call improbable." But, if the number is improbable, why report it? Perhaps in the hope that the inflated figure will be the one that sticks in your mind. You must be made to understand that Mexico is faced with a holocaust, not of babies like the more than 20 million we have aborted in the United States since *Roe v. Wade,* but of women who have died from illegal abortions.

And who is to blame for this? Ms. Ellison lays it on the line: "The search for a secret abortion, and the costs and risks of getting one are common trials for women of all economic classes in this Catholic nation." Mexico has an anti-clerical constitution and a record of persecuting the Church. "Yet Mexico is overwhelmingly a Catholic country. Top leaders go faithfully to Mass, priests have a strong, if subtle, influence, and laws reflect conservative morality."

The experienced reader asks himself why the *Mercury News* chose this moment to publish this report. He recalls that it appeared on April 11, two days after the Great Big Pro-Abortion Rally in Washington, D.C., which was meant to warn the U.S. Supreme Court that it had better not tamper with *Roe v. Wade.* Then it occurs to him that, just possibly, the *Mercury News* was helping the cause along with anti-Catholic horror stories from Mexico.

An Uncertain Trumpet

June 1989

There has been a sharp drop in vocations to the Catholic priesthood since Vatican II. One of the reasons for it may be confusion among priests themselves about what the priestly vocation is.

We have long had clerics who do not think that gaiety should be confined to the laity, and who therefore have dedicated their lives to fighting Jansenism by both word and example. Now we have priests who take it as their mission to relieve Catholics of their hangups on faith and morals by telling them how much of what the Church teaches they need not believe or do. Still others devote themselves to solving people's problems by, for example, finding ways for them to remarry after divorce. Yet others again concentrate on society's larger problems, and try to solve them through political action.

Some priests, particularly young ones, seem to be dubious about the significance of their own priesthood. I recall a concelebration of the Mass in which I once took part. The principal celebrant delivered a homily on the Eucharist in which there was much talk of bread and wine, but little, if any, of the Body and Blood of Christ. He referred to himself, along with the rest of us on the altar, as "presiding at the eucharistic liturgy." What that meant was not clear, since "Eucharist" seemed to be a warm and fuzzy feeling that embraced everyone and everything. But whatever it was, we were presiding at it.

Although there were at least fifteen priests on the altar, when it came time to distribute communion, that task was performed by a team of lay ministers, most of them women. It occurred to me, as I watched this, that if I were trying to attract young men to the priesthood, I would not go about it in this way.

But, of course, trying to attract young men to the priesthood is a sexist, pre-Vatican II idea rooted in an outdated ecclesiology. Since, as we now see, our real religion is democracy, and democracy means equality, recruitment to the priesthood must aim at women as well as men.

The priesthood to which we are to admit women, however, may not be what Catholics have previously understood the priesthood to be. Some years ago, for instance, I attended a symposium — more like a pep rally, as it turned out — on the ordination of women. The last speaker of the evening was a lady who since then has achieved a certain prominence as a newspaper reporter. But that evening she was a theologian, and offered a theological argument which in effect abolished the priesthood.

The conclusion toward which her argument steadily moved was that no one should be ordained, because the congregation does everything that is done in the liturgy. At the last minute, however, she remembered that she was there to argue for the ordination of women, so she concluded that women should be ordained. When she finished, I turned to an Episcopalian friend who was sitting next to me and said, "That lady may not know it, but she is not a Catholic." "Of course," he agreed, "that was straight Congregationalist theology."

I don't doubt but that some of those who advocate the ordination of women want them to be ordained to the traditional, sacramental Catholic priesthood. Others, however, seem to want to do away with that "magical" and "hocus-pocus" conception of the role of the priest. Not only does it elevate men above women, it confers on the clergy the privilege of exercising a divine power which is denied to lay people. But to give to some what others cannot have is to exclude the latter, and the idea of exclusion is offensive to pious democratic ears.

When someone brings up the subject of the priesthood, therefore, it is advisable to ask, What priesthood do you have in mind? It may be only a priesthood in which all can share because it can do nothing that any Christian cannot do. But then, is there anything Christians can do that non-Christians cannot also do? Must we not rather say that all of us, whether we know it or not — indeed, whether we want it or not — are children of the One God and can serve equally as instruments in his or her hands, without distinction of race, sex, or creed?

I know it sounds strange, but it is a fact, easily documented, that there is a certain amount of speculation in Catholic theological circles which questions not only the exclusive functions of the priesthood, but the exclusive claims of Christianity itself. We may no longer hold, these writers tell us, that Christ is uniquely the way, the truth, and the life; that no one comes to the Father but through him; and that there is no other name than his under heaven given unto men by which we must be saved. God wants all men to be saved, and all sincere ways of seeking him will lead us to salvation.

There is enough truth in that to make it an effective piece of sophistry. It is true that God gives every human being sufficient grace to be saved, and condemns no one for inculpable ignorance. But to draw the conclusion that therefore there is no one true religion is to reject Christianity with its undeniable exclusivist claim to be the saving truth revealed by God.

The number of priests who go that far is very small, but a larger number are manifestly uneasy about "triumphalist" claims to possession of the truth. The more widespread that attitude becomes among the clergy, however, the more difficult it will be to attract recruits to the Catholic priesthood. For if the trumpet gives forth an uncertain sound, who will gird himself for battle?

Papal Social Thought

August 1989

When John Paul II's encyclical *Sollicitudo Rei Socialis* (On Social Concern) appeared at the end of 1987, the *New Oxford Review* hailed it with delight as a socialist manifesto. More recently, in *Crisis,* Michael Novak has seen the encyclical as a belated papal discovery of what democratic capitalism has known all along, namely, the virtue of economic free enterprise. He quotes in evidence the passage (from section 15) of the encyclical:

> In today's world . . . *the right of economic initiative* is often suppressed. Yet it is a right which is important not only for the individual but also for the common good. Experience shows us that the denial of this right, or its limitation in the name of an alleged "equality" of everyone in society, diminishes, or in practice absolutely destroys the spirit of initiative, that is to say *the creative subjectivity of the citizen.* As a consequence, there arises, not so much a true equality as a "Leveling down." In the place of creative initiative there appears passivity, dependence and submission to the bureaucratic apparatus which, as the only "ordering" and "decision-making" body — if not also the "owner" — of the entire totality of goods and the means of production, puts everyone in a position of almost total dependence . . . similar to the traditional dependence of the worker-proletarian in capitalism.

But this is not quite so novel as Mr. Novak seems to think it is. In the line of "social encyclicals" that began with Leo XIII's *Rerum Novarum* in 1891 and has continued up to *Sollicitudo Rei Socialis,* there is a coherent tradition in which emphases vary but nothing is simply new. Thus, Leo XIII laid it down as a principle which "before all is to be considered as basic, namely, that private ownership must be preserved inviolate" (*RN,* no. 23). Seventy years later, in *Mater et Magistra* (no. 109), John XXIII reaffirmed that "the right of private property, including that pertaining to goods devoted to productive enterprises, is permanently valid" and "rooted in the very nature of things." The popes look upon private property as the spur to initiative and the source of wealth. "If incentives to ingenuity and skill in individual persons were to be abolished, the very fountains of wealth would necessarily dry up," said Leo XIII (*RN*, no. 22). Therefore, said Pius XI in *Quadragesimo Anno* (1931):

> Just as it is wrong to withdraw from the individual and commit to the community at large what private enterprise and industry can accomplish, so too, it is an injustice, a grave evil, and a disturbance of right order for a larger and higher organization to arrogate to itself functions which can be performed efficiently by small and lower bodies. This is a fundamental principle of social philosophy, unshaken and unchangeable, and it retains its full truth today . . . the true aim of all social activity should be to help individual members of the social body, but never to destroy or absorb them.

Every succeeding pope has confirmed this principle, which has become known as the Principle of Subsidiarity.

One will look in vain in the encyclicals for a condemnation of capitalism, the free market, or competition simply as such. Pius XI said of capitalism that "the system itself is not to be condemned" and "is not vicious of its very nature," although it has been seriously abused. Similarly, he said, "free competition" is "within certain limits just and productive of good results." So, too, Paul VI, in no. 58 of *Populorum Progressio* (1967), acknowledged that free trade's "advantages are certainly evident when the parties involved are not affected by any excessive inequalities of power: it is an incentive to progress and a reward for effort."

What, then, were the popes criticizing in the severe language that they so frequently used about capitalism? Paul VI expressed the thought of all of them when he deplored (*PP*, no. 26) "a type of capitalism . . . which considers profit as the *key* motive for economic progress, competition as the *supreme* law of economics, and private ownership of the means of production as an *absolute* right that has no limits and carries no corresponding social obligation." I have italicized the words which explain why Paul VI, like his predecessors, described this system as "unchecked liberalism" and later said (no. 58) that "the rule of free trade, taken by itself, is no longer able to govern international relations," adding significantly that "one must recognize that it is the fundamental principle of liberalism, as the rule for commercial exchange, which is questioned here."

As the Principle of Subsidiarity indicates, the popes are fully aware that the energies of society well up from below in the initiative and enterprise of individuals and private associations. What they reject is the classical liberal faith in the unfailing efficacy of the market. Social order is not and cannot be the automatic product of market forces, or of Marxian laws of history, or of any other mechanically functioning process. The just order which is the common good of society must be intended. It doesn't just happen if we set the autonomous individual free to pursue his own interest.

For that reason John Paul II can say (*SRS,* section 21) that both liberal capitalism and Marxist collectivism are "imperfect and in need of radical correction" (which, despite what some people have thought, is not to say that they are "morally equivalent"). He can also say (section 41) that the Church's social doctrine is not a "third way" between these two ideologies, because it is not itself an ideology but a moral theology which proposes the moral goals of human social life and the framework of moral principles within which men are to pursue those goals. The rest is politics, and "the church does not propose economic or political systems or programs, nor does she show preference for one or the other."

"Reason" and Abortion

September 1989

"The time of singing has come, and the voice of the turtledove is heard in our land" (Song of Sol. 2:12). In this land of America, as the prospect of abortion law being returned to the political process in the several states looms before us, the voice of the turtledove belongs to that political bird called a moderate.

Since we can no longer keep the regulation of abortion out of the legislatures, let us, he coos, take the abortion issue away from the wackos on both sides and reason together until we reach a sensible compromise. That was a song we never heard from the moderate while *Roe v. Wade* seemed to be firmly in place, keeping abortion law out of the grubby hands of the politicians and their constituents. But now that it appears the people may have something to say about the matter, the moderate has come out of the woods in flocks, covering the op-ed pages of newspapers and the columns of magazines with exhortations to reasonableness and compromise.

Which means that, since we may no longer be able to have abortion on demand, we should strive to keep as much legalized abortion as we can. If we must make concessions to the pro-lifers (who are all wackos by definition), let us concede as little as possible, while at the same time trying to persuade our own pro-choice wackos that at least some token concessions must be made, lest worse befall us and our cause.

Thus Michael Kinsley in a column published in *Time* shortly after the Supreme Court's decision in the Missouri abortion-law case. "America's abortion policy," he says, "could end up roughly where it is now: abortion on demand for the first three months (when more than 90 percent of today's abortions take place anyway), available only for certain weighty reasons in mid-pregnancy and generally unavailable for the last few weeks." That, he assures us, would be a "sensible arrangement."

I used to think that a moderate was someone who was willing to sell the pass, but only one yard at a time. Now I see that he has already given the whole pass away and is trying to persuade us that it was the only reasonable thing to do. Compromise, in the terms in which Mr. Kinsley proposes it, amounts to surrender: "A political compromise would deal with subsidiary issues, such as clinic standards and parental notification requirements, on their own merits," but it would have to leave the sacred right to abort substantially intact.

Politics is the art of the possible, as we all know and do not need moderates to tell us, and compromise is generally the only possible political resolution of divisive issues. But compromise is not in itself a goal to be achieved, and it works best when people have agreements that lie deeper than the matters on which they disagree. John H. Hallowell has explained in *The Moral Foundation of Democracy:*

> No one likes compromise for its own sake. . . . If a compromise is to approximate a solution to conflict, it must be made within a framework of goals and values commonly shared and mutually respected by all parties to the agreement. If it is to approximate a solution, moreover, it must embody what is best in all proposals, what will best promote the common good; and this can be determined only by appealing to those purposes and values that are shared.

A healthy democracy would work out its compromises on Prof. Hallowell's premises. The political battles over abortion, however, like the concomitant battles over euthanasia and "gay rights," are likely to reveal the extent to which basic values are not shared in this country. The compromise at which we shall arrive will be what political necessity dictates to people with sharply conflicting goals who have to live in the same community, and they will result, at best, from very hard-nosed bargaining.

Political necessity may well teach some of the more zealous opponents of abortion certain political realities. A reversal of *Roe v. Wade* by the Supreme Court will not of itself prevent a single abortion; it will only remove a judicially created obstacle to laws regulating, restricting, or prohibiting abortions.

Such laws will have to be passed by majorities in legislatures whose members are themselves elected by majorities, or at least pluralities, of the electorate. The laws that can win the assent of majorities will therefore fall short of what dedicated opponents of abortion want.

It will nonetheless be permissible and laudable to vote for such laws as the best we can get in a divided community in its present frame of mind. Compromise, in that sense, will be necessary, and ardent pro-lifers who cannot accept it will get nothing at all.

There is a still deeper reason than the mechanics of majority rule in a democracy for willingness to accept the results that can be achieved at any given time through the political process. It is that in the long run the laws cannot be much better than the people who make them and are governed by them. It is not enough to muster a temporary majority that can shove through a law. The political process must also be an educational process that convinces a substantial and lasting majority of the American people that abortion is a genuine human evil. If the process is nothing more than a political struggle, it will produce nothing more than temporary victories.

In the meantime there will be political battles, in the course of which the voice of the turtledove will try to lull us into acquiescence in "reasonable" liberal views on legalized abortion. When we hear that voice, let us keep three things clearly in mind: 1) These "men of reason" came to play. 2) The game they play is hardball. 3) They play to win — and we may profit by their example.

The Family Issue

November 1989

Some years ago, in the now-defunct *Center Journal*, the Methodist theologian Stanley Hauerwas put his finger on the radical flaw in the contemporary liberal theory of constitutional democracy. Constitutionalism means limited government as distinguished from government endowed with unlimited powers, and in America, he says,

> we have institutionalized the limited state. The state is understood only as one important actor in society; it does not replace the role or authority of other institutions such as the church, education or the family. This form of government is insured by basic rights guaranteed by law, such as assembly, speech, elections and assured transfer of power. Thus, democracies respect not only rights of individuals but of other institutions which are necessary to keep the state limited. In effect, the rights of the individual have become the secular equivalent to the church as the means to keep government in its proper sphere.

But, Hauerwas goes on to explain, relying solely on individual rights to keep government limited blinds us to the

> fundamental tension between our commitments to the rights of the individual, the preservation of intermediate associations, and the ability to retain a limited state. Indeed, the very language of "intermediate associations" already betrays liberal presuppositions which distort the moral reality of such institutions as the family. Whatever else the family is, it is not but another voluntary association. The very means used to insure that the democratic state be a limited state—namely, the rights of the individual—turn out to be no less destructive for intermediate institutions than the monistic state of Marxism. For it is the strategy of liberalism to insure the existence of the "autonomy of cultural and economic life" by insuring the freedom of the individual. Ironically, that strategy results in the undermining of intermediate associations because they are now understood only as those arbitrary institutions sustained by the private desires of individuals.

Or, as Christopher Lasch put it more recently in the *New Oxford Review*, "the family issue" came "to play such a large part in the politics of the 1970s and 1980s" because "liberalism now meant sexual freedom, women's rights, gay rights, denunciation of the family as the seat of all oppression, denunciation of 'patriarchy,' denunciation of 'working-class authoritarianism.'" The rights of the individual are now seen, not only as the bulwark against the power of the state, but as the battering ram to break down the institutions of society.

Last spring the Board of Supervisors of San Francisco passed, and Mayor Art Agnos signed, an ordinance allowing unmarried couples, both heterosexual and homosexual, to register their "domestic partnerships" at the County Clerk's office. The ordinance defines domestic partners as "two people who have chosen to share one another's lives in an intimate and committed relationship of mutual sharing, who live together and . . . have agreed to be jointly responsible for basic living expenses." To encourage commitment in such unions, the ordinance provides that a person who ends a domestic partnership must let six months elapse before registering again.

Those domestic partners who are city employees get the same sick leave, hospital visitation rights, and bereavement and maternity leave benefits as married couples. Stanley Hauerwas thinks that the family is not just another voluntary association, but in the city by the Golden Gate, it seems to be equivalent to just another domestic partnership, at least in the eyes of the law.

Such rights as this ordinance guarantees become claims, not only against government, but also against other individuals and private institutions. Last summer, for example, the highest court of the state of New York expanded the legal definition of a family in New York City's rent-control regulations to include persons living together in homosexual relationships. If one of those person dies, the survivor has the same legal right to remain in the rent-controlled apartment as a surviving wife, husband, or child, and the courts will enforce this right against the landlord.

"Legal and human-rights experts," according to the *New York Times*, have said that the state court's decision has implications far beyond rent control and could "affect everything from profound life choices, like decisions about partners and child-rearing to less significant matters, like whether people can compel insurance companies to compensate them for certain losses." The *New York Daily News* reported that civil-rights lawyers "now plan an assault on broader issues including homosexual marriages. 'Anywhere the word "family" is used — wills, inheritance, fringe benefits — we'll be there,' said William Rubenstein, the American Civil Liberties Union lawyer."

You folks out there in the Heartland may think that such things happen only in San Francisco and New York, but let me tell you, you've got trouble, right there in River City. Would you believe Wheaton, Illinois, site of Billy Graham's alma mater, Wheaton College? Two couples have brought suit against apartment-house owners there for refusing to rent to them because the couples are unmarried. "Nobody's going to tell me what to do," one of the unmarried ladies has announced, and who will venture to say that in this enlightened age the Illinois Department of Human Rights, which is investigating her complaint, will not agree with her? Or that it will remember that only a decade ago the Supreme Court of Illinois threw out a "palimony" suit on the ground that it is the public policy of Illinois to support the institution of marriage?

Taking Christmas Seriously

December 1989

Christmas is a scandal to the modern mind. It is not only that it has a child being born to a virgin; the greater scandal is that it has him born at all, as God entering the human race through a woman's womb. Christmas celebrates the birth of the incarnate God to a human mother whose name we know (Mary) in a place that is still there (Bethlehem), at an identifiable time in human history (when Caesar Augustus ruled the Roman Empire and Quirinius was governor of Syria). This immersion of God in historical particularity offends a mind for which, if there is a God, he should be above all that.

The Christ whose birth Christmas commemorates is presented to us as an historical figure who lived a real life in the real world, and at the end of that life was crucified, died, and rose again from the dead. The resurrection too, however, along with all the miracles in between, is intolerable to a certain type of intellectual who wants his religion reduced to a set of "meanings" unencumbered by embarrassing assertions of fact that cannot be true and must be taken as mythological.

That Jesus was born of a virgin mother is therefore translated into a symbolic way of saying that he was an important person. That he rose again from the dead is not denied — at least, not by theologians who want to go on teaching in Catholic faculties of theology — but it is "reinterpreted" in such a way as to take it out of history. To give but one recent example, the magazine *30 Days* for September 1989 quotes the Rev. David Coffey, president of the Australian Catholic Theological Association, as saying that "the resurrection is an event of grace not involving in any way the corpse of Jesus."

We must hold, that is to say, that Jesus in some sense rose from the dead (the Creeds force us to admit that much), but his dead body did not come back to life. The historical event of his death was not followed by the equally historical event of his returning to life in the body that died on the cross. Science tells us that a corpse cannot live again, and Fr. Coffey assures us that only "in a pre-scientific age" could one believe that a corpse did that. While we must believe in the resurrection, therefore, we must also believe that it means something other than that the dead body of Jesus rose again to physical life in this world.

If this kind of theological thinking is carried all the way through, it ultimately calls into question the incarnation itself, for it must seem strange that we can believe that God became man, but not that he was born of a virgin or that he rose from the dead. Liberal Christianity tends inexorably, as its history shows, toward Unitarianism, for which, as the quip has it, there is but one God at most. It not only takes Christ out of Christmas, it takes him out of history altogether. All that is left in the real world in which history actually took place is the man called Jesus who lived, taught, and was executed in Palestine two thousand years ago. The rest of the Christian faith is imaginative symbolism designed to convey insights into the human condition to a myth-making age. But in our age, whose only mythology is Science, the historical Christian faith just won't do.

The outburst of art, music, and liturgy that Christmas has produced during the Christian centuries was hardly inspired by this anemic and insubstantial liberal Christianity. People do not go to midnight Mass to celebrate a birth that is merely symbolic of whatever philosophical beliefs happen to be fashionable in theological faculties. Nor do men and women become Christians if that is all that Christianity has to offer. As C. S. Lewis wrote to his friend Malcolm, "did you ever meet, or hear of, anyone who was converted from scepticism to a 'liberal' or 'de-mythologized' Christianity? I think when unbelievers come in at all, they come in a good deal further."

Christmas is a season of joy because the Feast of the Nativity gives us something of supreme importance to rejoice about. It presupposes that we are a fallen race because of a real original sin, from the consequences of which we all need to be saved. Sin is not a popular subject, even in sermons, in an age in which religion is more and more a psychotherapy aimed at making people feel good about themselves. Yet we cannot fail to notice that the greatest horrors of our time are not the San Francisco earthquake, or Hurricane Hugo, or the tornado that ravaged Huntsville, Alabama. The worst evils we suffer are the ones we inflict on one another, on a scale we would consider massive if we had not become inured to it by seeing it every evening on the TV news.

We—all of us, and not only the obvious and flagrant bad guys—are weak, prone to sin, and in need of salvation. Without that conviction, Christmas makes no sense and gives us little joy. We rejoice because the real God became a real man and offered his life in expiation for our real sins, thereby giving us the chance to escape a real damnation and to win eternal life in a real heaven.

The tidings of great joy at Christmas are that "this day is born unto you in the city of David a Savior, who is Christ the Lord." With that announcement, Christ was born into this world. His last words to his apostles on leaving it were: "Go, therefore, and teach all nations, baptizing them in the name of the Father, and of the Son and of the Holy Spirit, . . . and lo, I am with you always even to the end of the world." Christ carries on his saving mission in historical time through his Church, and will carry it on until history comes to its appointed close.

All of these beliefs are implied in Christmas. If they are not true, the birth of Jesus from Mary in Bethlehem is insignificant. But if they are true, it is the most blessed event in history, on which the whole meaning of history turns. We have to take our Christianity straight, or it is not worth taking at all.

Doing Better for Lent

February 1990

In the coming season of Lent, the Church will ask us to reflect upon our sins and to do penance for them. While we are so engaged, we may also spare a thought for the dry rot that afflicts us collectively as the church in this country.

We may notice, for instance, that Lenten exhortations to do penance for our sins are not widely heeded among Catholics, because the sense of sin has faded among us, as it has among so many other people in the modern world. We may even be struck by the absence of Lenten exhortations, since the clergy are reluctant to upset us, or themselves for that matter.

In St. Mark's gospel (2:18-20), people asked Our Lord, "Why do John's disciples and the disciples of the Pharisees fast, but your disciples do not fast?" He replied, "Can the wedding guests fast while the bridegroom is with them? . . . The day will come when the bridegroom will be taken away from them, and then they will fast on that day."

That day has come, and has gone. Fasting in Lent was once a common Catholic practice, but no longer. Why, after all, should those who are not conscious of sin feel the need for penance? Even in some religious houses, no provision is made in the menu for those who might want to keep the Lenten fast. In the clerical circles in which I move, it is customary to joke about the ridiculous preoccupation we used to have with precisely how many ounces of food one could eat in a fast-day meal. We have got rid of that kind of scrupulosity, but we have done it by dropping fasting and the very idea of physical penance.

This shift of consciousness among Catholics helps to explain the phenomenon of whole congregations receiving Communion at Mass, even though most of them have not bothered to confess their sins or felt the need to do so. It also explains the demand for general absolution without the bothersome need for individual confession to a priest who might not agree with one's personal moral code. It throws light, too, on the outrage felt by liberal clerics when reactionary pastors announce from the pulpit that only Catholics should come forward for Communion. For many Catholics, it is apparent, the Eucharist has become a mere ritual, not a sacrament to be taken with utmost reverence.

The fading sense of sin also shows up in the growing Catholic acceptance of contraception, abortion, and divorce, and in our more tolerant attitude toward pornography, pre- and extra-marital sex, and homosexuality as an alternative lifestyle. The Catholic Church has always been keenly aware that ours is a fallen human nature, to the point where it sometimes scandalized pious Protestants by its readiness to forgive sins. The post-Christian world, however, is not only aware of fallen human nature but takes it as normative. Today, doing what comes naturally is not only what people do but what they have a right to do, and it is considered arrogant and unfeeling to ask them to do more than keep their quest for self-gratification within the bounds of moderation. That so many Catholics now take the same view of human nature reveals the dry rot that is eating away at the life of the Church.

For Christianity means nothing if it does not mean salvation from sin and from the disordered passions that lead to it. In the Christian view of man, all is not right with us, our nature is deeply wounded, and we need the constant help of divine grace through the Mass, the sacraments, prayer, and the practice of a Christian spirituality to live in a manner pleasing to God, and so to save our souls.

Catholics by and large once knew all that, even when they did not try to live it. But Christendom, the society in which Christianity could be taken for granted, has ended, has been coming to an end, in fact, for at least 300 years. With its final disappearance, we shall soon also see no more merely nominal or post-Christian Catholics. The gap between Catholicism and the general culture will be so wide and so inescapably visible that we shall all have to take our stand on one or the other side of it.

Critics may say that the only moral decline I can point to

(if it is a decline) is in sexual morals, and that today's Catholics are in fact better in other areas of life than earlier generations were — less racist, for example. But the sexually liberated Catholic who is a model of self-sacrificing Christian charity is a pipe dream. Conforming to the sexual mores of the post-Christian culture may make us more easygoing, tolerant liberal democrats, but it won't make us better Christians or even better citizens.

The end of Christendom will also manifest itself, as it is already doing, in the decay from within of Catholic institutions. In the larger Catholic colleges and universities, Catholicism will fade away like the Cheshire cat, leaving behind only a bland, reassuring, administrative smile. A similar process will take place in Catholic hospitals and social-welfare agencies, as both their personnel and the norms by which they are forced to operate become more and more secularized.

A magazine recently asked a number of prominent people, "What's Your Best Hope for the 1990s?" Walker Percy's answer was, "There will occur the spread of democratic societies, but of a certain sort: deeply informed by the values of the visual media, violence, pornography, standard network Brokaw-Rather ideology, Hollywood morality, and 10,000 Japanese car commercials. My hope is that we might do better." This Lent, let us hope the same for the American Catholic Church.

Civilization Is for the Civilized

March 1990

Civilization depends on the civilized imposing their standards on the uncivilized. But who decides who the civilized are? The civilized do, that's who. If you can't accept that, you are against civilization.

Does that go down too hard? Then consider this: science is what scientists say it is. And who decides who are scientists? Scientists do. They set the standards by which persons are recognized as doing properly scientific work, as distinguished from dilettantism, quackery, and magic.

Doesn't this mean that science itself is only what a self-constituted elite chooses to accept as meeting its own arbitrarily determined standards? No, it does not. It certainly is open to that abuse. But to say that science is what scientists accept as science is only to say that science, like every branch of human knowledge, consists of the judgments arrived at by human minds striving to understand some aspect of the real world.

If there is no real world to understand, obviously there is no science. Neither is there any science if there are no minds capable of grasping and agreeing upon the structure of the real world. There is no set of facts "out there" which speaks to us and says, "We are science."

Science depends on minds that can judge what is a fact, which facts constitute evidence, and when the evidence leads to a firm conclusion. It also requires a community of persons who, however much they may disagree on any particular scientific question, recognize each other as possessing the training, the self-discipline, and the intellectual honesty needed to take part in the pursuit of scientific knowledge. Science must be in that sense self-validating, but it is not therefore arbitrary.

Something similar is true of every profession. Lawyers, doctors, accountants, professors, and journalists must develop and enforce the standards for the practice of law, medicine, accounting, university teaching, and journalism. It does not follow that each of these professions is a law unto itself; each of them is subject, when necessary, to regulation by the general community which it serves. Nonetheless, at least in the first instance, those engaged in each profession must develop the standards of the profession and must judge who are the persons qualified to practice it. There is no escaping the need for human judgment and, therefore, the necessity of relying on human minds.

That is all very well, you may say, when we are dealing with judgments about facts that can be verified or falsified by experience and are subject to empirical proof or disproof. In those cases, the real world as we experience it controls our judgments. But such is not the case when we make judgments about what is good or bad.

Those "value judgments," as positivists call them, are not judgments about the real world, but expressions of our feelings about the world, nothing more. For that reason, moral judgments are all subjective and relative. To see that this is so, we need only look at the enormous variety of moral standards that have obtained among the cultures and civilizations of mankind.

Before we cave in, however, and accept this standard argument for moral relativism, let us pause and ask ourselves how relative our judgments about human good and evil really are. Take, for the sake of discussion, the following two lists (for which I pretend neither completeness nor any great depth of philosophical analysis):

life	death
nourishment	starvation
health	sickness
material well-being	destitution
community	isolation
respect	humiliation
friendship	enmity
marriage	celibacy
family	childlessness
knowledge	ignorance

| truth | error |
| meaning | meaninglessness |

If we compare each item with the item directly opposite it, is there any doubt about which of them is good in itself and capable of being chosen for its own sake, and which of them is bad or at least not capable of being chosen for its own sake? Yes, yes, I know that people do sometimes commit suicide — but only because life has become bound up with pain, misery, or disgrace which they find intolerable, not because they do not recognize life as in itself good and death as the end of that good.

Monks and nuns renounce marriage, family, and personal property, but only for the sake of a higher good, without which the renunciation would be senseless. No one pursues any of the items in the right-hand column as ends in themselves. If someone does choose one or another of them, we ask what good he hopes to obtain by choosing something not choiceworthy in itself. We do not ask that question about people who choose life, health, friendship, marriage, knowledge, or truth.

What makes these things desirable is not merely the statistical fact that most people desire them, as if they could just as well desire the opposite. It is that these objects of choice answer to basic needs of human nature, without the satisfaction of which it cannot survive or flourish. The goods in the left-hand column can furnish a society with a list (a partial one, to be sure) of its goals. But a society which took the right-hand column as its goals would be unendurable and would in fact not long endure. The civilized are those who are capable of understanding that.

The Devil We Know

April 1990

John Cardinal O'Connor, the archbishop of New York, created something of a sensation earlier this year with a Sunday sermon in his cathedral on the subject of Satanism. He got headlines for denouncing an increase in Satanic practices which he said were encouraged, particularly among teenagers, by heavy-metal rock music. What most grabbed attention, however, was his evident belief that Satan truly existed and that there are real, though rare, instances of demonic possession that require exorcism.

The press at once telephoned a number of experts for opinions on the cardinal's sermon, including those theologians who can be counted on to give a modernist answer to any question. Thus *Time* reported on March 19, 1990:

> Father Richard McBrien, chairman of the theology department at the University of Notre Dame, dismisses the idea of a personal archdemon as "premodern and precritical." Individuals tend to personify evil, he explains, "because we see it in people." But for sophisticates acquainted with sociology and other disciplines, says McBrien, "sin is now seen as something systemic, institutional and structural, as well as personal."

When I myself am asked if I believe in a personal devil, I always reply: "Of course. How else could one account for the liberal mind?" As you may imagine, this answer is not well received by sophisticates acquainted with sociology and other disciplines, and I must admit that it is a bit flippant. I am not concerned here, however, to defend my belief, but to ask another and more important question: Why is it taken for granted that, in the modern world, no intelligent person can believe in a personal spirit of evil or in non-human spirits of any kind?

For example, on the TV program *The McLaughlin Group*, moderator John McLaughlin asked a panel of four men what they thought of Cardinal O'Connor's sermon. Two of them dismissed it out of hand, but the other two were unwilling to do that. There is a spirit of evil in the world, they said, some rock music panders to it, and we should recognize Satanism as capable of doing genuine harm to young people—but they did not regard this spirit of evil as a person.

But how do we know that unseen personal agents do not act on human beings to tempt them to evil? To reject that possibility seems strange in Christians who profess to believe that the unseen grace of God is indispensable for good deeds and the avoidance of sin, and that unless God acts within us to enlighten our minds and move our wills, we cannot faithfully serve him. What, then, makes them so sure that all impulses to evil arise solely from ourselves? Is it really obvious to any thinking man that the horrors of the twentieth century are attributed exclusively to the base inclinations of the human heart?

To push the question further, is our understanding of the human psyche so exhaustive that we can fully explain all the motives that actuate human beings? Well, no, we have to admit that much work remains to be done in the science of psychology. But we must also insist that it is a science and that, in principle, it can explain the whole of human motivation. We may therefore be confident that some day it will do so, because what science cannot, even in principle, explain is not real.

This attitude reflects a certain view of the world that is derived from the spectacular triumphs of science in early modern times, which have continued to the present day. Science not only explains the world, it will eventually explain it entirely. Seen in this perspective, the world is a vast and complicated machine in which everything that happens can be reduced to prior and knowable causes. In such a machine we know that everything has a "natural" explanation, and there is no room for "supernatural," personal, non-mechanical causes.

But, of course, we do not *know* that; we can only believe it. Scientism, that belief that all phenomena, including human actions, can be explained by the method of the natural sciences, is as much a faith as any taught by a church. It is no less a faith because the multitudes who have been raised in it take it as unquestionable scientific truth. They rely, as Thomas Spragens remarks in *The Irony of Liberal Reason,* "on a credulous interpretation of scientific reason that has become the principal superstition of modernity." Those who are steeped in this superstition reject diabolic possession, not because there is no evidence for it, but because they are convinced that the evidence must have some natural explanation.

Will Rogers used to say, "The trouble with this country is that too many people know too many things that just ain't so." Our problem is not that we do not believe enough, but that we believe far too much, on no better ground than that it is what "everybody knows." A certain skepticism is therefore in order for men and women of Christian faith. Sheldon Vanauken has put it well in *Under the Mercy:* "There is only one wisdom for Christians: to look with a cool and very skeptical eye at all the things their own age is precisely *most certain* of. Especially is this true of the certainties that contradict what has been believed by wise Christians down the centuries."

Wise Christians have believed down the centuries in fallen angels. We may therefore do so, too, and need not be overly impressed by theological sophisticates. After all, as the Anglican writer Harry Blamires has said, "We do not need a horned devil, scattering lies, to lead us astray. A theologian, speaking selected truths, can do it just as easily." Especially if the theologian doesn't believe in the devil.

Handling the Easy Cases

May 1990

What would I do about abortion if I had the power? The first answer to that question is that I don't have that power, I am never going to have it, and I don't want it. In a constitutional democracy, no one, and no single group of persons, has the power to make and enforce laws. Under a constitution and within its bounds, democratic government is government by the consent of the people acting by majority, which is presumed to be the larger and sounder part of the people, at least in the long run.

That consideration should take care of the liberal cant about not imposing our moral beliefs on others. I cannot impose my moral beliefs on anyone, and most certainly not living, as I do, in the city of New York, where no candidate has a chance of election to high public office unless he lays his hand on his heart and vows never to do anything to restrict in any way the sacred right to abortion. Nor could all American Catholics together impose their beliefs on an unwilling people, even if we were a monolithic bloc, as we obviously are not.

Let us rephrase the question, then. What would I do about abortion if I were in high public office as, say, the governor of a state or the mayor of a city, or the majority leader of one of the houses of a state legislature? I would carry the people with me as far as I could persuade them to go in restricting abortion. More than that I could not do, and my task would be one of persuasion, not of imposition.

I don't mean, of course, that I could do nothing until I had persuaded Molly Yard, or the American Civil Liberties Union, or the editorial board of the *New York Times.* They are only part of the American people, and not by definition the larger and sounder part. Like the rest of us, all they can do is to try to persuade their fellow citizens, at least if the U.S. Supreme Court follows through on the indication it gave last summer that it is now willing to let the people have something to say on the legality of abortion.

In my effort to persuade, I would begin at the beginning, not at the end. I would not start, that is, by proposing a constitutional amendment to prohibit or restrict abortion. Such a proposal will be successful, if ever, only at the end of a long process of getting the American people to face and to think seriously about what abortion is and what we have done (or have had done to us) by the present legalization of abortion on demand.

To begin at the beginning is to talk about the existing situation: one and a half million abortions every year, which terminate almost a third of all pregnancies, and have killed more than 20 million babies since *Roe v. Wade*. If I were asked, as I surely would be, what I would do about pregnancies due to rape or incest, I would reply by asking another question: are you willing to do anything to reduce the 1.5 million abortions performed in this country every year?

If not, why not? Even according to Planned Parenthood's research arm, the Alan Guttmacher Institute, rape and incest account for only about one percent of all abortions; they are not the major issue in the abortion controversy. If, however, you agree that abortion on demand should be reduced, then work with us to put some effective limits on it. When we get to the end of the line and face the "hard cases," we can disagree — but let's get there first and, in the meantime, stop talking as if rape and incest were the only reasons for abortion.

One advantage of beginning at the beginning is that it breaks the abortion issue down into more specific issues on which it is possible to get the people to support legislation. William McGurn has explained in *National Review* (December 22, 1989):

> Most Amercians would be suspicious of a politician who favored allowing their 13-year-old daughters to have abortions without the parents' consent when these same girls can't get their ears pierced without parental permission. Most Americans would look askance at a candidate who opposed giving American women the same extensive information about abortion that they can get on every other operation. Most Americans would be horrified by a

candidate who believed it was okay for someone to have an abortion if she was hoping for a boy and proved to be carrying a girl. Most Americans would not give their vote to someone who argued for abortion into the late stages of pregnancy. Above all, most Americans would find something extreme in a party that was shown to oppose all these restrictions on abortion.

The second and more important advantage of taking this approach is that it keeps the abortion issue alive. Abortion is at bottom not merely a legal, or even a constitutional issue, but a moral one. Richard John Neuhaus has concisely stated it in the new monthly journal, *First Things:* "Who shall live? Who shall die? Who does, and who does not, belong to the community for which we accept common responsibility?" That is an issue of the most profound *public* moral importance.

But it would fade out of the consciousness of many people as an issue of public morality if we passively accepted the present legal situation, in which abortion is a purely private choice. To keep it in the public forum as a moral issue that involves the community as such, it is necessary to make it a legal and therefore a political issue, however much politicians wish it would go away. To make it a political issue, it is further necessary to propose the kind of legislation to which the larger and sounder part of the people are now, at this moment, willing to agree, and with which politicians will find it difficult to disagree. When the leaders of the people won't lead, the people have to get behind and push them.

Our Liberal Censors

Last fall I attended a talk given by Midge Decter, in the course of which she posed two questions: In an era in which contraception has become about as efficient as it can be, why are there so many abortions? In an age of almost complete sexual freedom, in which real bodies are readily available for sexual encounters, why is there so much pornography?

She did not pause to answer her questions, but simply put them out for our consideration. To my mind, the questions answer themselves. Take the lid off the cauldron of sexual passion, and it boils over on all sides, not only on the side on which a refined and liberal mind would like to see it overflow. When we liberated the id, we should have recognized that it was the id we were liberating.

But that is a facet of reality with which the liberal mind finds it difficult to deal. For it is a mind that has been schooled to look upon human nature as tame, reasonable, and well disposed, once it has been freed from the trammels of superstition and prejudice. This view of human nature received typical expression last year from my confrere, the Rev. Timothy Healy, S.J., when he wrote: "Literature and the arts, like scholarship, are essentially self-correcting. Give the critics and scholars time to do their sorting and, sooner or later, work that panders to titillation and debases human dignity will end up on the ash heap." *Magna est veritas et praevalebit* – truth is great and will prevail in a bit.

One must recall that Fr. Healy was until recently the president of Georgetown University and is now the president of the New York Public Library, and that academics and librarians are notoriously immune to the more intense human passions. So, too, are the editors of the *New York Times,* in whose pages Fr. Healy's plea for artistic and academic freedom appeared. Admirable as their view of human nature may be, however, we may doubt if it has much relevance to life outside the ivy-covered halls of academe, libraries, and editorial board rooms of the nation's more sedate publications. Indeed, we may wonder how much relevance it has even inside them.

Fr. Healy's column in the *Times* was provoked by Senator Jesse Helms' effort to prohibit the use of federal funds to subsidize "obscene or indecent materials" or work that "reviles a person, group, or class of citizens." Senator Helms, in turn, was moved to action by an exhibition funded by the National Endowment for the Arts that included explicit photographs of homosexual acts by the late Robert Mapplethorpe and a picture by another artist, entitled "Piss Christ," which portrayed a crucifix immersed in urine.

When the exhibition opened in a Cincinnati museum this spring, the museum director was indicted on charges of criminal obscenity. *Time,* the Weekly News Magazine (which in recent years has evolved into the Weekly Journal of Liberal Opinion) reported the incident under the caption, "battling Bluenoses." The indictment, according to *Time*'s reporter, exemplified "the hard-shell moral conservatism that has dominated Cincinnati for 30 years," and has made the city "a spawning ground for the national anti-abortion movement and the headquarters for the National Coalition Against Pornography." Hard-shell conservatism engenders opposition to both abortion and pornography, from which we may infer, in answer to Midge Decter's questions, that hard-shell liberalism inspires support for both pornography and abortion.

It is no easy thing, however, to be a consistent hardshell liberal. Charles Krauthammer has pointed out in one of his columns that "when Dan Rather reports on the banned-in-Cincinnati exhibit . . . he does not show the homoerotic, pedophilic or sadomasochistic pictures." Nor does *Time* print the photographs which it sneers at Cincinnati for trying to suppress. The media, says Krauthammer, practice censorship by classification: they defend the right to exhibit in theaters and museums, or to view in the privacy of one's home, what they themselves will not publish.

The issue, therefore, is not simply whether we are for or against censorship, but the more complex one of what sort of thing we wish to exclude from what places and media of communication. For all of their condescension to benighted Cincinnati, liberals are not consistent in their opposition to censorship, because they cannot be.

The liberal dilemma becomes more acute when factors other than sexual titillation enter the argument. A two-story-high sculpture of the black musician Duke Ellington is planned for the northeast corner of New York's Central Park, where it borders on Harlem. It has aroused controversy because it portrays the Duke and his piano standing on a platform which rests on the heads of nine nude women. Columnist Bob Herbert has no objection to the nudity, but to the fact that "the piano and the Duke are standing on the women's heads." That is raw sexism, male domination of women graphically depicted and carved in stone. What is worse, "the city plans to spend up to $450,000 to install the sculpture, and improve the area surrounding it." Bob Herbert was unable to get any city official to condemn this expenditure of money. "They want it both ways," he commented. "They want to oppose sexism but they don't want to be perceived as anti-art or pro-censorship."

Sins against the liberal light will not be forgiven. Sexism is one of them, racism and "homophobia" are others, but pornography is not. The next time you hear a liberal bleating about censorship, press him a bit and make him tell just what he is willing to censor, and why.

To Whom Shall We Go?

July 1990

The man who wrote the books of the Bible that recount the exodus of the Israelites from Egypt and their subsequent wanderings in the desert was a master storyteller. He had a hero, Moses; behind him the superhero, the Lord God; and a villain, Pharaoh. The people of Israel were cast in the role of the archetypal Common Man, sensual, shortsighted, and a born grumbler.

"Were there no graves in Egypt, that you had to take us out here into the desert to die?" they asked Moses when they saw Pharaoh's army pursuing them. After Pharaoh's army perished in the Red Sea, their complaint was: "Would that we had died by the hand of the Lord in the land of Egypt, when we sat by the fleshpots and ate bread to the full, for you have brought us out into this wilderness to kill us with hunger." When God gave them manna to eat, they tired of it and wailed: "O that we had meat to eat! We remember the fish we ate in Egypt for nothing, the cucumbers, the melons, the leeks, the onions, and the garlic, and there is nothing here but this manna."

Human nature has changed little, if at all, since their day. I thought of those early Israelites recently when I read the results of a poll taken among Catholics in New York for that city's *Daily News.* New York, of course, is not the United States, and polls are to be taken with more than one grain of salt (this one was based on answers to telephone calls to only 447 "current Roman Catholics" in the largest archdiocese in the country). But — and this is my point — if we were to accept the data of the poll at face value, the major difference that would emerge between the People of God in the time of Moses and the People of God today would be that then they were crying for food, while now they are more concerned with sex.

Thus we are told that 62 percent of Catholics do not think

that sexual intercourse by unmarried couples is morally wrong, 59 percent do not disapprove on moral grounds of listening to heavy metal rock music and videos, 38 percent do not see "homosexuality" as immoral, 83 percent would approve of a married woman using birth control pills, and 93 percent would approve of using a condom to prevent the spread of AIDS.

On the abortion issue, the question posed was: "Should a woman be able to get an abortion for any reason?" To this question 63 percent of Catholics answered "Yes." What that answer meant, however, was not clear because it is not clear what the question meant. It seems to have referred, not to the morality of abortion, but to making it legally permissible. Even in the latter sense, the question could mean, "Is there at least one ground, e.g., saving the life of the mother, that would justify allowing a legal abortion?" Or it could mean, "Should the law allow a woman to have an abortion for any reason she wants?" Since the question, as phrased, was ambiguous, what the Catholics who gave it an affirmative answer meant remains unclear. I find it hard to believe, however, that nearly two thirds of Catholics, even in New York, are in favor of abortion on demand.

On the other hand, when asked, "How much are you guided by Cardinal O'Connor's public statements on abortion, birth control, homosexuality, and AIDS?" 41 percent answered, "Not at all," and 60 percent said that their local parish clergy better represented their views on moral and religious issues than did their cardinal archbishop.

Why the local clergy are preferred to the cardinal on moral and religious issues appears in the answer to another question, to which 54 percent of Catholics replied that they would prefer "an independent American Catholic Church that would maintain symbolic ties with the Vatican, while placing the final decision-making power in the hands of the American clergy" (not, however, in the hands of Cardinal O'Connor, who is perceived as the pope's man).

Nancy Q. Keefe, a columnist in the Gannett newspapers that circulate in the suburbs north of New York, summed up this sentiment when she wrote: "Pope John Paul II is closing in on many things that the church never put under the mantle of infallibility, mainly moral teachings, where the whole matter of sexuality comes in. Dissent is still possible, but for how long? An Ursuline nun, who taught me theology many years ago, told me this last month: 'It's not dissent but creeping infallibility that's going to kill us.'"

If you can't get a Jesuit to tell you what you want to hear, get an Ursuline nun. It doesn't greatly matter from whom you get it, so long as the result is a sexual morality that people feel they can live with. The argument is that, since so many Catholics do not accept what the Church teaches, the Church must change her teachings. But whether a weak religion, soft at the core and sticky around the edges, can keep them in the Church is at least questionable. The recent history of the independent churches of England and Scandinavia, and of the Episcopal Church in the United States, does not offer us much reason for believing that it can.

Neither does the gospel give us any encouragement in that direction. When Jesus told the people, "Unless you eat the flesh of the Son of Man and drink his blood, you have no life in you," many of his disciples said, "This is a hard saying, and who can listen to it?" They went away, but he did not run after them and promise to change his teaching. Instead, he turned to his twelve apostles and asked them, "Do you also wish to go away?" Peter answered for them all, "Lord, to whom shall we go? You have the words of eternal life." The question is the same today: To whom shall we go?

Temporary Popularity

August 1990

Sometimes the throwaway line, the casual remark made tangentially to the writer's main subject, says more than a set treatise. Thus, in a recent issue of *Time,* two writers made passing comments on this country that revealed more about its moral condition than a sermon or an editorial would have done.

They were both writing about Scott Turow, a Chicago lawyer and author of best-selling novels. One of them wrote about the man himself, the other about his latest book. One of these writers referred to "the present moment, when moral authority is collapsing and the law has become, for better and worse, the sole surviving arena for definitions of acceptable behavior." The other alluded to "an America where the seven deadly sins are taken as seriously as the Seven Dwarfs." That is all they said on this point; they neither applauded nor deplored, but only stated as a fact that moral authority is collapsing in this country and that the idea of sin has vanished among us.

I do not mean to exaggerate the importance of their remarks. Two journalists writing about a novelist do not speak with the authority of, say, the Rev. Andrew Greeley explaining the Catholic Church to us. It nonetheless strikes me as significant that in a middlebrow, mass-circulation, liberal magazine, two writers should mention the collapse of moral authority in our culture as something known to everyone (except, of course, to theologians of a progressive cast of mind).

Whether they are conscious of it or not, Americans today are the intellectual heirs of John Stuart Mill, who promised in his famous essay *On Liberty* that, if society would free every individual to think, say, and do whatever he thought right (short of direct, tangible harm to others), the result would be a steadily developing consensus on higher levels of truth and more elevated standards of conduct. More than a century later, we are still waiting for that consensus to emerge, but we still believe in Mill's idea of liberty, whether or not we have read his essay or even heard of it. As Gertrude Himmelfarb has said, "we imbibe its 'truth' by osmosis, so to speak, from the culture at large."

Instead of a consensus we have a steadily progressing disintegration of commonly accepted moral standards and a growing tolerance of what we previously regarded as deviant conduct. Even those who still hold to traditional moral norms are often cowed into regarding them as merely personal, idiosyncratic beliefs, not to be imposed on others. Society as a whole now forbids only what the law forbids, and the law with increasing insistence concentrates on forbidding discrimination. As moral authority collapses, the freedom of the individual to choose his own moral standards is the highest social good, and discrimination is the only deadly sin.

This mentality has infected the Church as well as society at large. In the course of a lifetime I have met very few people whom I considered wicked and evil, but the Church today is full of "good people" who are convinced that, in everything that seriously affects their lives, their own sweet will is heaven's will. They do not rob, rape, mug, maim, or kill, and you could trust them with both your wallet and your wife. But let the Church's teaching of God's law conflict with their felt needs, and they begin to talk about "man-made laws": "My son needs a divorce." "My daughter needs an abortion." "I need to make a living." About these matters, they will make up their own minds and will feel free to disregard the Church's "man-made" laws.

In the current issue of the *New Oxford Review*, Fr. Jonathan Foster, O.F.M., tells us that, as far back as 1978, a Gallup poll reported that

> Eighty percent of its respondents expect to arrive at their beliefs, not through what the churches believe, but independently of them. The church is an institution, not where common vision and truth are found, but where the primary concern is for an experience of being comfortably at home. Even Catholics, presumably more doctrinally oriented, manifest this concern.

Or, as Cardinal Ratzinger wrote twenty years ago, the Church "has become in an entirely unprecedented way the Church of pagans: she is no longer, as she once was, the Church of pagans become Christians, but the Church of pagans who still call themselves Christians and in reality have become pagans."

There are two possible responses to this situation. One, favored by theologians of a progressive cast of mind, is to say, "If you can't beat them, join them." We must, that is, adapt the teaching to those taught and not insist on telling them what they don't want to hear and will refuse to listen to.

The other response, reactionary and unenlightened though it may be called, is more realistic. It is to follow St. Paul's advice to Timothy (2 Tim. 4:2-3), and "preach the word in season and out of season." For, while it is true that "the time is coming when people will not endure sound teaching, but having itching ears, will accumulate for themselves teachers to suit their own likings," that time will not last. It is at least a sound bet that the day will come when many people in our society will become so sick of the results of the collapse of moral authority that they will be eager to listen to a Church that teaches, as Jesus Christ did, with authority. As Perry Miller once said, "the price of popularizing for contemporaries is temporary popularity." Realism suggests that the Church cannot survive on temporary popularity.

The Customer's Rights

September 1990

$\mathbf{P}$eople who are in favor of a constitutional right to abortion on demand do not describe themselves as pro-abortion but as pro-choice. Abortion is what they want to protect, but they manage to defend it without talking about it by reducing it to a woman's right to choose.

A typical example of this kind of thinking is Justice Thurgood Marshall's opinion, partly concurring but mostly dissenting, in the case of *Hodgson v. Minnesota*, which the U.S. Supreme Court decided last June 25. The case concerned a Minnesota law which provided that no abortion should be performed on a woman under 18 years of age until at least 48 hours after her parents had been notified of her intention to have an abortion. But the teenager could bypass notification of her parents if she could convince a judge that she was "mature and capable of giving informed consent to the proposed abortion," or that an abortion without notice to her parents would be in her best interest.

I am not going to summarize what the court decided or why Justice Marshall disagreed with it. I want only to pluck a handful of passages from his opinion, to let the reader taste the flavor of his argument and so get some sense of how the pro-choice mind works.

To begin with, we get no indication from the opinion of what an abortion is or what it does. Marshall says repeatedly that it terminates a pregnancy, but we are left with the impression that pregnancy is a condition, like a bad cold, in which girls sometimes find themselves, and which they understandably want to get rid of without having to ask permission of uncaring parents or an uncomprehending public authority. There is no hint that a pregnancy involves any physical life other than the girl's or that the purpose and effect of an abortion is to kill the living being in her womb. That question, you see, was disposed of in *Roe v. Wade*, where the court said, "We need not resolve the difficult question of when life begins." Once that was said, the prenatal life in a woman's womb went off the court's radar screen, and all that the court's pro-abortion majority could see was a woman's "fundamental" right to decide "whether or not to terminate her pregnancy."

From that point on, it was the court's duty to defend this right against all contenders, be they the father of the child, or the woman's parents, or the public authority of the state. "No person," says Marshall, "may veto *any* minor's decision, made in consultation with her physician, to terminate her pregnancy. An 'immature' minor has no less right to make decisions regarding her own body than a mature adult."

Moreover, forced notification of parents "can be extremely traumatic for a young woman, depending on the nature of her relationship with her parents." Having to notify a parent may cause a girl to delay her abortion, with increased risk to her health. Some girls would even "forgo an abortion entirely and carry the fetus to term." But parents must not be allowed to deter their daughters from having abortions:

> The exercise of parental authority in some instances will take the form of obstructing the minor's decision to have an abortion. A parent who objects to the abortion, once notified, can exert strong pressure on the minor — in the form of disapproval, withdrawal of financial support, or physical or emotional abuse — to block her from getting an abortion. . . . In such circumstances, the notification requirement becomes, in effect, a consent requirement.

But, you may say, the Minnesota law provides a "judicial bypass": the pregnant teenager can avoid letting her parents know by going to a court and getting a judge's permission for the abortion. According to Marshall, however, that too is "unconstitutional because it gives a judge an absolute veto over the decision of the physician and his patient." It is also intolerably heartless because "the bypass procedure can be extremely traumatic for young women." He quotes with approval the words of the lower court which first passed on this case:

> The experience of going to court for a judicial authorization produces fear and tension in many minors. Minors are apprehensive about the prospect of facing an authority figure who holds in his hands the power to veto their decision to proceed

without notifying one or both parents. Many minors are angry and resentful at being required to justify their decision before complete strangers. Despite the confidentiality of the proceeding, many minors are left feeling guilty and ashamed about their lifestyle and their decision to terminate their pregnancy.

On the next page, Marshall cites authorities who say that, anyhow, the bypass procedure is a mere formality: very few petitions for abortion are denied, and the hearings typically last less than 15 minutes. The judicial bypass therefore is unconstitutional because it is useless. With this one-two punch, he knocks out the bypass procedure as being at once both traumatic and perfunctory.

Besides, Marshall asks, how can a judge "know more about a woman's medical needs or psychological makeup than her doctor?" When we reflect that the doctor to whom a teenage girl goes for an abortion without notifying her parents is very often an abortionist operating in an abortion clinic, we must wonder in what sense he is "her doctor," and how much he knows or cares about her "medical needs or psychological makeup." He will, of course, give her a physical examination before performing the abortion, in order to protect himself against a subsequent malpractice suit. But his attitude as a professional abortionist is likely to be, "You want an abortion? You've got it!" In this kind of medicine, as in department stores, the customer is always right.

"Man-Made Laws"

I have had occasion before in this space to remark on the ease with which Catholics today dismiss as "man-made laws" any moral teaching of the Church that they don't want to live up to. On no subject is this tendency of theirs more obvious than divorce and remarriage. Part of the blame for this, I must admit, lies with the clergy's habit of talking about marriage primarily in terms of canon law, a habit to which I myself have too often yielded.

The Church does have a sizable body of canons regulating marriage. Yet her teaching on divorce and remarriage cannot be reduced to laws that the Church has made and could remake. In its basic lines, Catholic teaching on this matter comes to us directly from the gospels, in the words of Jesus Christ. Since, as Christians, we believe that Jesus is God, we must accept his teaching as the law of God, not of men.

What the gospels tell us is familiar enough but it bears repeating, today more than ever. The clearest text is found in St. Mark (10:2ff.):

> And Pharisees came up and in order to test him asked, "Is it lawful for a man to divorce his wife?" He answered them, "What did Moses command you?" They said, "Moses allowed a man to write a certificate of divorce, and to put her away." But Jesus said to them, "For your hardness of heart he wrote you this commandment. But from the beginning of the creation 'God made them male and female.' For this reason a man shall leave his father and mother and be joined to his wife, and the two shall become one flesh. So they are no longer two but one flesh. What therefore God has joined together, let not man put asunder."

When his disciples questioned him about this teaching, Jesus said to them, "Whoever divorces his wife and marries another, commits adultery against her; and if she divorces her husband and marries another, she commits adultery."

The same account occurs in St. Matthew (19:1ff), with this variation, "whoever divorces his wife, except for unchastity, and marries another, commits adultery." In another place (5:32), Matthew adds, "and whoever marries a divorced woman commits adultery." St. Luke repeats the same words of Christ, but without the phrase, "except for unchastity" (16: 18). St. Paul adds (1 Cor. 7:10), "To the married I give charge, not I but the Lord, that the wife should not separate from her husband (but if she does, let her remain single or else be reconciled to her husband), and that a husband should not divorce his wife."

This commandment of Christ, that marriage is for life, and that people may not marry after divorce, is not difficult to understand, hard though it may be to accept. Those who are professionally skilled in explaining words away can no doubt explain away these words, too. The least that can be said, however, is that the burden of explanation lies on them, and not on the Catholic Church. All that she has to do is to point to the teaching of Christ and say, "That is my teaching, and that is where I got it."

Reciting what Jesus taught, of course, will not slow the emancipated modern Catholic down. He will simply refuse to believe that Jesus could possibly have meant what he said. There has been a revolution in sexual morals in this country, and the liberated Catholic has welcomed it, cheered on by dissenting theologians. As Russell Shaw wrote a few years ago in *Our Sunday Visitor*, "Wittingly or unwittingly, theological dissent has provided Catholics with a rationale for joining this revolution with clear consciences. The message is that one can be a good Catholic while rejecting what the Church teaches in favor of what American secular culture holds." As for the words of Christ, we'll leave it to theologians to dispose of them.

It is now a commonplace that about half of American marriages end in divorce. *Time* recently remarked, "It is probably no coincidence that even as women make gains in the workplace, more than 50 percent of new marriages today end in divorce." Women who are intent on getting into the fast lane to the executive suite stand an even greater chance of their marriages breaking up. It is also reported that couples who lived together before marriage have divorce rates 80 percent higher than those who have not done so. The reason for this, according to Neil G. Bennett of Yale University, is that "those who live together premaritally are simply less committed to traditional institutions and more committed to individualism than those who do not. These factors are also associated with a greater inclination to divorce."

As belief in "traditional institutions" wanes, and divorce and remarriage are accepted as normal, the very way in which our culture understands marriage necessarily changes. It has therefore become questionable, at least to me, how many young Catholics, raised in such a culture, are capable of contracting a valid marriage. They may pronounce the words, "until death do us part," but can they mean them? Can they even understand them? If not, how can they consent to an indissoluble marriage?

Talk to a priest who works on one of the Church's marriage courts, and you begin to see the dilemma with which those courts are faced. People are free to marry, but many of them don't know and cannot comprehend what Christian marriage is, hence the flood of annulments. Products of the American secular culture, they are more post-Christian than Christian. Making genuine Christians of them will necessarily include persuading them to take Jesus Christ seriously when he says, "What God has joined together, let not man put asunder."

How to Write Libspeak

November 1990

Would you like to know how to write like a liberal? You wouldn't? Well, then, at least let me tell you how to read and understand the liberal language which, for brevity's sake, I will call Libspeak.

As our Libspeak text, we shall take an article that appeared in the *San Francisco Bay Guardian* on August 22. The author was Bill Kenelan, whose position as West Coast correspondent of the *National Catholic Reporter* guarantees his credentials as a Libspeaker. The article was what, to avoid calling it a hatchet job, I will describe as an unfriendly criticism of Fr. Joseph Fessio, S.J., whom Mr. Kenelan accuses of nearly destroying the Jesuits' University of San Francisco (USF).

My acquaintance with USF is slight, and with Fr. Fessio even slighter. You will understand, therefore, that I do not vouch for the accuracy of the charges that Kenelan makes against him. I am interested only in the language in which he makes them so that you, the reader, may learn to recognize Libspeak when you see it.

But, first, who is Fr. Fessio? He is 49 years old and comes from a middle-class family on the other side of San Francisco Bay. But, says Kenelan, throughout his career, he "has been helped by the rich and powerful" (whose financial support Jesuit university presidents have been known to seek with, it must be admitted, uneven success). Aided by these sinister people, Fessio was able to found the St. Ignatius Institute as a kind of "great books" program within USF, and to dedicate it to what he would call Catholic orthodoxy but which, since we are trying to be evenhanded here, we will call conservative Catholicism.

From this base, Fessio pushes his "reactionary ideas" into "the mainstream of campus life," and has "transformed a respected Catholic university into a hotbed of radical right-wing dogma." Previously it "wasn't exactly UC Berkeley, but for a Catholic university, USF had a decidedly intellectual bent."

But, alas, no more. The student newspaper, *The Foghorn*, has been taken over by Fessio's admirers and has "defended South African apartheid as a bulwark against communism, faulted campus AIDS education efforts, and opposed gay student organizations." One of its editors proclaimed the paper "pro-papal, pro-life, and pro-U.S." *The Foghorn* has become the Catholic equivalent of the "venomously conservative" *Dartmouth Review.*

Fessio's followers in the student body also campaigned "to close down university health services that distributed contraceptive information," to forbid "law students from disseminating abortion-rights information on campus," and "to prevent speakers whose opinions they opposed — including U.S. Supreme Court Justice Harry Blackmun — from appearing at USF." A member of the Campus Ministry team says, "They have effectively stifled the atmosphere of inquiry and imagination that a university needs to thrive" (words which one hopes are remembered if anyone should ever invite Jeane Kirkpatrick or Jesse Helms to speak at USF). A Methodist student adds, "The Catholic Church needs to realize that being open is how you find the truth" (as, presumably, the United Methodist Church has done).

Fessio's greatest sin, however, is keeping liberal theologians out of the faculty of the St. Ignatius Institute. When he refused to hire a member of the USF theology department "because of his less-than-reactionary views," the theologian filed a complaint with the labor union that represents USF's unionized faculty (but didn't get the job). Although he has not administered the Institute for the past three years, Fessio somehow "continues to choose rigid conservatives over USF faculty for teaching posts at the Institute," and the Institute continues to emphasize "such esoteric topics as ecclesiology, patristics, mariology."

How comes he, then, to wield such power? He is protected by his friend and former professor, Cardinal Joseph Ratzinger, "the Vatican's front man in its current assault on liberation theology in Latin America and progressive priests in Western

Europe and the United States." Thus shielded, Fessio has created a "climate of fear" at USF.

Although his Institute enrolls only one or two hundred students out of about 3,500 on campus, they control not only the student newspaper but the Student Senate as well. How do they do it? A student who opposes them explains that USF students by and large are reactionary: "I couldn't believe how many Bush-Quayle signs I saw on campus during the elections." As a member of the Campus Ministry team says, at USF "McCarthyism is alive and well."

Fessio's other enterprise is the St. Ignatius Press, whose books, says Kenelan, "rail against secular humanism: Women are best off barefoot and pregnant or locked in a convent. Liberation theology is bad. Nuclear weapons are good. Overpopulation is a liberal myth. Gay people are better off dead." I happen to have a brochure of the St. Ignatius Press before me as I write. I find that it republishes books by Hans Urs von Balthasar, Etienne Gilson, Cardinal John Wright, Adrienne von Speyr, Mother Teresa, Josef Pieper, John Henry Newman, Louis Bouyer, G. K. Chesterton, Ronald Knox, Thomas Merton, Jacques Maritain, and even, God help us, Thomas à Kempis. It also publishes more recent authors, none of them in the same league as Rosemary Radford Ruether, but none of them likely to fit Kenelan's description above.

But a niggling concern with accuracy does not bother a Libspeaker. When reading Libspeak, just remember that liberal, progressive, and intellectual are synonyms, and liberals are open-minded seekers after truth who are in the mainstream. In contrast, those who oppose them are reactionaries, sometimes venomously conservative, but always intent on imposing right-wing dogmas in order to stifle thought. Remember, too, that liberals are never happy unless they see themselves as victims of McCarthyism.

Why Squirrels Can't Sing

December 1990

On the Fordham University campus, we have a lot of squirrels, probably because we have so many nuts. Since I am not a zoologist, I have never made a professional study of these cute little beasts. But I have been observing them in a casual way for some decades and have formed certain impressions of them in my mind.

One is that the round of activities squirrels engage in is very limited and that, consequently, all squirrels do pretty much the same things. As Spiro Agnew might have said, if you've seen one squirrel, you've seen them all. Most of their time seems to be spent in looking for food, though some of their running about may be merely playful. They eat, they drink, they sleep, and in the mating season, they mate. I presume they build nests of some sort to shelter the young when they're born. All squirrels do these things, and they do them in the same way from generation to generation.

I have never seen a squirrel do anything out of the ordinary, like play a violin, or paint a picture, or write a poem, or study the stars through a telescope. No squirrel, so far as I know, has ever addressed God and asked "What is squirrel that Thou are mindful of him or the son of squirrel that Thou dost care for him?"

Squirrels don't talk to God because they cannot conceive the idea of God. In this sense, your squirrel is a total agnostic who lives in a world without fantasy, myth, or meaning. He does not try to answer the ultimate questions because he cannot ask them. The world he lives in is the world of direct and immediate experience.

The squirrel is therefore also the perfect empiricist. The only world he knows is the one he experiences through his senses. If he cannot see it, hear it, smell it, taste it, or feel it, it does not exist for him. But if he can perceive it through his senses, he responds to it instinctively with desire or fear. As well as an empiricist, the squirrel is a complete hedonist.

You now see why the nuts among us humans want to be squirrels. To live without guilt or anxiety, with few desires (and those easily satisfied), is a prospect that entrances the modern, post-religious mind. Thus, a lady named Ann Giudici Pettner writes to the *New York Times:* "During the happy years I served in Kenya as adviser to the Ministry of Health and lived in close association with people from a number of tribal groups, it was my impression that sex was as natural as feeding (as opposed to eating or dining) and without the ego involvement and acceptance-rejection that plagues our culture. I admit to envy of their lack of anxiety."

Bliss was it in that Eden to be alive, but to be young was very heaven. There is, however, a snake in every paradise, and in Africa its name is AIDS, the spread of which is taking the edge off happy, joyous, and free promiscuity. Nonetheless, the dream of a guilt-free, anxiety-less culture persists and reaches beyond mere sexual freedom. At the heart of the dream lies a craving for the kind of freedom that is proper to brute animals, not to human beings. Despite their incessant clamor for freedom, what emancipated moderns want is an escape from human freedom with its necessary connotations of responsibility, praise or blame, and guilt.

An American theologian, Zachary Hayes, O.F.M., in *Visions of a Future*, has called attention to

> the modern tendency to wash out any strong sense of personal responsibility for the decisions we make in human life. It is easy to explain away the evil done by human beings as signs of psychological immaturity or emotional instability. In such a context, it is difficult for many to be convinced that moral choices are far more important than certain psychological categories would seem to indicate. A moral choice is an exercise of human freedom, and the quality of our choices has far-reaching consequences. Only if we have a human sense of responsibility for our actions can we find a meaningful basis in our experience for speaking of the religious reality of judgment. If we take the human awareness of responsibility to one another as the starting point for reflection on judgment, then it is possible to move to significant reflections on our responsibility in the presence of that Other whom we name God.

Such reflections, if indulged in, will lead us to awareness of the unpleasant realities of sin and guilt, but also to acceptance of grace, forgiveness, salvation, and the promise of eternal happiness. Of course, that acceptance requires us to recognize that we cannot both have the cake and eat it too, but must choose, surrendering one to have the other. Choice, however, is precisely what we'd like to avoid.

So, as C. S. Lewis said in the preface to *The Great Divorce*, we cling to "the belief that reality never presents us with an absolutely unavoidable 'either-or'; that, granted skill and patience and (above all) time enough, some way of embracing both alternatives can always be found; that mere development or adjustment or refinement will somehow turn evil into good without our being called on for a final and total rejection of anything we should like to retain."

It is a comforting belief, but it leaves us with no cause for rejoicing at Christmas and no reason for singing, "God rest ye merry, gentlemen, let nothing you dismay, for Jesus Christ our Savior was born on Christmas day." Squirrels cannot sing that song, and nuts who would rather be squirrels refuse to sing it, because they won't admit that there is anything to be saved from.

Downhill Passions

January 1991

Water naturally runs downhill. So do our human passions. There seems to be a psychological law of gravity that exerts a downward pull on our human inclinations, as physical gravity acts on material bodies.

I thought of this when I watched a videotape of a talk show on abortion that the Public Broadcasting System had once put on. It pitted a Catholic priest against a pro-abortion ex-nun, but the priest soon learned that he had two adversaries: the ex-nun and the moderator. Towards the end of the program, a third opponent was brought in, a young man who informed the priest that the Catholic Church was losing credibility because of its opposition to contraception, abortion, divorce, pre-marital sex, and homosexuality.

His choice of the word "credibility" puzzled me. If he had said that the Church was losing popularity, I would have understood him, because chastity has never been popular. But why did he say that the Church was losing credibility, i.e., the ability to be believed?

Belief, one would think, means accepting something as true, and requires an act of the mind rather than of our sex glands. Gonads are not organs of thought. Vitally important parts of human nature though they are, we can't think with them. They arouse strongly felt passions in us, and are an unfailing well-spring of song and story. But we cannot use them to arrive at reasoned convictions.

Yet this young man found it "incredible" that the Church should ask him, or anyone else, to restrain his sexual urges. In this he was a typical product of contemporary liberal culture, a culture perhaps best symbolized, on its popular level, by Madonna prancing about in her underwear, singing raunchy songs.

Liberalism marches on, and at the head of its column it

carries a banner with a strange device: Contraception — Abortion — Divorce — Fornication — Sodomy. If I were marching in that column, I would want to state my cause in terms less revealing and embarrassing. My banner would proclaim my devotion to Freedom — The Right to Choose/Personal Autonomy — or even (if I were candid) The Primacy of the Self. A flag bearing those phrases would give the boys something to rally 'round. But Sodomy? Promiscuity? Etc.? No; I would want to put a better face than that on what I stood for.

But liberalism in the United States today has come more and more overtly to stand for precisely what the young man blamed the Church for condemning. This was only to have been expected, however, as the final stage in a development that began centuries ago in the breakdown of medieval Christendom.

The late David I. Sarnoff reportedly was fond of saying, "There are three drives that rule most men: money, sex, power." What he said was nothing new. We have known from the beginning of time that material wealth, sexual intercourse, and the exercise of authority, all of those things good in themselves, easily become the objects of compulsive drives. But our Christian forebears recognized the need to restrain the lust for wealth, sexual gratification, and domination. They also honored, even when they did not imitate, the three vows of religious orders — poverty, chastity, and obedience — that renounced the satisfaction of these desires, even in their legitimate forms, as a salutary example to a fallen world inclined to sin by excess. The dechristianization of Western culture in the modern era, however, has progressively removed the moral bonds on these drives.

Modernity's revolt against the moral restraints on appetites was rooted, of course, in the appetites themselves. But it got its theoretical justification from writers like Machiavelli in the sixteenth century, who separated the lust for power from subjection to moral law, and Locke in the seventeenth, who furnished an argument for the unlimited acquisition of money. It was reserved for the final decades of our century to take the wraps off sexual desire. As Professor Joseph Cropsey has observed, "If a leading insight of modernity was that men do badly so long as they try to stifle rather than to compound with the passions, then surely the modern project must be said to have lain in a state of incipience until the sexual appetite . . . was itself at least reported on the surface."

That day has arrived: sex is now on the surface and up front, along with money and power, and is even more clamorous in its demand for recognition and approval by society. We now have, properly speaking, no sexual morality. Having uncoupled sexual activity from procreation, we discover that we have also uncoupled it from marriage and even from union with the opposite sex. We no longer see any natural structure or purpose intrinsic to sexual intercourse from which norms of right and wrong sexual conduct can be derived.

The only moral norms that we now accept are very general ones such as tolerance and respect for other persons, which a liberal theologian would call the Christian law of love. In regard to sex, this law tends to reduce itself to the precept: be sure to use a condom and never force your attentions on an unwilling partner.

It is a morality that has flowed, like water, downhill to its lowest level. In the nineteenth century, even that great exponent of liberal freedom, John Stuart Mill, could still declare: "It is better to be a human being dissatisfied than a pig satisfied; better to be Socrates dissatisfied than a fool satisfied." Today the satisfied pig declares Socrates to be lacking in credibility.

Salvation One by One

February 1991

How odd of God to choose the Jews, said Hilaire Belloc. He said that because he did not like Jews. But even if we discount his anti-Semitism, we can't help thinking that it was odd of God to choose the Jews or any other group as his vehicle of revelation and salvation. Steeped in egalitarianism as we are, we instinctively feel that it was unfair and, worse yet, undemocratic to single out one people, in preference to all others, as God's chosen one.

To our way of thinking, God should have offered salvation in the same way and on the same terms to all human beings everywhere and at all times. But, for one thing, there is no evidence that God has done that. For another, in the biblical and Christian account of salvation, he has acted in a very different way. He has chosen to act through particular human agencies to bring men to the knowledge of himself.

It is Catholic doctrine that every human being is given sufficient grace to save his soul, and nothing I say here calls that into question. But that is not the only Catholic doctrine, nor does it tell us how God acts in human history to lead men to know, and love, and serve him, and so to achieve the purpose of human life.

He does not do it through some universal illumination, or advertising campaigns, or mass movements that sweep all before them. Still less does he do it through military conquests. Rather, he works through personal contacts and individual conversions. We are saved one by one.

So it was at the beginning of Christianity. When John the Baptist saw Jesus walking by, he pointed to him and said, "Behold the Lamb of God." Two of John's disciples thereupon went after Jesus. When he noticed that they were following him, he turned and asked them what they were looking for. They said, "Teacher, where are you staying?" "Come and see," he replied.

So they went with him and spent the day with him.

As a result of that meeting, one of the disciples, Andrew, went and brought his brother Simon to see Jesus. Simon was the man whom Jesus renamed Peter and later made the head of his church. The following day, Jesus met Philip, and Philip in turn went to his friend Nathanael and told him that he had found the Messiah, Jesus of Nazareth. Nathanael sarcastically asked, "Can any good come out of Nazareth?" and Philip replied, "Come and see." Nathanael came, saw Jesus, and promptly became his disciple.

We notice in these passages from the Gospel according to John (1:35-51) that Jesus made disciples one by one, through personal contact with them. This individual, personal call to discipleship runs all through the New Testament. Jesus was sent, first of all, to preach to the people of Israel and, through them, eventually to convert the Gentile nations. In his ministry in Israel, he often preached to large crowds, and with great immediate effect, but in the end the crowds abandoned him. His final and effective appeal was to the individual person who responded in faith and love.

Out of these original disciples, he chose twelve men as his apostles. Very ordinary men they were (not a Ph.D. or a CEO in the lot of them) and, after his resurrection, he sent them out to convert the world. That work still goes on, and its method is still, "Come and see." Some refuse to come; others come, and having seen, go away; but some come, see, and believe. This is how God has chosen to save mankind, one by one, as individuals respond to his invitation, conveyed through his Church: "He who hears you hears me, and he who rejects you rejects me, and he who rejects me rejects him who sent me" (Luke 10:16).

For Jesus was absolutely intransigent on that point. The invitation had to be accepted, as all the parables about invitations to the heavenly wedding feast indicate. So also do his severe denunciations of the religious leaders who refused to accept him as the promised Messiah, even after the miraculous works he performed to verify his mission from God. They had sinned against the light and therefore would not be forgiven: "I say to you, all sins will be forgiven the sons of men, and whatever blasphemies they utter; but whoever blasphemes against the Holy Spirit never has forgiveness, but is guilty of an eternal sin" (Mark 4:28-29). As he said in his last words to his apostles in St. Mark's Gospel (16:15), "Go into all the world and preach the gospel to the whole creation. He who believes and is baptized will be saved; but he who does not believe will be condemned." Jesus offers us salvation, but each of us has to accept it or reject it, for himself.

All men receive sufficient grace to save their souls. If they respond to it, they seek for God, but often in dark and distorted ways, as their various cultures influence them to do. Presumably the continual human sacrifices of the Aztec religion were more a hindrance than a help to Aztecs seeking God. In our own day, I once turned on my radio and came in on a sermon just as the preacher was saying, "In our church, we're so liberal that we don't know that we believe." I didn't pause long enough to find out what church that was, but I doubt if it was much help to sincere seekers after God.

The Christian message is that, not only do men seek God, he comes to them with a full and final revelation of himself. He does it in history and through human instruments, therefore not everywhere at the same time, but through the mission of his Church as it is carried on in historical time and space.

As we are fond of saying today, we are the Church, not just the clergy, but all of us — and that is true. It follows, however, that we are all among the instruments whom God has chosen to bring men to the knowledge and love of himself. Even in this ecumenical age, we cannot shirk that task: someone's salvation may depend on it.

Celibacy and Contempt

March 1991

Any stick is good enough to beat a dog with. Or, as Ronald Knox put it, any stigma is good enough to beat a dogma and especially, these days, if the "dogma" is Catholic sexual morality. A recent example is a book by a German lady, Uta Ranke-Heinemann, which Doubleday published late last year under the title, *Eunuchs for the Kingdom of Heaven.* Its thesis, I gather from reviews, is that the Catholic Church for centuries has inculcated a "pleasure-hating, celibate contempt for marriage and a maniacal cult of virginity." She documents this thesis with every anti-sex statement she could find by any Catholic cleric in the history of the Church. Since that history is now nearly two thousand years long, she has come up with more than a few sticks to beat the ecclesiastical dog with.

There is, however, more than one way to read the same history. One might, for instance, take Harold J. Berman's *Law and Revolution: The Formation of the Western Legal Tradition,* which the Harvard University Press published in 1983. Berman is a professor of law at Harvard and a distinguished legal historian. Being of Jewish ancestry, he is presumably free of pro-Catholic bias. Yet he paints a very different picture of the Church's attitude toward women and marriage from the one that Ranke-Heinemann presents in such glaring colors.

Berman's thesis is that in the late eleventh and twelfth centuries, the papacy centralized the Church's authority in Rome and, through its "new canon law," founded the Western legal tradition. This canon law, he says, was the first modern Western legal system, on which later secular legal systems were modeled at all levels of government. He calls this great change in medieval society the Papal Revolution of 1095-1122.

According to Berman, the Papal Revolution was very much a reform movement, intended not only to free the Church from domination by emperors, kings, and feudal lords, but also to humanize and Christianize society. It is not that Christianity had previously had no effect on law and social custom. On the contrary: "Gradually, between the sixth and eleventh centuries, Germanic law, with its overwhelming biases of sex, class, race, and age, was affected by the Christian doctrine of the fundamental equality of all persons before God: woman and man, slave and free, poor and rich, child and adult. These beliefs had an ameliorating effect on the position of women and slaves, and on the protection of the poor and helpless."

Under the influence of the Abbey of Cluny, various synods in France issued peace decrees which "forbade, under pain of excommunication, any act of warfare or vengeance against clerics, merchants, Jews, women, and peasants, as well as against ecclesiastical and agricultural property." But the development of a universal canon law for Christendom greatly broadened and strengthened these reform movements.

The Church had long promoted "the idea of monogamous marriage by free consent of both spouses" in previously pagan societies "in which polygamy, arranged marriages, and oppression of women predominated." But "this idea had to do battle with deeply rooted tribal, village, and feudal customs," so "children continued to be married in the cradle, and family relations continued to be dominated by the traditional folkways and mores of the Germanic, Celtic, and other peoples of Western Europe." It was only the Papal Revolution that "made it possible to effectuate to a substantial degree ecclesiastical policy concerning marriage and the family."

Thus, "canon law offered considerable protection — as contrasted with the folklaw of the society in which it first developed — to the female partner in the marriage." In the words of another historian, whom Berman quotes, "Before God, the two parties to marriage were equal and the doctrine of equality was first taught by Christianity. In practice it meant, above all, that the obligations, especially that of fidelity, were mutual." The husband was recognized as the head of the household, and the Church for the most part accepted the severe restrictions which the secular law placed on women's property and other civil rights. But, says Berman, "to protect the widow it insisted that no marriage could be contracted without a dowry, that is, the establishment of a fund which could not be reduced in value during the marriage." The indissolubility of marriage was another bulwark of a wife's security.

Canon law "also strengthened the protection of the surviving spouse and children against disinheritance by the testator" (i.e., the husband and father). Under canon law, "the part that could not be taken from the wife and children was also the part that they inherited without a will; and all other kin had no right of inheritance at all unless the decedent had named them in a will."

The Papal Revolution also "pursued policies that were favorable to peasants." For one thing, the Church, which was "by far the largest proprietor in Europe, . . . often attracted peasants from other estates by offering more favorable conditions of life and work." It "generally emancipated the slaves on its own domains and thereby, as well as through other means, contributed to the virtual elimination of peasant slavery throughout most of Europe in the eleventh, twelfth, and thirteenth centuries." Slaves became serfs, and "Pope Hadrian, himself of humble birth, declared that the marriage of a serf, with or without his lord's consent, was valid and indissoluble." The disappearance of slavery was followed by "the widespread emancipation of the serfs in the thirteenth, fourteenth, and fifteenth centuries."

When we consider that the canon law, which played so large a part in these reforms, was entirely framed by celibate clerics we must marvel at how well they managed to keep their celibate contempt for marriage under control.

Just a Matter of Taste

April 1991

St. Patrick's Day, 1991, has come and gone, and now is, as they say, as dead as yesterday's newspaper. But there are lessons to be learned from what happened in New York on that day that will be worth remembering long after the scent of lavender has gone from the wearing of the green.

One is that there actually exists an Irish Lesbian and Gay Organization. I had always thought that an Irish queer was someone who preferred women to whiskey. But now it appears that there are real, practicing homosexuals among the Gaels, they are organized, and they insisted on marching as a unit in the world's largest St. Patrick's Day parade.

The Ancient Order of Hibernians, which runs the parade, tried to wriggle out of letting them in by claiming that there was no room for them in the number of units that could march within the time limits set for the parade by the city. At that point, David N. Dinkins, the mayor of New York, intervened and said he would extend the time allowed for the parade. A "compromise" was reached, by which the homosexuals could march, if they did not carry banners, and Mayor Dinkins promised to march with them instead of in the Mayor's traditional place at the head of the parade. So he did, too, to an angry chorus of boos all the way up Fifth Avenue.

From this incident we may learn something about David Dinkins, still more about the city of New York, and even something about the political culture of the United States. First, why did David Dinkins jump into this controversy when he didn't have to and had very little to gain by it? He did it because he is a black political leader who has fallen for the delusion that the defense of black civil rights depends on an utterly undiscriminating opposition to discrimination of any kind, against any group.

Anti-discrimination is a seamless garment and requires a

rainbow coalition of all groups that feel oppressed. As the mayor explained, "What happens in New York goes around the world immediately and we ought not to be seen as a city that discriminates." To understand Mayor Dinkins, it is necessary to see that he really believes that.

The only issue that his mind can grasp is discrimination, which is BAD. It matters not what the ground of the discrimination is, because there is no public standard of judgment, moral or legal, that can justify discrimination on any ground. All persons (and, some people would now add, animals) who are discriminated against have achieved what Joseph Sobran calls Accredited Victim Status and have a common cause. They are all one in the only essential aspect, that of being victims of a discrimination which must be attributed to blind bigotry, because there is no other possible explanation for it.

That was the line taken by editorial writers in the *New York Times* and *Daily News,* and by the usual gaggle of ex-Catholic columnists, but from them we had to expect it. With Mayor Dinkins, however, it is a sincere belief. After the parade and the reception he got from the onlooking crowd, he said in an op-ed column in the *Times* that he was "deeply saddened, and quite frankly surprised, by the outbursts at the parade." All that he could see in those outbursts was "a fearful rage of intolerance" and "a fear of a lifestyle unlike their own." In his eyes, nothing was at issue but a lifestyle, and as we all know — do we not? — all lifestyles are equal, none being better than another.

In New York today, the equality of all human beings has become, in George Will's apt phrase, the moral equality of appetites. There is no common human nature that furnishes us with common standards of human goods and founds a community with a common public morality. Everything is a matter of taste. Some like chocolate, some like vanilla. Some like Beethoven, some like rock. Some like girls, some like boys. Some prefer the stolid security of marriage, some seek more free and flexible arrangements. Some enjoy family life, some can't stand it. That the family is the foundation of society, and that the homosexual lifestyle is a direct attack on it is neither here nor there, because it is only an opinion and a matter of taste, like all of the above. Public authority, therefore, must treat all of them with even-handed impartiality, intervening only to see to it that no one discriminates, not even the Ancient Order of Hibernians in organizing a St. Patrick's Day Parade.

Mayor Dinkins is significant only insofar as he symbolizes the moral and intellectual bankruptcy of official New York. His predecessor, Mayor Edward I. Koch, tried to force religious agencies running social service programs under contracts with the city to hire homosexual workers. The city's courts have undermined the legal status of the family by broadening its definition to include any group of people living together in a long-term relationship. The chancellor of the city's public schools, having announced that 80 percent of their high school students are "sexually active," recently persuaded the Board of Education to approve of providing the students with free condoms. (Having thrown money at a social problem, we now throw condoms.) In New York, anything goes, so long as it doesn't discriminate.

And not only in New York. Keep an eye on Washington, and when you hear of a civil rights bill before Congress, ask yourself what principle Congress is trying to implement, and what social consequences it will have.

The Prophet Motive

May 1991

A darkness is spreading over the Catholic Church. So says Father Richard McBrien, chairman of the Theology Department of Notre Dame University, in one of his syndicated columns. His column was once widely published in the Catholic press, but not so widely any more, since a number of bishops have decided to drop him and other columnists who have what he calls "a genuinely critical approach to ecclesiastical issues" from their diocesan newspapers. The pre-Vatican II Dark Ages, he therefore fears, are upon us again.

Not that all is lost. He assures us that the Vatican's attempt to control the Catholic universities has failed. With a few glaring exceptions, Catholic universities in this country have retained their liberal credentials: "institutional autonomy and academic freedom." Nor has this caused any real harm to our faith and morals.

Despite the cries of alarmists, the Church is not "dangerously divided over matters of doctrinal and moral substance." No respected Catholic theologian that Fr. McBrien knows denies or questions "first principles of morality or the core of the Catholic faith." Theologians have aroused alarm only by their dissent from Catholic teaching on such matters — serious, to be sure, but not of primary importance — as "birth control, papal authority, Mary, abortion, homosexuality, feminism, clerical celibacy and the like."

Fr. McBrien furnishes us with a list of beliefs which lie "closer to the core of Christian and Catholic faith." It is too long to reproduce here, but one item in it will suffice for comment: "the redemptive value of his [Christ's] life, death, resurrection and ascension." I daresay no Catholic theologian who wants to keep his job will challenge that proposition. But if we ask a theologian what resurrection and what ascension he has in mind, we may discover that he derides the notion that, as

229

one theologian has elegantly put it, "a corpse came back to life." The resurrection, on which St. Paul tells us all our faith and all our hope depend, was not a bodily resurrection, but a spiritual and symbolic one. But not to worry: we're all Catholics here and the core of our faith has not been touched.

The deeper issue raised by Fr. McBrien's theology, however, is not what this or that theologian holds about a particular doctrine, nor whether certain doctrines stand nearer than others to the center of our faith. Granted that there is a hierarchy of Catholic beliefs, some being more essential than others, the question remains, where is the court of last appeal on what doctrines are at the core of Christian faith and what doctrines, whether core or not, does the Church authoritatively teach as true.

The question is hardly a new one. Sir Leslie Stephen remarked on it years ago in *English Thought in the Eighteenth Century*. (Stephen, best known as the father of the novelist Virginia Woolf was ordained in the Church of England, but lost his faith and became an agnostic.) Once Western Christendom had splintered into a multitude of sects, he pointed out, "the true faith must be that residuum which was common to all so-called Christians. In the language of the time this problem thus presented was to make out a list of fundamentals — of articles of faith, that is, which were necessary to salvation; and the difficulty of accomplishing the task supplied the Catholic controversialists with many taunts against their adversaries." This is a problem that is not solved by moving it into the Catholic universities and leaving it to the theologians. They have their function, and discussion and debate have their place, but the authority to define what the Catholic faith is and what the Catholic Church teaches belongs, as it must, to the hierarchy headed by the pope.

Furthermore, the much-touted value of "dissent" is much exaggerated. Here a word from Leslie Stephen's brother, Sir James Fitzjames Stephen, will be instructive. Like Leslie, James eventually rejected Christianity altogether, retaining only a robust Protestant dislike of Catholicism. But, as the saying goes, he lost his faith but not his reason, and thought that John Stuart Mill was wildly optimistic in believing that opening all subjects to public debate would result in a convergence of minds on higher levels of truth. On the contrary, said Stephen:

> The notorious result of unlimited freedom of thought and discussion is to produce general scepticism on many subjects in the vast majority of minds. . . . It seems to me that to publish opinions upon morals, politics, and religion is an act as important as any which any man can possibly do; that to attack opinions on which the framework of society rests is a proceeding which both is and ought to be dangerous. I do not say that it ought not to be done in many cases, but it should be done sword in hand, and a man who does it has no more right to be surprised at being fiercely resisted than a soldier who attacks a breach.

Dissent is no sure high road to truth, and its results in contemporary religious bodies have not been encouraging. Speaking of the mainline Protestant churches in America and their steady loss of members, *Time* has said: "Not only are the traditional denominations failing to get their message across; they are increasingly unsure just what that message is." When Robert Runcie resigned as Archbishop of Canterbury in "the Church of England [which] is fast fading as any kind of force in the nation's life," *Time* remarked that "his successor will confront the same passionate left-right disputes — not only over women clergy but homosexuality, remarriage after divorce, modernization of *The Book of Common Prayer*, and assaults upon the belief in Christ's virgin birth and the bodily resurrection."

These issues may not touch the core of the Christian faith as Fr. McBrien understands it, but they are wrecking the Church of England. We may profit by its example.

Family Is as Family Does

June 1991

It was bound to come, I suppose. For generations polygamists have been quietly tolerated by law-enforcement officials in small towns along the Utah-Arizona border. Now, however, according to the *New York Times*, polygamists "have begun a virtual public relations campaign to achieve tolerance, respect, a greater following, and ultimately legal protection." The American Civil Liberties Union has joined them by adopting a policy resolution calling for the legalization of polygamy.

I don't foresee polygamy sweeping the nation. Now that Justice William J. Brennan has retired from the Supreme Court, there is no danger that a majority of the justices will declare it a constitutional right. But in this country we have left ourselves with no logical ground on which to reject the polygamists' demand for equal respect and legal protection. As the mayor of one of the desert towns, who himself has five wives, has pertinently observed, "In this liberal age, with all the alternative life styles that are condoned, it is the height of folly to censure a man for having more than one family."

We have reached that height because of our previous folly in translating the statement in the Declaration of Independence, "All men are created equal [and] are endowed by their Creator with certain unalienable rights," into the proposition that "all lifestyles are equal." They are equal in our eyes because we no longer recognize any natural and objective standard by which we could judge any one of them superior or inferior to any other one. The rights with which the Creator has endowed us—not that we really need a Creator—come down to the right to live as we please, so long as we don't stop others from living as they please. That is, as Mr. Norman Lear might put it, the American Way, or in other words, the established liberal orthodoxy of the United States.

This is the height of folly we have reached, and now there

may be no remedy for it but to laugh at it so loudly and so long that even university professors, judges, journalists, and politicians will begin to feel foolish. We shall need good lungs, however, because there is an awful lot out there to laugh at.

For an opener, let us take a letter to *Time* which scolded the magazine for having "insulted each woman of the Mustang Ranch bordello by labelling her a 'floozy.' Professional prostitutes prefer to be known as 'pros.' You owe the women of the Mustang Ranch, and all pros, an apology for your careless designation."

Silly, of course. But is it any sillier than the sensitivity of umbrage-taking individuals and organized groups that are constantly on the lookout for language to take offense at? Or than the following passage which the late Justice William O. Douglas wrote in dissenting from a Supreme Court decision which upheld a conviction for publishing obscene literature?

> Some of the tracts for which these publishers go to prison concern normal sex, some homosexuality, some the masochistic yearning that is probably present in everyone and dominant in some. Masochism is a desire to be punished or subdued [which] may be expressed in the longing to be whipped and lashed, bound and gagged, and cruelly treated. Why is it unlawful to cater to the needs of this group? . . . Another group [fetishists] represented here translates mundane articles [e.g., shoes] into sexual symbols. . . . But why is freedom of the press and expression denied them? Are they to be barred from communicating in symbolisms important to them?

Granted, Justice Douglas was a droll fellow and not to be taken seriously. But the view he expressed — all lifestyles are equally deserving of respect — has been gaining ground since he left us and went wherever good liberals go when they die. For example, in a number of states, lesbians are battling each other in court over child-custody and visitation rights. Before the relationship between these women broke up, one of them conceived a child by artificial insemination; the other took the role of the child's "father," and is claiming a father's rights, now that the "marriage" has ended. Such lawsuits raise the question, what is a family in the eyes of the law? They are part of a larger drive to dissolve the traditional definition of the family as a married couple and their children, and reduce it to any long-term relationship among people living together, on the premise that all relationships are equal. In California, people not related by blood are registering with the state as families, under a law originally written for another purpose, in the hope of eventually winning the legal benefits enjoyed by families. Two years ago, New York State housing officials redefined the family to allow the surviving partners of homosexual or other unmarried couples to get the benefit of rent-control laws.

Earlier this month, the General Assembly of the Presbyterian Church (U.S.A.) had before it the report of a study committee which recommended that the church drop its prohibition of sexual relations outside of marriage. To its credit, the Assembly rejected the report and, anyhow, it was little worse than a similar report submitted to the Catholic Theological Society of America some years ago. But we surely have not heard the last of pleas that churches should not condemn sexual relations, married or unmarried, hetero or homosexual, which are characterized by genuine equality and mutual respect. After all, equality and mutual respect are what America is all about, and what Christianity is about, too.

At this point you can laugh or cry. Laughing is easier, and may even do more good, if you laugh long enough and loudly enough.

When the Magic Is Gone

July 1991

The two sexes have an intoxicating effect on one another, but eventually they sober up. When they do, their tendency today is to walk away from each other, explaining that the magic has gone out of their relationship. Those who do not walk away settle down to a real married life, often successfully.

One reason for the frequency of separation is that people expect marriage to do for them what nothing on earth can do: make them happy. We may think that we are marrying a goddess (or a god, as the case may be, but I have never understood what women see in men). In fact, however, we can only marry another human being, with whom we have to learn to live. It can be done, and often is, but it takes a determination on both sides to make the marriage work. It does not happen automatically.

Yet successful marriages are in accord with human nature, not against it. God made men and women to form lasting couples. As Pope John Paul II said in his encyclical *Sollicitudo Rei* (On Social Concern), "the transcendent reality of the human being . . . is seen to be shared from the beginning by a couple, a man and a woman (cf. Gen. 1:27), and is therefore fundamentally social." We are by nature social creatures, and our sociality is rooted in our natural division into two sexes. All of human society grows out of that basic natural fact.

Marriage is a freely chosen union between equal persons, and their equality must never be forgotten or denied. But if it is to last, marriage must be understood to be a union between persons of opposite and complementary sex, not only physically but psychologically. Clasp your hands before your face, look at them, and reflect that you can't do this with two right hands or two left hands, but only with opposite and facing hands. So, too, with marriage. It won't work if each partner insists on being a right hand.

It struck me during a recent concert by the tenor Frank Patterson that men write love songs about women but, although women commonly return more love than they get from men, they seldom write songs about them. Their failure to do so may betray a lack of musical talent, but more likely it reveals the natural polarity of the sexes. Woman is the flame and man the moth that is attracted to it, so men write the songs and women listen to them (without, one hopes, believing every word of them).

Given this natural polarity, we must acknowledge that there are different roles for men and women in marriage, in the family, and even in the workplace. The idea of distinct sex roles goes against the individualistic and egalitarian grain of American thought. We are not supposed to see men and women as different and complementary, but as identical and competitive, in a society in which a person's worth is judged by his/her job. But that is an illusion we shall have to get over if we are to have a viable society.

I have no universal formula for the working roles of men and women in the society of the future, and I doubt if there is one that can be carved in stone. In the pre-industrial age, when people lived on farms or, when they lived in the cities, in buildings which were at once their homes and their workplaces, women were closely engaged in their families' enterprises. But they did not perform the same functions as their menfolk. Industrialization revolutionized the role of women by separating the workplace and the home, not always with good effects. As we move into the post-industrial age, it is impossible to predict with certainty what the economic structures of the future will be, or how men and women will fit into them and combine them with their family lives.

This much, however, we can say: one of the ill effects of the separation of the workplace and the home has been our increasing acceptance of the idea that a woman can develop her potentialities, contribute to society, and justify her existence only through a full-time job that takes her outside her home for several hours a day. On that premise, women are victims of injustice if they do not have equal access with men to jobs, promotions, and salary increases. To expect a woman to make her primary role that of having and rearing children, and being the center of a family and a home, is to demand that she subordinate her life to her husband's.

I gather from my married friends that a successful marriage, out of which a strong family comes, requires a good deal of subordination to one another on both sides. But this is not to adopt the Swedish ideal of the equal responsibility of man and wife for earning the family income and performing identical roles in raising the children. The rate at which marriages and live-in arrangements break up in Sweden indicates that something is missing in that ideal, namely, a common-sense human understanding of what a couple is.

In this country, the *New York Times* has reported: "An unusual alliance of conservative Republicans and liberal and moderate Democrats is pressing the Federal Government to adopt policies that members say will reverse the decline and breakup of American families." The alliance includes persons as diverse as Phyllis Schlafly and Patricia Schroeder, Gary Bauer, who worked for Ronald Reagan, and William Galston, who worked for Walter Mondale. According to the *Times*, "both sides of the coalition agree that strengthening the family is the best way to make progress on a number of domestic ills from drug abuse to poor achievements in education."

The measures they propose include a bill to lessen the tax burden on families and "permit more parents, generally mothers, to spend more time at home with their children, rather than having to work full time." They are also "talking about encouraging the states to revise divorce laws to discourage couples with young children from separating." These proposals represent what William Galston calls "second thoughts about a value system oriented toward individual freedom." They may flower in a rediscovery of that divine idea, the married couple.

Anything Goes, Almost

August 1991

Last spring date rape was a big topic of discussion in the media, which very properly condemned rape, but did not question a woman's right to be "sexually active" if she so chose. In their view, not merely the only crime but the only sin that could be committed was to force sexual intercourse on a woman against her will.

As one feminist writer put it, a woman has the right to say no at any point in the process leading up to intercourse, and the man who does not obey her ought to be punished. In the world of feminist fantasy, the sexually active woman is a sacred cow, and should not have to put up with a minotaur — half man and half bull — who doesn't understand that he must desist the moment she says, "Stop!" Which is to say that anything goes, except rape.

The feminist fantasy is intelligible, however, only in the larger context of the liberal fantasy. In that imaginary world, the individual is autonomous and sovereign, bound by no moral norms to which he has not agreed. It follows that the only norm of morality is consent. No action is wrong if all parties involved have freely agreed to it, because the only thing that could make it wrong is the lack of consent by one or other of the parties.

This liberal morality has obvious attractions for persons intent on consummating a meaningful relationship, but it cannot be confined to fornication, and inevitably extends itself to other actions. Thus we have a member of the New Hampshire legislature who voted for a bill inviting the French manufacturer of the abortion pill, RU-486, to conduct a trial of the pill in that state. She explains, "I'm a Republican, a Catholic, and a mother of six. But what I support above all else is an individual's right to personal choice." Or, as a woman in Poland who disagrees with the Catholic Church on abortion proclaims,

"Every Catholic has the right to choose."

That means, in effect, that moral right and wrong do not govern choice; instead, choice governs morality. That is a position, however, in which it is difficult to be consistent. Women have been prosecuted for using hard drugs while pregnant because, as the plague of "crack babies" shows, drug use can severely damage an unborn child. Such prosecutions face the liberal society with a dilemma: can it hold that these women have no right to harm their unborn children, while maintaining that they have the right to kill the children by abortion?

On this point the National Organization for Women seems to have made up its mind and resolved the dilemma. At least, when the New York State legislature passed a bill requiring sellers of alcohol to post signs warning pregnant women that drinking alcohol could cause birth defects, the president of NOW's state branch objected on the ground that the bill would set a precedent for upholding the rights of the unborn against the rights of pregnant women. We may credit NOW with being consistent: a woman's right to choose is supreme, and prevails over all other considerations.

Further questions continue to arise about the limits of choice. In California, doctors have transplanted bone marrow into a 19-year-old girl, who was dying of leukemia, from her baby sister. The parents of the baby girl say that they conceived her precisely so that she could be a donor for her sister. They are the first parents to admit publicly that they had a child for that reason, but many others have done it privately. "Some parents," according to the *New York Times,* "have sought prenatal diagnosis to insure that the fetus had genetically compatible tissues necessary to serve as a donor, intending to abort it if not." This degree of freedom of choice bothers even some ethicists.

It would be hard to establish a relationship between freedom of choice and certain recent statistics published by the U.S. Census Bureau, but one can't help wondering if there is not some connection between them. In the past twenty years, there have been dramatic increases in the following percentages: of women who have never married, people who live alone, children in single-parent families, and divorced persons. I certainly do not imply that these are all bad people who have done bad things. But we may ask whether there would be quite that many people in those categories if our society were not so dedicated to the ideal of the autonomous individual who chooses his own norms, follows his own conscience, and regards his own sweet will as heaven's will.

Let us give the last word to that less than Delphic oracle, Madonna. *Time* has said of her, "Every fresh outrage is a soaring career move." But she claims that, while she indeed makes money at what she does, she is also shouting the battle cry of freedom and leading a revolt against an oppressive patriarchal society: "My rebellion is not just against my father but against the priests and all the men who made the rules while I was growing up."

All that she and many another in our culture can see are "the rules," which they regard as a sheer imposition on their sovereign wills. It would not occur to them that "the rules" may embody the lessons of countless generations of human experience, express fundamental needs of human nature, and reflect the divinely established order of the world. The ability to choose is part of our nature, and we cannot avoid using it because human life is a series of choices. The question at issue is whether there are given standards — divinely revealed, naturally known, or humanly evolved — that govern our choices, or does each of us create his own moral universe?

A God to Live For

September 1991

It is common knowledge among Catholics that there is a "crisis" in vocations to the priesthood. There is no common agreement, however, on the causes of this sharp decline in the number of vocations. The most convincing explanation that I have read is that it is rooted in a crisis of faith.

I don't mean a total loss or outright rejection of the faith held by the Catholic Church, but something more subtle. In a perceptive article which is well worth reading, in the August 1991 *Commentary,* Irving Kristol remarks that "though many people still go to church or synagogue for psychological reasons (consolation, hope, fear), very few educated people actually think that their immortal souls are at stake as a result of their beliefs or actions. Man's immortal soul has been a victim of progress, replaced by the temporal 'self.'" Nor has this occurred only among avowed secularists. "Christianity and Judaism have been infiltrated and profoundly influenced by the spirit of secular humanism."

Mr. Kristol does not hail this development. On the contrary, he says that we are witnessing the

> collapse of secular humanism as an ideal, but not yet as an ideological program, a way of life. . . . If one looks back at the intellectual history of this century, one sees the rationalist religion of secular humanism gradually losing its credibility even as it marches triumphantly through the institutions of our society — through the schools, the courts, the churches, the media. . . . Secular humanism is brain dead even as its heart continues to pump energy into all of our institutions.

The future of the Catholic priesthood is not a matter of concern to Irving Kristol (whose article is entitled "The Future of American Jewry"), and he does not mention it. But I believe that he has put his finger squarely on the deepest reason for the waning desire of young Catholic men to become priests:

they do not actually think that men's "immortal souls are at stake as a result of their beliefs or actions." Consequently, they cannot take their religion seriously enough to consider committing their lives to its priesthood.

For Catholicism is a religion of redemption and salvation, in which the stakes for which we live our lives are enormously high, being nothing less than eternal life or eternal damnation. Without that belief, our religion becomes a soft sentimentalism, which believes that everyone is saved because it is unthinkable that God should let anyone go to hell. If we can't believe that comforting doctrine, we replace it with a *hard* sentimentalism, which declares that, since hell is impossible, so is heaven, too, and we are here as on a darkling plain, etc. Neither view is likely to attract candidates to the priesthood.

In the Catholic view of the world, as Pope Paul VI stated it in *Profession of Faith,* "in Adam all have sinned, which means that the original offense ommitted by him caused human nature, common to all men, to fall into a state in which it bears the consequences of that offense." The most radical of those consequences is that without the special help of God, called grace, none of us can consistently live in accordance with God's will. We cannot save ourselves by our own intelligence and willpower alone.

From this situation we are redeemed by the life, death, and resurrection of Jesus Christ. Through the grace that he has won for us, we can win heaven and save ourselves from that eternal separation from God which is hell. Catholicism is therefore a religion of hope, based on the love that God has shown us in sending his eternal and only-begotten Son "not to be served, but to serve, and to give his life as a ransom for many" (Matt. 20:28, Mark 10:45). But redemption presupposes that there is a fate from which we need to be saved, that of hearing from the same Son of God the dread words, "Depart from me, you cursed, into the eternal fire prepared for the devil and his angels" (Matt. 25:41).

We are endowed by God and nature with intelligence and free wills. While they are not sufficient to save us, they are indispensable to our salvation, for God will not save us without our consent or against our wills. As St. Angela Merici said,

"God has given everyone liberty, and therefore He compels no one, but only points the way, calls, and persuades."

Jesus Christ came, as he said, that we might have life, and have it more abundantly (John 10:10), but he will not force it on us. We must choose it, accept the gift of grace, and cooperate with it. It is within our power to reject it out of self-will, and so choose to be damned. Seen in that light, human life is an interaction between God and man, and a drama whose outcome is salvation or damnation.

A distinguished French theologian once remarked that it is not necessary for us to know how many people go to hell. It is enough if we remember that, in the words of the Epistle to the Hebrews (9:27), "it is appointed for men once to die, and after death comes judgment." That alone should make us believe that our freedom really matters and regard life as a serious business.

A man who takes it seriously may feel called, not only to save his own soul, but to dedicate his life to helping others to save theirs through the ministry of the Church. But no one will accept that vocation who has been seduced by modernity into believing in what a lady in Los Angeles has called, in a letter to *Time*, "the God that I always knew existed: the nonjudgmental God, the loving God, the God who has no requirements, no prejudices, and no restrictions." The therapeutic God, for whom no one really lives, and certainly no one is willing to die.

The Court of First Resort

October 1991

On Tuesday, October 8, 1991, shortly before the U.S. Senate was scheduled to vote on the nomination of Judge Clarence Thomas to the U.S. Supreme Court, Senator John C. Danforth of Missouri took the floor and denounced the way in which the Senate was handling the nomination. "This whole confirmation process," he said, "has been turned into the worst kind of sleazy political operation, with no effort spared to assassinate the character of Clarence Thomas." What Senator Danforth said contains an element of truth that far transcends the fate of Clarence Thomas.

After he spoke, the Senate postponed its vote on the nomination until its Judiciary Committee could hold special hearings on the sensational testimony of Anita Hill and Judge Thomas's reply to it, as well as listening to other witnesses. What I write here implies no judgment on which of these two persons was telling the truth. The point I make is only that the process by which the Senate confirms or disconfirms nominees to the Supreme Court has become a thoroughly partisan political process. It may not always be a sleazy one (though in this case it certainly was one because of the calculated leak to the media), but it is always in danger of becoming a no-holds-barred fight to the death.

The reason for the fight being so intense is that the stakes are so high, and they are so high because the power that the court now claims and exercises is so great. Historians of a liberal bent of mind will tell us that the court has always been a political body in the sense of being a law*making* body, because those who can interpret the law with final authority make the law. There is some validity in that argument, inasmuch as a constitution that is meant to last for ages cannot always be so clear and unambiguous in its terms that there is no room left for interpretation. But if the argument is pressed to the point where the court has authority to give the force of constitutional law to such undefined concepts as liberty and equality, we destroy constitutional, i.e., limited, government.

The major source of such unlimited power in the court is the due process and equal protection clauses of the Constitution. Prior to the Civil War, the court made little use of the Fifth Amendment's clause that no person "shall be deprived of life, liberty, or property without due process of law." After that war, the Fourteenth Amendment imposed similar restrictions on the states: "No State shall deprive any person of life, liberty, or property without due process of law; nor deny to any person within its jurisdiction the equal protection of the laws." Even then, however, the court was slow to expand the meaning of those clauses, declaring that it did not want to be "a perpetual censor on all legislation of the States."

At the turn of the century, however, the court discovered a right of "freedom of contract" in the word "liberty" in the due process clauses, and used it regularly to strike down labor legislation, such as minimum-wage and maximum-hour labor laws. Professor (later Justice) Felix Frankfurter was thereby moved to declare, "The due process clauses must go." They did not go, but in 1937, under the pressure of the Depression and the New Deal, the court noted that "freedom of contract" occurred nowhere in the Constitution, and abandoned it as a basis for decisions.

In the second half of this century, the court has returned to the due process and equal protection clauses, and has found in them an ever-welling source of new constitutional rights. As a consequence, a constitutional historian, Leonard W. Levy, has remarked that now, "the States in our federal system can scarcely act without raising a Fourteenth Amendment question." The court has reduced the due process and equal protection clauses to the concepts of "liberty" and "equality." Since the Constitution itself does not supply the meaning of those concepts, the court furnishes their meaning from whatever ideology the court's majority can be persuaded to accept. The court has thus become a secular Holy See, with the law school professors as its theologians, and exercises a degree of power over our public morality and public policy that the Holy See in

Rome would hardly dare claim.

That, I believe, is what Judge Robert Bork had in mind when he wrote, "I am far from denying that there is a natural law, but I do deny that we have given judges the authority to enforce it, and that judges have any greater access to that law than do the rest of us." The question is not whether there is a natural law that binds us all, but whether the Constitution gives judges power to enforce natural-law principles that are not written in the Constitution.

In recent decades, a series of liberal justices (by no means all of them appointed by Democratic presidents) have carried out a constitutional revolution by writing their notions of liberty, equality, and justice into the Constitution. Liberals today, having accomplished so much of their agenda through the courts, now understandably want to protect the constitutional revolution. They have in that sense become conservatives who try tenaciously to preserve the revolution's gains by blocking the appointment of new justices who may undo them. Some of them, it is now evident, will stop at nothing to do so, and have thereby turned the Senate's confirmation process into the sleazy political process that Senator Danforth called it.

I myself agree with Felix Frankfurter that we should get rid of the due process (and equal protection) clauses, or at least rewrite them so that they will no longer be the unlimited grant of power that the court has made of them. But I know that that cannot be done. We might at least, however, make a beginning by getting over the idea that all of society's ills can be cured by the decisions of the Supreme Court.

The Sex Taboo Teens Need

November 1991

Dr. Bruno Bettelheim, a psychoanalyst, committed suicide last year. He was 86 years old, his wife had died, a stroke had impaired his ability to write, and he had been moved into a retirement home. Feeling that his life was no longer worth living, he ended it by his own hand.

I mention this sad fact only because it suggests that Dr. Bettelheim was a man of solidly secular views and free from religious hangups. We may therefore listen to him with respect when he tells us, as he did in the *New York Times Magazine* on April 13, 1969:

> If a society does not taboo sex, children will grow up in relative sex freedom. But so far, history has shown that such a society cannot create culture or civilization; it remains primitive. Without sex repression, there is no prolonged span of intellectual learning.

Yet that seems to be the direction in which American society is now going. As a lady who was watching a Gay Pride parade said to a reporter, "Everybody's got a right to be what they want to be." Or as Marla Maples (you remember Marla?) explained, "I've learned you can't take the Bible literally and be happy." On what is presumably a higher level of intellectual discourse, Senator Joseph Biden of Delaware said during the hearings on the nomination of Clarence Thomas to the U.S. Supreme Court, "We must never forget that the central natural law commitment made by this country is the commitment to individual freedom."

We therefore dream of a mythical Polynesia, where the boys and the girls copulate without shame or guilt beneath the palm trees, and everyone is idyllically happy doing what most pleases him. But it is only a dream. A world in which no one ever does anything for which he need feel ashamed or guilty is not the world we live in. There are people, of course, who experience

247

neither shame nor guilt, no matter what they do, but they are few and are found in limited circles such as organized crime. The world they live in is not an idyllically happy one.

Yet we cling to the Polynesian dream. We live in a popular culture which regards sex as candy for big children and celebrates complete sexual freedom, while denouncing date rape and sexual harassment, and apparently sees no connection among them.

We also have a popular religion to support us in our freedom. I have been reading what I am told is a widely read novel called *Joshua*. Its author is Father Joseph F. Girzone, about whom I know nothing except that he is listed in the *Catholic Directory* as "retired," and has an obvious resentment against authority. But he seems to be telling people what they want to hear.

His Joshua is Jesus of Nazareth come back to earth again to free God's children from organized religion. This Jesus never forgives sins because in this book no one ever sins, except the clergy. Their sin is to impose rules on people, instead of letting them follow their consciences. Those rules, as you might expect, are the Church's legislation on marriage. The mission of Jesus is not to save us from our sins, but to relieve us from feelings of guilt induced by "rules." Jesus Christ Savior turns out to be Jesus Christ Therapist.

If we look around us at the world we actually live in, however, we may begin to doubt religion as therapy. As Dr. Bettelheim said, without sexual repression, there is no prolonged span of learning — and that may have something to do with the present state of public education.

When the chancellor of New York City's public schools tells us that 80 percent of the students in his high schools are sexually active, we might infer that those students are not learning at their highest potential. We might also suspect that the flight of businesses from the city is due to the difficulty that employers find in getting literate, competent employees. But the only problem that concerns the chancellor, the Board of Education, and the mayor of New York is checking the spread of AIDS by distributing free condoms to students, with no allowance made for parents to forbid distribution to their children.

The rate of sexual activity among New York's teenagers does not seem to be much higher than the nationwide rate, according to reports I have read in the press (which, however, may be Planned Parenthood propaganda designed to promote the use of contraceptives by the young). However that may be, we have had in recent decades a marked increase in teenage pregnancies, abortions, and illegitimate births. We also have a high divorce rate, and the net result of all of the above is a large number of single-parent (usually female-headed) families.

These realities cannot be eliminated by reliance on contraceptives, and they have social consequences beyond poor performance in school. Social philosopher Myriam Miedzan comments that "boys raised without caring and involved fathers in the home are at a higher risk for violent, antisocial behavior than those who have such a father."

Such a society, as Bettelheim said, cannot create culture or civilization, nor can it long maintain them where they already exist. The future of civilization depends on forming the young to a belief in freedom as responsibility and habits of self-restraint. That task cannot be left solely to churches and schools, but requires the cooperation of families and such institutions of society as the press and the courts. The success of those efforts will in turn demand a thorough rethinking of the meaning of freedom by churchmen, educators, parents, journalists, judges — and entertainers. More is at stake than our national commitment to individual freedom.

The Culture of Death

December 1991

We all know the wonders that technology has wrought in enabling people to avoid conception while having sexual relations. Now, it seems, we are witnessing similar revolutionary advances in making it possible for previously infertile couples to have children.

Women can be made to conceive through artificial insemination, either by injecting sperm into the womb or even directly into the egg. If a woman is incapable of carrying a pregnancy through to term in her own womb, she can use another woman's womb in surrogate motherhood. Or, conversely, she can bear a child in her womb, using an egg supplied by another woman (there are now healthy young women who are willing to sell their eggs for a sufficient price). The egg is fertilized in vitro (in glass) and injected into the womb or Fallopian tube of the prospective "mother."

Before being implanted in a woman's body, embryos conceived in vitro can be tested for genetic defects and destroyed if found defective. Unfertilized eggs, and even embryos, can be frozen and later thawed out for use when a child is wanted. If not wanted, they can be thrown away.

Implicit in the use of these techniques is a view of the human body as manipulable matter, of which we are the owners and masters. As C. S. Lewis said in *The Screwtape Letters*, "Much of the modern resistance to chastity comes from men's belief that they 'own' their bodies." The same can be said of the notion that they are free to use their bodies in whatever way will achieve a desired result, be it preventing or bringing about the conception and birth of a child.

This belief in turn entails an idea of the human being as a conscious self dwelling in a body which is an appendage to and an instrument of the person, rather than a constituent element of it. What is meant by this statement will become more clear if we contrast it with something that a Methodist theologian, the late Paul Ramsey, said in his book, *Fabricated Man:* "We need the biblical comprehension that man is as much the body of his soul as he is the soul of his body."

In the biblical view of man, his body is not a mere material possession which he may use as he will to accomplish whatever purposes seem good or necessary to him. On the contrary, his body is a natural and essential part of himself, which he cannot abuse without dehumanizing himself and thereby offending his Creator. The secularized modern mind denies, or at least prescinds from, this understanding of human nature and the law inscribed in it by God.

This mind, particularly if it prides itself on being "scientific," knows no such thing as a soul, but it does recognize a conscious self. Some scientists would deprive us even of that: Daniel C. Dennett, in his recent book, *Consciousness Explained*, acknowledges consciousness as a phenomenon in that supercomputer, the brain, but no ego or self that is conscious. But the idea of man that concerns us here situates human personality in the consciousness of a self that dwells in a body and depends on it for its own existence, but for which the body is a mere instrument and piece of property.

It was this view of man that lay behind liberal Catholic criticism of the encyclical *Humanae Vitae* for being based on "physicalism" and "biologism." Moral norms, it was said, cannot be derived from biology or anything merely physical. It now appears, however, that to reject or downgrade our physical bodies as normative constituents of our human nature has implications that are far more vast.

An enthusiastic evolutionist claimed in a letter to the *New York Times* on October 9, 1991, "The future of humanity is unlimited because it is now within the means of the species Homo sapiens to create its own successor species." But, as C. S. Lewis pointed out back in 1947 in his little book, *The Abolition of Man*, the idea of Man as Self Creator really means that some men "create" other men according to what they want humanity to be.

That thought ought to bother us, but it probably won't, because the pragmatic American mind will see no more in biological engineering than a tool for solving people's problems. Some people want children, others don't, and technological mastery of the human body will solve either problem, and many others besides.

Suffering, for example, can be regarded as a problem that must be solved. It is a delicate moral question when and in what circumstances it is permissible to withdraw medical treatment and allow a person to die in peace, and I offer no answer to that question here. But to the pragmatic mind the patient is just as dead whether the doctor stops treatment or gives him a lethal injection: therefore, the distinction between killing and letting die is, as one bioethicist puts it, "superstitious." And, anyhow, we own our bodies and have a right to dispose of them when they stand in the way of the conscious self and its flight from pain. If enough Americans come to think this way, we may establish a culture of death.

"And the Word was made flesh and dwelt amongst us." He did not take on the mere appearance of human flesh, as an ancient heresy taught. Nor did he assume a body as the earthly vehicle of an inner core of consciousness. He became living human flesh, a single human being composed of body and soul, truly man as well as truly God. In these waning years of the twentieth century, Christmas Day, on which a child was born unto us, has an ever more urgent significance for our lives in this world.

Faith as a Burden

January 1992

The Church is full of Catholics who regard their religion as an inherited burden rather than a God-given blessing. It tells them too many things they don't want to hear about what to believe and how to live. For these reluctant Catholics, ignorance would have been bliss if only God or Fate had left them in it. Far from seeing any reason to spread the Catholic faith, they think it would be kinder to let the pagans continue in their guiltless, carefree, and happy ignorance.

One would think that the daily news would have destroyed that illusion. Willie Smith and Patricia Bowman (whichever of their stories you believe) acted like pagans and seem to be free of feelings of guilt.* But neither of them comes across as carefree and happy. Rather, they remind one, or me at least, of Matthew Arnold's comment on the ancient world:

> On that hard pagan world disgust
> And secret loathing fell.
> Deep weariness and sated lust
> Made human life a hell.

Catholic semi-pagans, however, do not see that, and therefore resent the Church's claim to speak in the name of God. They object to Vatican II's statement: "Whosoever, knowing that the Catholic Church was made necessary by God through Jesus Christ, would refuse to enter her or to remain in her could not be saved." If they were to read the New Testament, they would reject as undemocratic its flat assertion about Christ as Savior: "There is no other name under heaven given among

---

* At the time this column was written, William Kennedy Smith, a nephew of President John F. Kennedy, was on trial for the alleged rape of Patricia Bowman. The accuser and accused met one night at a Palm Beach bar, where Kennedy invited Bowman to his family's mansion. Bowman alleged he sexually assaulted her at the home after they had been drinking together for hours. The trial ended with an acquittal. — *Ed.*

men by which we must be saved" (Acts 2:12). They would also get angry at the judgment it pronounces on those who abandon Christ: "The last state has become worse for them than the first. For it would have been better for them never to have known the way of righteousness than after knowing it to turn back from the holy commandment delivered to them" (2 Pet. 2:20-21).

If that be so, then many feel that it would indeed be better never to have heard of Christ and to be able to live in happy pagan freedom. On this notion several comments are necessary.

The first is that, while ignorance may excuse people from guilt, it does not save them. Only good living does that. Christ came, not to condemn us, but to save us and show us the way to life. But living well requires a knowledge of the truth about living, just as health depends on knowledge of what maintains health. Many a person has died because in all innocence he did not know the rules of health, but he is just as dead as if he had been guilty.

Secondly, life is growth, and in human life growth inevitably involves effort, self-denial, and some pain. Pagan sages knew this, but pop paganism does not. In its modern form, it sees in self-denial only a surrender of our freedom of will, and therefore seeks the easy way out. That way makes for neither physical, mental, nor spiritual growth.

So far is the Catholic Church from denying our freedom that it insists on it. Cardinal Ratzinger, for instance, has spoken of "God's unconditional respect for the freedom of His creature." Pope John Paul II has said: "All of God's action in human history respects the free will of the human 'I'." In Catholic teaching, only God can save us, but not without our free consent.

We need salvation, not because our wills are not free, but because they are weakened by sin: by not only our personal sins, but by the long history of sin which from the beginning has shaped us and the world into which we were born. As St. Augustine says in *On Grace and Free Will*,

> It is certain that we can keep the commandments if we so will; but because the will is prepared by the Lord we must ask Him for such

force of will as to make us act by willing. It is certain that it is we who will when we will, but . . . it is He who makes us act by supplying efficacious power to our will.

It is Catholic doctrine that Christ died for all men, and that all receive sufficient grace to save their souls, be they pagans or even atheists. "Aha!" says the semi-pagan Catholic mind, "so there is an easy way out. You can be a pagan and save your soul." Yes, but not by being a pagan, and not by seeking an easier and softer way. You do it, as everyone else does who achieves salvation, by responding to the grace of God as it is given to you and wherever it leads you. Paganism, moral relativism, atheism, and modern nihilism make that response harder, not easier. The burden of sin (or, in more modern terminology, the bondage of self) is hard enough to shed without religions and philosophies that urge us to cling to it.

Christ came to free us from that burden, so that we might have life and have it more abundantly. There is, of course, a penalty for refusing his invitation, just as there is for refusing proper medical care or insulting our friends. But it is a mistake to look upon his invitation as a threat of punishment rather than a promise of life and an opportunity to grow into greater fullness of life. Faith in Christ, membership in his Church, and participation in her sacramental life give us more grace and lead us on to more and higher life.

In an age that makes so much of "choice," it is worth remarking that Christ and his Church present us with the most fundamental choice of all—and it is our choice. God invites, but does not compel; he helps, but does not force our wills; he knocks at the door, but leaves it to us to open it. Salvation is for those who want it and do not merely need it.

A Veto on Morality?

February 1992

We live, as we are endlessly reminded, in a pluralistic society. Moreover, our pluralism steadily grows deeper, especially on moral issues. As Terry Hall remarked five years ago in *Crisis,* among professional and academic people rational discussion of these issues has become almost impossible:

> It is not simply that there is disagreement. More seriously, there is hardly any common ground between us. We confront one another as visitors from another planet. A shared sense of moral perspective has virtually vanished.... The argument gets nowhere because it never really gets started.

We may describe this situation as the dilemma of liberal pluralism: on what basis can people of radically conflicting views on issues of profound importance for human life live together in one society and in peace? One solution which is popular in liberal circles is the neutral state. A simple way of explaining what that means would be that all functions of government are like its role in building and maintaining highways. Government may regulate their use by setting speed limits and forbidding driving while intoxicated, but beyond that it may not go. The highways are there to enable people to get rapidly to wherever they want to go. Where that may be and why they want to get there is no business of government.

From a moral point of view there is a difference between using a highway to rush one's wife to a hospital and using it to rush someone else's wife to a motel. But the moral judgment is not one that government should make. If you ask why this should be so, a common answer is that (1) moral judgments are not ones that are universally shared throughout the pluralistic society, and (2) there is no ground on which they can be universally shared. We no longer have a common religion and we have lost our faith in the ability of reason to establish valid moral norms. Not only do we have no common morality, we have no hope of arriving at one. It is well that we do not, for now there is no basis on which any group can claim the right to impose its morality on the rest of us. Moral relativism, as Arthur Schlesinger, Jr., would have it, is the firm foundation of liberty.

Arguments along this line, however, end by imposing certain morality and a philosophy behind it as the public orthodoxy of the pluralistic society. To choose but one example out of many, H. Tristam Englehardt, Jr., in *The Foundations of Bioethics,* first leads us, as he says, to "the brink of nihilism" by destroying every ground in which any particular moral standard could be proposed as a public morality. He then offers what he considers to be a valid and viable alternative: "a procedural ethic, based on respect of the moral agents involved," to which people of diverse and conflicting moral beliefs can subscribe.

Since we do want to live together in peace in a common society, and we have no rationally verifiable moral basis for doing so, we are driven back upon agreement on procedures which we commit ourselves to respect as authoritative. "If authority cannot be acquired through sound arguments, or through the conversion of all to a single moral viewpoint, it can be acquired through mutual agreement," says Engelhardt. "The moral world can be fashioned through free will, even if not on the basis of sound rational arguments." We create our own moral world by an act of will, and accept procedures to which we consent as the necessary condition of living together in peace in a pluralistic society. Nothing more is needed.

Engelhardt has smuggled into this allegedly neutral model of society a number of philosophical assumptions on which as a matter of fact not everyone agrees: that human beings are endowed with free wills, that they are therefore moral agents and persons, and that human society is a merely contractual agreement among sovereign individuals. But let that pass. We need only note that in Engelhardt's society, public decisions cannot be made by any procedures "unless *all* can be presumed to have agreed in advance to such procedures." But that presumption has limits. There are certain rights "that one can never presume individuals to have ceded, without threat of force, to a social organization." Thus, "one might think here of individuals wishing to acquire contraceptives, have abortions, take hallucinogens, or end their own lives."

This philosophy would foreclose in principle all rational discussion of the substantive moral content of public policies (discussion of which, as Terry Hall pointed out, is already extremely difficult). It would give every group and even every individual a veto of any public policy that embodies a moral view of what human beings are and what is good for them. It would thereby constantly subordinate any understanding of the common good of society to the will of dissenters. It would limit public policy decisions to such supposedly neutral matters as building and maintaining highways. And it would be a confidence game in which, in the name of neutrality, we would be tricked into agreeing to a secular liberal agenda.

There is no reason to believe that all or most Americans have accepted or will accept this as our public philosophy. Pluralistic as our society undeniably is, and inevitable though we know half-measures and compromises to be in the democratic decision-making process, we do not consent to have our moral concerns systematically ruled out of that process. We can and we will insist on talking about the moral content of public policies. Democracy is an act that others besides secular liberals can get into.

What Dr. Freud Knew

It is strange how quickly and how thoroughly we have forgotten what we all once knew. Not long ago our culture took for granted the following:

> The abandonment of the reproductive function is the common feature of all perversions. We actually describe a sexual activity as perverse if it has given up the aim of reproduction and pursues the attainment of pleasure as an aim independent of it. So, as you will see, the breach and turning point in the development of sexual life lies in its becoming subordinate to the purpose of reproduction. Everything that happens before this turn of events and equally everything that disregards it and that aims solely at obtaining pleasure is given the uncomplimentary name of "perverse" and as such is proscribed.

Sigmund Freud wrote those words for a lecture that he gave in 1917 under the title, "The Sexual Life of Human Beings" (you may find it in *The Complete Psychological Works of Sigmund Freud*, ed. James Strachey, vol. 16, pp. 303-319). Freud was an atheist and in this lecture took the stance of the detached scientific observer, who said of perversions, "What we have here is a field of phenomena like any other." But he knew what a perversion was and why it was one.

He listed as perversions homosexuality, fetishism, exhibitionism, voyeurism, masochism, and necrophilia. All these and other activities he described as "pathological forms of sexuality," as distinguished from "normal sexual life."

Yet within the same century in which Freud wrote, we have been seduced into accepting the proposition that no sexual activity is a perversion. We have agreed so readily, of course, because we were eager to justify contraception, the purpose of which is to prevent sexual acts from achieving reproduction. Having done that, however, we find it difficult to explain why sexual acts must be confined to the use of organs of generation.

We are also discovering that our redefinition of sexual morality leads to a redefinition of the family. Earlier this year the city of Santa Cruz, California, held a public hearing on an ordinance prohibiting discrimination against persons on any of several grounds, including sexual orientation. Some Christian fundamentalists appeared to say that they did not want to be forced to rent their premises to couples who were violating the laws of God. (Who but fundamentalists would object today for that reason?) At that a lesbian stood up and declared: "We are all equal in the eyes of the goddess." The goddess teaches the equality of all preferences, cravings, and lusts. For her, it is unjust to grant legal protection only to "the family" composed of married men and women, and not to all "families" of whatever composition.

The same issue has arisen in Washington, D.C., where the city government has passed an ordinance that allows unmarried, including homosexual, couples to register as domestic partners and to receive expanded health services if one partner is a city employee. Congress reviews city ordinances, however, and some congressmen want to repeal this measure. Rep. William E. Dannemeyer (R., Calif.) says: "Since this is a direct effort to redefine the American family, I think it is appropriate for Congress to consider whether we want to go down this road."

The issue has appeared in a somewhat different form in the state of Georgia, where a lesbian lawyer has brought suit against Attorney General Michael J. Bowers (of *Bowers v. Hardwick* fame) because he rescinded a job offer when she disclosed that she planned to marry another woman. It has come up in still another form in Bay Ridge, a backward, benighted, and bigoted section of Brooklyn, N.Y., where people still believe in God, marriage, family, and church on Sunday. The New York City Board of Education sent out an optional list of books which local community school boards could adopt for use in their schools. Bay Ridge rejected *Heather Has Two Mommies, Gloria Goes to Gay Pride*, and *Daddy's Roommate* as "inappropriate" for gradeschoolers. They felt, in particular, that some of the language in *Heather* was too graphic for first-graders (and graphic it was, but I would hate to try to explain to the tots what that language meant).

All of the above are attempts to persuade or to force changes, not only in the public's attitudes, but in the community's laws. Ostensibly they intend to privatize sexual morality, leaving it entirely to the consciences of individuals. In fact, they mean to substitute a new public morality for the traditional one. Everyone will remain free to believe in his heart that there is a difference between what Freud called pathological forms of sexuality and normal sexual life. But the whole weight of public law and policy will be thrown against speaking or acting on that distinction in the public forum. When the community acts in regard to marriage, the family, and education, it will have to grant the same status to deviant forms of sexuality as to the normal one.

As we have seen in more than one city on St. Patrick's Day, a private organization is now told that it cannot even hold a parade on a city street unless it admits "gay and lesbian" groups to join the march. In New York, the Ancient Order of Hibernians, which sponsors the parade, argued that, as a Catholic organization, it should not be obliged to admit a group openly opposed to the Church's teaching. It won its case in court, but it is a symptom of New York's moral degeneracy that the AOH could not simply say that it recognizes homosexuality as a perversion and did not want people flaunting their perversion in its parade.

Madness in the Courts

January 2000

The courts are running wild, and not only in these United States. The *New York Times* reported on January 19: "Parents who smack their children on the head or beat them anywhere on their bodies with objects like canes or belts could face jail under a new law being formulated by the [British] government. Britain has to bring its laws into compliance with decisions outlawing corporal punishment by the European Court of Human Rights, despite polls showing that most British parents are against the changes."

I can't recall it ever happening, but I am sure that if I dared to call my mother Kate, I got a slap and an instruction on how little boys should address their mothers. But that is beside the point I want to make. I don't know on what ground the European Court made this decision, but I would bet that it was some vague general word or phrase that the Court seized upon to turn spanking a backside with a hairbrush into a violation of a basic human right (thus defending the end against the means).

The latest outrage in this country is a decision by the Vermont Supreme Court under its state constitution. The court informed the state legislature that it must provide to homosexual couples the same benefits and protection that it gives to heterosexual couples. In a burst of generosity, the court left it up to the legislature to decide whether it would do this by legalizing same-sex marriages or by adopting a domestic partnership law. The generosity may have been only seeming, however, since in its report on this case the *Times* quotes a member of the Democratic majority in the state senate as saying that it would be much easier to get votes for domestic partnerships than for full-fledged gay marriages.

But where in the state constitution did the Vermont court find the basis for its decision? In a phrase stating that government "should be instituted for the common benefit, protection and security of the people, nation and community." That sounds very much like an introductory remark that states the general purposes of government, similar to the Preamble to the Constitution of the United States. The U.S. Supreme Court, however, has never taken the Preamble as "justiciable," that is, as a basis for judicial decisions.

The U.S. Supreme Court, of course, has no need of the Preamble to arrive at the results it wants: the words "liberty" and "equal protection of the laws" in Section 1 of the Fourteenth Amendment are sufficient for its purposes. The mark of a true ideologue is that he can take a broad and undefined concept like liberty or equality, spin it out to its most remote implications, translate them into binding rules of law or goals of public policy, and impose them on the people of the nation or a state as the meaning of their constitution.

Thus the Supreme Court in *Roe v. Wade* found a right to abortion to be implicit in the idea of ordered liberty. In *Bowers v. Hardwick* it came very close to finding a right to sodomy. In *Romer v. Evans* the court denounced Colorado's refusal to allow homosexual anti-discrimination laws as "inexplicable by anything but animus toward a class that it affects."

Homosexuals in fact already have a right to marry, but do not choose to exercise it. They do not want to engage in the sexual intercourse that marriage enshrines, but in facsimiles of it, and to have society call that marriage. If society will not go that far, then the Vermont court tells its legislature to pass a domestic partnership law that will confer on homosexual couples, in the words of the *Times* report, "the myriad benefits, from inheritance rights to health insurance to tax breaks, that accrue to heterosexual couples."

This is a rejection of marriage as the basic institution of civil society, which is basic because it joins man and woman in a lasting union that engenders children and founds families. The legal privileges of marriage are not for the sake of the married persons as individuals but for society's need of the family. The demand that the same privileges be extended to other persons is inspired by a radical individualism and a concept of equality pushed to the utmost limits.

In the dissenting opinion in *Bowers v. Hardwick*, Justice Harry Blackmun declaimed that "individuals define themselves in a significant way through their intimate relationships with others," and "much of the richness of a relationship will come from the freedom an individual has to choose the form and nature of these intensely personal bonds." Choice determines the structure and value of a sexual relationship—including marriage. This "choice" rhetoric turns up in numerous subsequent court decisions, federal and state, e.g., in euthanasia cases.

Democratic equality, so understood, demands that whatever benefits the law confers on heterosexual married couples be extended to all couples (and why only couples? why not trios, quartets, and quintets, if they love one another?). The net result is to devalue marriage as a social institution and to raise the question why it and all other unions should not be totally privatized and deprived of all social benefits.

Paying Our Dues

February 2000

A lady whom I know once told me that her daughter no longer goes to Mass because "the Catholic Church makes me feel guilty." The same lady also told me that a friend of hers had assured her, "If something helps you and makes you feel good, for you it is good."

That is not a true doctrine, but it is a consoling one and understandably popular. For such people (and their name is legion), Lent can have little meaning. Unburdened by guilt and free to do whatever makes them feel good, they see no need of repentance or penance. Those of us, however, who are not so sure of the purity of our hearts and thoughts, words, and the deeds that flow from them, are given this penitential season to reflect, ask God's pardon, and do some penance for our faults and sins.

We all have faults which become sins if we knowingly choose to act on them. Even if they are "only venial sins," they are nonetheless sins. And none of us has a lifelong, ironclad guarantee that we shall never have a temptation so serious that to give in to it would endanger the salvation of our souls.

Daily experience tells us that the spirit may be willing, but the flesh is weak. Who among us, to take a medical example, consistently follows a diet prescribed by a doctor? I am on a cholesterol diet, which allows me to feel the thrill of living dangerously by eating a chocolate-chip cookie. We mean well, but we frequently yield to the impulse to judge rashly, make unkind remarks, refuse to do services to others that we could and should do, to beat others out and, in general, act on purely selfish motives, sometimes in small matters, but sometimes in large ones. All of this reveals a disorder in our souls.

We have minds that understand and wills that choose. We also have a raft of impulses that are hard to control. They traditionally have been called the seven capital sins: pride, greed, lust, anger, envy, gluttony, and sloth. These are not sins until carried into action, but they are the sources from which all sins flow. As Our Lord put it in the gospel (Mark 7:20), it is not what a man eats that defiles him but what comes out of him: "From within, from the heart of man, come evil thoughts, fornication, theft, murder, adultery, coveting, wickedness, deceit, licentiousness, envy, slander, pride, foolishness."

The root of all these disordered impulses is our selfishness, which leads us to put our desires and fears ahead of what we owe to God, our Creator and the giver of all our gifts; ahead of what we owe to others; and even ahead of our own long-range good, which God intends for us and we ourselves would want if we did not weakly yield to disordered impulse.

Salvation in this world as well as in the next requires us to learn to control these impulses by self-denial. Lent gives us an occasion for practicing some small degree of it by fasting and in other ways. (I am thinking of following the diet rigidly.)

There are other and higher reasons for self-denial. One is to show that we really repent of our sins by doing penance for them. Merely telling God that we are sorry is not enough.

Giving up some legitimate pleasure, suffering a little pain, and doing good deeds that cost us something, show God that we are serious about doing his will rather than our own.

Higher yet is a motive that does not register on many modern minds. It is to vindicate the moral order of God's world. The purpose of the criminal law of the state, for example, is generally considered to be deterrence of further crimes and, ideally, the rehabilitation of the criminal. Yet, whether punishment rehabilitates the criminal or deters other persons from crime, it is vitally important that justice be vindicated by being done and seen to be done.

Punishment is not revenge, although the relatives of victims of murder too often demand that it be that. God is not vengeful. He demands that sin be punished because it is fitting, right, and just that it be, not because he wants to take revenge on mankind. On the contrary, he so loved the world that he sent his only-begotten Son to become man, suffer, and die in order to atone for our sins. Sin is such a violation of the moral order of justice that it had to be atoned for, and the only one who could do that adequately was God the Son.

There have been men and women so keenly aware of the sins, either of their past lives or of this fallen world, that they lived lives of penance in order to make up for them. We ourselves need not wait for Purgatory to pay our dues; a bit of reparative penance in Lent to make up for the wrong that we have done would be appropriate and pleasing to God.

Middle-School Sex Mess

April 2000

I grow old. I am getting tired of seeing one generation after another of teenagers arrive, each a new Columbus discovering an America its parents didn't know was there, each finding the sweet mystery of life for the first time in human history, each supremely confident that no one over 21 had anything to tell it. Yes, yes, I know, we all went to high school and must be tolerant — but the sheer repetition does become boring.

Besides, sexual activity is beginning at ever earlier ages and has now reached down into middle school, grades 5-8, ages 10-13. I'll grant you, my acquaintance with the fast set in middle school is limited. But, if I can believe what I read in the *New York Times* (and if you can't trust the *Times,* whom can you trust?), the kids, boys and girls together, are already at it hot and heavy in middle school.

A *Times* report on this subject appeared in the Styles section on April 2, written by Anne Farrell in a low key but with genuine concern about what is going on. She does not think it is good for children to have begun their sex lives so soon. Since national studies of sex activity among teenagers look only at high-school students, the evidence on middle schoolers is largely anecdotal. But Ms. Farrell has interviewed a swath of psychiatrists, psychologists, psychotherapists, physicians, and other health professionals, from whom she got her data.

The data indicate that the percentage of middle-school students who engage in sexual intercourse is increasing and predictably will continue to do so. The experts give many reasons for this phenomenon, including "the rising divorce rate, inattentive parents, the availability of condoms and the earlier onset of puberty. But the most frequent explanation is that today's culture sends a very mixed message to its young." May I add the reluctance of the clergy to preach on chastity, lest we disturb the faithful, who hate controversy?

The mixed message is that preteens and early teenagers are taught in their schools, public and private, that sexual intercourse is dangerous to their health, transmitting AIDS and other diseases (and, of course, causing pregnancy), so that the only safe course is abstinence. On the other hand, the culture is sex-saturated, portraying sexual intercourse on TV and movie screens, on the Internet, and in rap music, as what people normally do. The young naturally push the envelope.

A favored substitute for sexual intercourse in the middle schools is oral sex, wrongly thought to be less likely to transmit sexual diseases, but certain not to cause pregnancy. Oral sex has the additional advantage of lessening emotional involvement. Ms. Farrell reports that "the anecdotal evidence points to increased sexual activity, often of a detached, unemotional kind." A boy no longer has to persuade a girl that if she loves him, she will oblige him. Oral sex has taken the place of a goodnight kiss.

This is not surprising in a teenage generation that witnessed the Clinton-Lewinsky affair, and heard adults say, "It's only sex and it's consensual." Now the boy tells the girl, "This is safe and fun and O.K., and you have nothing to worry about."

But the experts whom Farrell interviewed do worry. One psychologist is quoted as being disturbed by "a new, casual, brazen attitude" toward sex: "The kids don't even look at each other. It's mechanical, dehumanizing. The fallout is that later in life they have trouble forming relationships. They're jaded." This unfeeling hedonism is particularly hard on girls, who do tend to take sex seriously and still think of it in relation to marriage in the future.

Although the experts consulted in this report are sincerely concerned about what the middle schoolers are doing to themselves and each other, there is no hint among them of any belief that premarital sex is immoral. Teenage sex to them is a health problem, not a moral one. To their credit, they see the problem as one of emotional as well as physical health. Preaching abstinence to the kids "doesn't work," however, so as Planned Parenthood's research wing, the Guttmacher Institute, advises, the schools go in for sex education and distributing condoms. But that does not solve emotional problems.

One psychologist at a private school for girls proposes discussion as a solution: "Do I really like this person? Or am I just doing this to be popular? These are the questions the kids need to learn to think about and ask." Enlightened self-interest of that kind may be the best that those who don't believe in God can offer. Others of us may think of faith, moral training, prayer, and the sacraments. Given fallen human nature, that won't always work either, but as St. Paul so often pointed out, it gets better results than paganism.

Home Swede Home

June 2000

I remember reading an article by an Englishman in which he sarcastically referred to his own country as "this scepter'd isle, this other Sweden." Sweden is not a fully socialist state, but we may take it as the prototype of the modern social-democratic welfare state, the one that has gone farthest toward realizing a certain ideal of equality.

I say a certain ideal because it takes democracy as meaning more than political equality and extends it to all aspects of social life. I have recently paged through a Swedish government publication entitled *Sweden: The Equal Way,* written by Gunilla Furst, a researcher into working life, and distributed in translation through the Swedish Information Service in New York. Gender equality, as Ms. Furst calls it, "entails women and men having the same rights, obligations and opportunities."

But why call it gender equality when it means the equality of the two sexes? The first meaning my dictionary gives for gender is sex. A secondary one is "a subclass within a grammatical class in a language that is partly arbitrary but also partly based on distinguishable characteristics." One could see in the use of the term gender, rather than sex, a belief that, despite some obvious physical differences between men and women, the distinction between them is not a natural given but mainly an arbitrary social construct.

Ms. Furst says as much. In the debate over sex roles, she says, "it is not a question of roles predetermined by nature but of roles shaped by the pressure of economic and political change." In Sweden from the 1960s on, "the old view of women and men complementing one another was replaced by the notion that the sexes were basically similar." Once equality was understood in this way, promoting it in public life, in the workplace, and in the home became a matter of justice and was made a primary object of public law and policy.

Although productive property in Sweden is largely privately owned, the ideal pursued by law and policy is a socialist one. It regards men and women as interchangeable entities entitled to equal individual status in the labor market. It contemplates women's financial independence and their engagement on equal terms with men in public and private employment. Laws and ordinances are framed in gender-neutral terms. Spouses have the same obligation to contribute to the family income, and are equally responsible for housework and childcare (which in the two-income family tends to be daycare).

Another document distributed by the Information Service informs us that in the early 1990s, the Swedish welfare state was in an economic crisis, with heavy welfare costs and declining employment. A crisis agreement between the then-governing non-socialist coalition government and the opposition Social Democrats was arrived at in 1992.

In the discussions leading up to this agreement, the Christian Democrats proposed offering payments to parents to stay at home and take care of their children. But their coalition partners, the Liberals, and the Social Democrats "objected that this was a thinly disguised attempt to reverse progress in breaking down the sexual division of labor." So the proposal was rejected.

In the 1990s power issues came to the fore: women must be equally present with men "where vital decisions are being made in public life." This goal has been almost fully achieved. According to the letter from the Swedish Information Service that accompanied *The Equal Way,* "Women hold half of the cabinet posts in the Swedish government and 45 percent of the seats in the Riksdag."

Yet the overall results of the drive for equality have been disappointing, at least to Gunilla Furst. Gender equality is now taken for granted in Sweden and is thought to have been achieved — but wrongly so. "The ideology is equal but the reality is segregated. . . . A large proportion of women work part-time and run the home." This lowers their personal earned income and, since the Swedish social insurance system is based on individual income, women are left behind men in financial independence.

Part of the solution to this inequity would be to persuade men to share housework and childcare equally with their women, but this men are unwilling to do. Another Information Service document in the 1980s reported that Swedish law requires employers to give a year's parental leave, with pay, upon the birth of a child. It could be taken by either parent or divided between them. But the great majority of men took none of this leave — and the women didn't want them to.

Boys will be boys and girls will be girls. Besides, who wants to be married to someone who gets up every morning and recites the Declaration of Independence before breakfast? Serious, lifelong marriage would be a better fate than that.

The Ideological Mind

October 2000

The ideological mind thinks only in extremes: every issue is either-or, all-or-nothing. The needle on the gauge always stands at either zero degrees or 180 degrees, because there is no convincing reason for it to stop at any of the 179 degrees in between.

That way of thinking makes for intransigent politics and bad lawmaking. For, as Edmund Burke once explained, "the decisions of prudence (contrary to the system of the insane reasoners) . . . almost all . . . are determined on the more or the less, the earlier or the later, and on a balance of advantage and inconvenience, of good and evil." Or, as he had said on an earlier occasion, "It is no inconsiderable part of wisdom to know how much of an evil ought to be tolerated; lest, by attempting a degree of purity impracticable in degenerate times and manners," we may make the situation worse than it already is.

On the abortion issue, for instance, we find some ideologues on the pro-life side, people for whom nothing short of a constitutional amendment banning all abortions will do. But they are vastly outnumbered by the extremists on the pro-abortion side, for whom any restriction on abortion-on-demand must be resisted to the last ditch.

A recent example is Hillary Clinton's campaign in New York for a seat in the U.S. Senate. One of her aides quoted her as saying "unequivocally that she would oppose a Supreme Court nominee who opposed *Roe v. Wade* and would vote to overturn it." Her pro-choice allies ran an ad attacking her opponent for refusing to say the same.

Would she vote to confirm the appointment of a justice who might support banning partial-birth abortion? Not likely, because to the ideological mind, any limitation on abortion puts the whole "pro-choice" position in danger.

For an even clearer example, take Dr. LeRoy Carhart, the abortionist who successfully contested the constitutionality of the Nebraska law banning partial-birth abortion. On the day the case was argued before the U.S. Supreme Court, he appeared on the *NewsHour* with Jim Lehrer and said that if they can ban that kind of abortion, they can ban the abortions he regularly performs by "cutting the fetus to pieces" in the womb.

The words in quotation marks are ones that I clearly remember, because it struck me as remarkable that a doctor would barefacedly tell a nationwide audience that he made his living by cutting babies to bits in the womb. Yet neither he nor the majority of the court saw anything remarkable in it.

Such minds seem to function in a world of pure abstractions: a constitutional right must be defended, no matter how revolting the exercise of the right may be. It is a matter of principle from which conclusions may be spun out to the last extreme, by judges who refuse to know what everybody knows.

On the abortion issue, as on several others that seriously affect human life, we live in what Burke called degenerate times. Moral principles are involved, from which we may never deviate. But what we can do, or should even try to do about translating them into law in the existing situation is another question. If abortion is presented to the American public as a choice between abortion-on-demand and no abortion at all, there is no doubt about which of the two the public will choose. Therefore prudence forbids offering that stark choice at the present time.

Better to put pressure on the politicians to enact some limits on abortion that the public will support, and to continue to try to awaken the public conscience to the evil that it now accepts.

That will not be easy. We are up against ideologues who wield power in the media, the universities, the courts, and even in some churches. The great middle of the public will say in polls that to some extent or other they are pro-life. But the majority of them do not rank abortion as a major issue in politics.

They either secretly want to keep it in reserve as a way out of difficult situations, or they have been brainwashed into believing that they have no right to "impose their views" on other people who do not share them. That is why they so tamely submit to the rhetoric of "tolerance" and "equality," not only in regard to abortion but to homosexual relations, divorce, euthanasia, and other practices that eat away at the fabric of society. But by accepting this we let the ideologues shape the social and cultural world we all have to live in.

We have both the right and the duty to insist that our beliefs have as much place in the public forum as those of the ideologues. We have no obligation to remain silent. What, after all, is the public forum for if not to allow all citizens to express their convictions on matters that fall within the state's jurisdiction?

And what is the state for if not the protection of life, along with liberty and the pursuit of happiness?

"Does New York Believe Anything?"

January 2001

The demand for school vouchers to allow parents to choose the schools they want their children to attend is spreading throughout the country. So far it has not been successful in places where it has been defeated by the public education lobby or overruled by judges acting on interpretations of the Constitution favored by the American Civil Liberties Union and similar organizations.

The arguments they use are generally legalistic: separation of church and state, public money for state-operated schools only, etc.; sometimes sociological: non-public schools are divisive and elitist, etc. But there has been little consideration of one great reason for parents wanting to take their kids out of today's public schools.

The usual assumption is that the reason parents remove their sons and daughters from public schools is that the schools are academically inferior. But where that is the case, it is argued, it can be corrected by spending more public money on public education, with higher salaries for teachers, smaller classes, more and better equipment, etc. But there is an unavowed reason for objecting to vouchers, especially when they are used in religiously affiliated schools.

It is that the "civil-libertarians" want all children to get a simon-pure secularist education untainted, not only by denominational religion, but by what is now called traditional morality, sexual morality in particular. Teaching young people that sexual abstinence is the most effective way of avoiding pregnancy or sexually transmitted diseases is said to inculcate a religious doctrine. You might think that the effectiveness of abstinence is something that anyone with eyes and even half a brain could see for himself. But no, it is and can only be a dogma to be accepted on faith. We must instead give the youngsters a solid sex education plus free and easy access to contraceptives, and they will have all they need to avoid the undesirable consequences of sexual freedom.

Therefore the time now has come to offset this type of argument by raising the question whether, in our increasingly divided culture, the state is capable of giving an education. In a book, *Education Between Two Worlds*, published in 1942 by Harper & Bros., Alexander Meiklejohn stated the issue: "The city of New York, or San Francisco, or Middletown, has schools whose task it is to prepare young people for living. What do those cities believe about living? What lessons do they teach? Does New York believe anything? Has it any values or convictions out of which a scheme of teaching may be made?"

Does New York believe anything? A good question (about San Francisco, the less said the better). But I live in New York, and my impression is that New York officially believes in tolerance of all views and ways of living, that is, in what George F. Will has called the moral equality of appetites. But can a city make a scheme of teaching out of that?

Meiklejohn advocated what he called a civil religion. It was not to be the establishment of any of the traditional religions based on what they claimed to be divine revelation. But it would give the public schools the mission of passing on to the rising generations a general set of moral principles that was accepted by all or by far the greater part of the population. However possible that may have been in 1942, when the public school was still widely regarded as the common school of a predominantly Protestant culture, it is hardly possible today, in our age of an intensifying culture war.

To the secularist mind, the solution to the problems of the sexual life of the young is to be sought in technology, not in moral virtue. A solid secular sex education, along with easy, preferably free, access to condoms, is all that is necessary. The same attitude will apply across the board in other areas of morality, provided only that we do not impose our beliefs on others.

One result of that approach, however, is that as you drive out of the schools all morality that can be traced in any way to religion, you inevitably drive out the parents who want something better for their children. Insofar as public education judges fostering physical and psychological health to be its only permissible moral obligation, to that extent a growing part of the population will find it inadequate as a way of preparing the young for life.

I am not proposing that public schools should offer a purely civil, let alone a religious, moral education. On the contrary, I think that we must now openly raise the question whether the state can function as an educational institution if it serves no higher goal than equipping the young for making a living. Is that really a satisfactory preparation for life?

Happy Family Ties

April 2001

The purpose of the public services is to serve the public, right? No, silly, wrong. The purpose of the public services is to create jobs for members of the public, and the jobs must be distributed evenly among the groups that make up the public.

For example, in a column in the *New York Daily News* last January, the authors complained that in the New York Police Department, "only 15% of new officers are women, who are half the population." We are a democracy in this country, you see, and the basic rule of democracy is equality. Therefore 50 percent of the police force ought to be composed of women. The same goes for the armed forces.

It would not occur to an ideological mind to ask how many women want to be police officers or soldiers. Still less to wonder how many women would prefer to have their lives and limbs protected against attack by male cops 6 feet tall weighing 190 pounds rather than by female cops 5 feet 6 inches tall weighing 130 pounds. Or to contemplate the desirability of training women to go into battle and kill people with bombs and guns.

I do not mean that there is no role for women in police forces; I can see a need or at least a genuine use for women detectives. But their number would be proportionate to the service they performed for the public, not to an abstract principle of equality. The same would apply in the armed forces, and across the board in the work force.

I have no statistics, but I presume that women teachers outnumber men in elementary schools, perhaps even in high schools, and this for good reasons. But it is not an injustice crying out for remedy by anti-discrimination laws that men outnumber women in the ranks of college and university professors.

Nor am I sure that the growing number of anti-discrimination laws and court decisions is a net gain for society. Such laws are sometimes necessary in situations where a government is dominated by a racial, religious, or ideological faction that monopolizes jobs, and regularly finds superior merit in members of its own group. But these laws ought to be temporary, to be phased out over time. Otherwise they become entitlements that freeze certain "victim groups" in protected positions, in the name of equality. Think, for example, of the efforts still being made to force the Boy Scouts to accept homosexual scoutmasters.

Linda Chavez (of happy memory) has written in *Crisis*: "The feminists' solution to female vulnerability is to replace the role that men have traditionally played in women's lives — that of provider and protector — with government. It is as if the feminists are quietly conceding that they have failed in masculinizing women to be totally self-sufficient."

But it is not good that women should be totally self-sufficient, because the world needs wives and mothers more than it needs career women. Note that I say "more than," *not* "instead of." The Church has always honored virginity and celibacy, and women have well served both Church and State in many careers. But no generation has anything more important to do than to raise its own next generation, and that requires wives and mothers who make raising their children their primary mission. To the extent that the feminists have succeeded in convincing young women that sacrificing a career to marriage and motherhood is a renunciation of their personal worth and dignity, they have ill-served both women and society.

Before they marry, men and women are free and equal individuals. But when they marry, they form a family, which Leo XIII in *Rerum Novarum* called "a very small society indeed, but a true one, and older than any polity." Now, in any society there must be some locus of authority and a division of roles. In the family formed by the union of man and woman, with the children they beget, there will be sex roles. (Any small child knows, without having to be told, that he relates to Mommy and Daddy in different ways, although they both love him.)

Ultimate authority will and normally should be held by

the male parent. I have known strong and intelligent women who were determined that their husband would be the head of the family, even if they had to prop him up, because he had a necessary role in the family, and they wanted him to perform it.

This goes down hard in our egalitarian society. But if we remember that authority is not for the benefit of those who hold it, but of those who are subject to it, and if we get rid of the idea that subjection to authority is demeaning, we'll find that families last longer and—if the parents truly love each other—they can even be happy, strange as that may seem to the modern mind.

Our Pluralist Sea

May 2001

We are drowning in a pluralist sea. In an article in the March 2001 *Commentary,* Jack Wertheimer explains that "increasing tolerance and equality [are] the twinned ideals that in our age seem to trump all other competing values." All beliefs in the good, the true, and the beautiful must yield, in the name of the tolerance that is now taken as the meaning of democratic equality. Democratic liberty guarantees the right to hold whatever beliefs one chooses, but in private, not in the public forum. There all beliefs and lifestyles must be treated as equal in value, because all are the results of individual choices — and all choices are equally deserving of respect.

Mr. Wertheimer is Jewish and is concerned in his article with the devastating effect that intermarriage between Jews and Gentiles is having on the continued existence of the Jewish people. But his concern should also be the concern of other communities in that community of communities that is America. As he says, "For any community determined to ensure the survival of its own island in the pluralist sea, the very minimum required is that it be willing to assert without apology the absolute worth of its traditions and beliefs."

Making that assertion raises the hackles in our egalitarian culture, in which any claim to have a truth is seen as an attack on freedom. The claim may be tolerated if it is confined to one's community, which is composed of voluntary members who are free to leave if they so choose. But the alleged truth must be kept out of the public forum if it is asserted as valid for all persons.

Tolerance, you see, is based on the primacy of choice. A woman's famous "right to choose" is now enshrined in our constitutional law. The rights to choose assisted suicide and to engage in homosexual acts, perhaps even gay marriage, still lie down the constitutional road. Those who are interested may read the opinion that the late Justice Harry Blackmun wrote in the 1986 case of *Bowers v. Hardwick*. Dissenting from a Supreme Court decision that upheld a state law that made sodomy a crime, he declared that "the fact that individuals define themselves in a significant way through their intimate sexual relationships with others suggests . . . that much of the richness of a relationship will come from the freedom that an individual has to *choose* the form and nature of these intensely personal bonds." (The italics are his.) With those words Blackmun threw out human nature as a norm and made individual choice the supreme norm in sexual relationships.

It is true that Blackmun's was a dissenting opinion, but there were four dissenters in that case and, after his retirement from the court, Justice Lewis Powell announced that on second thought, he should have voted with them, thus making them the majority and establishing a constitutional right to homosexual acts. There is nothing in Blackmun's rhetoric, or in that of several other justices for that matter, that would prevent the court from going farther — to making polygamy a constitutional right, for instance.

Beneath the level of constitutional law there is the level of an increasingly fragmented culture in which transcendent truth is unavailable, freedom is taken to mean personal autonomy, every man has the right to create his own conception of what is good, so long as he does not "impose his beliefs on others," and nothing is wrong unless one personally thinks it is wrong.

Lying beneath that is a view of humanity according to which man is the creature whose nature it is to have no nature. Other animals have natures that confine them within certain ranges of activity. But man is the free creature who can remake the world and, so far as possible, is free to make himself whatever he wants to be. Thanks to recent advances in modern science, he is on the verge of being able to make embryonic human beings into whatever he wants them to be. In other words, man is a free and *sovereign* will that creates its own good.

The biblical, Christian, and Catholic tradition presents a radically different concept of human freedom. The Church recognizes that man is by nature free, but is not the creator of the moral universe. Every individual must save his own soul, but on God's terms and only with the help of God's grace.

According to *The Catechism of the Catholic Church*, "The act of faith is of its very nature a free act." But the act does not define the faith; it freely assents to it. According to the Church's canon law, marriage is an act freely performed by a man and woman who declare, in the presence of a priest and two witnesses, their free consent to take each other as man and wife — but they do not *define* marriage; they consent to enter into it.

Does choice create the good, or is the good antecedent to choice and does it morally oblige consent? The difference between these two views of human freedom is the root of our present cultural crisis. When we sing "Sweet land of liberty," let us make up our minds about what liberty we mean.

Seen and Unseen

July 2001

Life is an unending series of miracles. Or so we are told by the wise and educated among us. I have read articles by intelligent men who assure me that a tadpole is not a frog, but "turns into" a frog (and this, mind you, without being kissed by a beautiful princess; it just happens, miraculously). Others say that a caterpillar is not a butterfly but turns into one (again, no princess is involved; indeed, no princess would consider kissing a caterpillar, because it's icky). I also recall a column by an author who offered as a decisive argument that a fertilized human ovum (the zygote) is not a human being, because it is no bigger than the period at the end of this sentence.

You see, a thing is what it looks like. If it does not look like a frog, or a butterfly, or a human being, it isn't one. That is a very American way of thinking, steeped as our culture is in the empiricist philosophy of John Locke, for whom we never know the nature of anything, but only the impression it makes on our senses. That has a profound impact on our thinking, our morals, and our politics.

For example, Connie Mack, a former U.S. senator from Florida, wrote a column in the *Wall Street Journal* (June 19) in favor of government funding of experiments with stem cells (cells not yet differentiated as parts of specific organs) derived from fertilized human eggs. The eggs would be fertilized in glass in laboratories and, at the time that the stem cells were subject to experiments, would be tiny clusters of cells no bigger than the head of a pin.

Senator Mack professes to be a practicing Catholic and a pro-lifer, and I see no reason to doubt his word. But he suffers from the common delusion that a thing is what it looks like, and neglects to ask why it gets to look like what we eventually recognize it as being. If a fertilized ovum implants itself in the womb, it moves steadily toward becoming an unmistakable human baby. Why does it do this? Because it was a human being from the beginning.

At this point the debate turns into an argument over when the zygote, embryo, or fetus becomes a person. I have read enough articles and attended enough conferences to know that there is a multitude of definitions of a person and of when a conceived being in the human species becomes a person, and therefore the subject of a right to life.

I also have the impression that the definition of a person is often chosen to establish the point prior to which it is permissible to kill the zygote, embryo, or fetus. Thus, some argue that it is permissible to kill an embryo before the primitive streak appears, or before the point at which it is capable of feeling pain. Some go so far as to say that a child that is already born may be killed (painlessly, of course) before it is some weeks, months, or years old, or before it reaches the use of reason. All of these are definitions of when a developing human being acquires the traits that constitute personhood.

These arguments all assume that if certain human traits are not visibly present, we are not dealing with a person and may therefore kill it (for worthy purposes, of course). That conclusion leads naturally to the question of the point at which someone who has been a person for a full lifetime ceases to be person. A visit to a nursing home will reveal that even the brightest and the best among us may lose their eyesight, hearing, memory, and apparently even their awareness of who they themselves are. Enters now Dr. Jack Kevorkian or any licensed doctor in the Netherlands. Does personhood depend on the demonstrable possession of certain perceptible human traits or does it rest on the possession of a common human nature? An empiricist culture that does not recognize common natures has already answered that question.

The U.S. Supreme Court spoke in *Roe v. Wade* of the fetus to be aborted as a "potential" human life, and overlooked the fact that it was very much alive and actively striving by an inner force for the actualization of its further potentialities. Furthermore, the potentialities were inherent in the fetus. Its mother and father gave it life and its genetic inheritance and, if it were allowed to live, would give the upbringing they and the surrounding culture would contribute to its development. But they can only develop what was already there in the fetus.

A living being grows and develops in a certain direction according to its nature, and the higher the nature, the longer the development takes. But what it develops is the nature that it already has. As Aristotle said, we judge the nature of a horse by a mature and fully grown horse, not by a newborn colt. The colt may grow up to be a weak and sickly horse, but it will never turn into a giraffe. A baby, being human, may turn out to be a gangster, but it will be a morally distorted human being, not a cat or a dog. In either case, the horse or the human being, the standard by which we judge it deficient or distorted will be our knowledge of what that kind of creature is in its mature and fully developed form. Saying that a member of the human species is no bigger than the period at the end of a sentence or the head of a pin is merely to describe a stage of life that every single one of us has gone through, and would not be here if we had not gone through it.

All of this, however, is beside the point to the proponents of embryonic-stem-cell research. They are utilitarians for whom the greater good of society overrides the sanctity of mere life, which they see as all that a newly conceived human being has. Generating and destroying fertilized human eggs and zygotes is justified, we are told, because it may, and probably will, lead to discoveries that will prevent or cure devastating diseases. But that argument avoids the issue, indeed several issues.

If human life does not begin at conception, how do we explain the fact that, left to itself, the being in the womb will regularly "turn into" a baby, a child, a teenager, and an adult? If it was not a human being at conception, how do we determine when it becomes one? If our standard of judgment is utilitarian, i.e., its ability to contribute to the community, can that standard protect all of us, or only the fit, the capable, and the productive? On what basis, then, do we found universal human rights? It gives one to think. Or so let us hope.

Democracy's Disease

December 2001

Every form of government has its characteristic disease. Monarchy's disease is the desire of monarchs for absolute power. Aristocracy's is the drive to monopolize the goodies of society and to turn them into absolute privileges. Democracy's disease is the craving for absolute equality.

Carried far enough, democracy's disease becomes the Marxist dream of a classless society, where all productive property is owned by everyone in common, everyone is called comrade, everyone gives according to his abilities and gets according to his needs, and the state and political power wither away. Curiously, every attempt to implement this theory and put it into practice has resulted in a dictatorship resting on a bureaucratic aristocracy (which the Soviet Union called the nomenclature), and the masses remained the masses.

We in America have not gone that far, and I doubt if we ever shall. But we have given way to a creeping egalitarianism that makes us suspect inequalities of being unjust and undemocratic. Not all inequalities, of course: it does not bother us that star athletes earn money in the millions of dollars.

We are a nation of sports fans and rejoice that some men are superlatively better baseball players or golfers than others. Topflight women tennis players now draw huge crowds and huge amounts of money. When it comes to sports, one hears little talk of glass ceilings. That's because Americans take sports seriously. Either you can hit the ball out of the park or put it through the hoop more often than less talented athletes — or you can't. No excuses are accepted. If we want a winning team — and what could be more American than that? — we of necessity want winning players. The same attitude prevails in the business world, where big money is also taken seriously.

When it comes, however, to what are now considered personal beliefs and preferences, we think in terms of individual rights. Criticism of diverse tastes and behaviors is condemned as "judgmental." Interference with a person's acting on his beliefs is alleged to violate his civil rights. The equality of all persons before the law has come to mean the equality of all appetites, beliefs, and lifestyles in the eyes of the law — and of public opinion.

The assumption behind this understanding of equality is that differences of opinion and conduct are of little or no importance to society at large. If a husband and wife are not getting along together, the law must provide for divorce, division of property, and custody of the children, made as free of strife and bitterness as possible. If a pregnancy is unwanted, legal abortion must be available. Homosexuals must be protected by anti-discrimination laws and given the benefits, if not also the legal status, of marriage. If sexual promiscuity is prevalent among students (as we are told that it is even in middle school), condoms must be provided.

That health is good is one of the few things it is presumed that we all agree on, and a life free from pain is about as high an ideal as the nation can ambition. Many Americans would stoutly deny that they believe that, but when it comes to questions of public policy they put up little resistance to it, because they don't want to impose their beliefs on others.

Religion must be kept out of public life, not only in its denominational forms, but even in the most general terms. The attack on the World Trade Center brought forth a flood of religious sentiment and memorial services in this country. Unbelievers protested that these expressions of religious faith "shut them out." They could have organized their own meetings, open to the public, in which they thanked whatever gods may be for their unconquerable souls and praised the resilience of the human spirit which would triumph over the evil that religious fanaticism had inflicted on us. But, no, they want a public life from which religious belief and expression have been shut out.

If everything that offends secularists were banned from public life, it would leave us with a democracy modeled on the French Third Republic, in which there was "no God and no master" and René Viviani could declare in the Chamber of

Deputies, "We have put out lights in heaven that will never be lighted again." Governing a pluralistic society is indeed a difficult task, but we have no reason to accept the premise that the public square is open only to expressions that do not wound secularist sensitivities. That attitude claims to exclude no one but in fact leads to a flattened-out society in which the only norms of acceptable speech and conduct are ones set, in the name of equality, by the most secularized and individualistic among us.

Having denied that moral standards taught by religious institutions may have any effect on public custom or public policy, they go on to tell us that there are no rational norms of human reason that a society may recognize and uphold against individual preferences. For example, militant feminists assert that human sexuality itself is not something determined by nature. There are certain physical differences between men and women that cannot be wished away, but beyond that sexual differences are social constructs. Womanhood and manhood are whatever a particular culture says they are. This argument pushes us toward the masculinization of women and the feminization of men, making men and women equal because they are nearly as possible identical. But is that democracy or is it democracy's disease?

"Tell Us What You Want!"

February 2002

The campaign against Pope Pius XII continues, and is now expanded into an attack on the papacy as such. The two most recent books that I know of in this campaign are by a Jewish author, David Kertzer, *The Popes Against the Jews*, and a Catholic one, Thomas Cahill, *Pope John XXIII*, in which he presents that pope as the one good apple in a papal barrel of rotten ones.

I call this a campaign, but I do not imply that a group of men sat around a table and planned it. Propaganda campaigns often spring up spontaneously when something happens that offers an opportunity for one. An example is the campaign to legalize abortion that spread rapidly in the media after the U.S. Supreme Court found a constitutional "right to privacy" in a contraception case in June 1965. The event that let loose the flood of condemnation of Pius XII was *Der Stellvertreter* (The Deputy) by a German playwright, Rolf Hochhuth, in 1963.

Prior to that play, Pius XII had been the object of high praise by Jewish leaders such as Golda Meir and organizations such as The World Jewish Congress. But with Hochhuth's play a number of people saw their chance to express feelings and views they had previously kept bottled up, by blaming Pius for not doing enough to help Jews during the Holocaust, or doing nothing, or even collaborating with the Nazi extermination program.

Now, I am able to understand attitudes that I disagree with. I may think them misguided, but I find them understandable. I remember a rabbi saying, "I have to tell you that my constituents would rather live under an atheistic government than under a Christian one." Given the history of Christian-Jewish relations, I can see why Jews feel that way. I am not impressed by minds that can look at 2,000 years of Christian history and see nothing but the persecution of Jews. But the persecution was real when it happened and was not only physical or economic. One example of what we might call social persecution is Christopher Marlowe's play, *The Jew of Malta* (1633), which drips with contempt for Jews and must have aroused a resentment that does not die.

Jews therefore understandably hailed the Enlightenment, because it freed them from Christian domination: the enemy of my enemy is my friend. The Enlightenment, however, had its own mode of persecution. According to Peter Gay in *The Enlightenment: An Interpretation* (I :59), "The most militant battle cry of the Enlightenment, *écrasez l'infâme*, was directed against Christianity itself, against Christian dogma in all its forms, Christian institutions, Christian ethics and the Christian view of the world." It is equally understandable that Christians, Catholics in particular, regarded the friend of their enemy as being also their enemy. That goes some way toward explaining why Catholics and Jews lined up on opposite sides in regard to the Dreyfus Affair and the Bolshevik Revolution in 1917.

It is not my intention to defend Pius XII against his accusers. That has been done by persons better qualified than I, for example, Professor Ronald Rychlak, in *Hitler, the War, and the Pope*, and Rabbi David G. Dalin in "Pius XII and the Jews" (*The Weekly Standard,* February 26, 2001). What I want to do here is to put a question to the accusers: What are you getting at? What is your objective? What do you hope to accomplish by these charges? What do you want the Catholic Church, or the papacy, or the general Catholic body to do for you? (These questions are all really one.) Please don't just repeat accusations against Pius XII or other popes — *tell us what you want!*

It seems clear to me that the campaign against Pius XII is a guilt trip, laid on to get some result. For the liberal or ex-Catholics it is to get the papacy out of the way and to lead the Church into modernity or post-modernity with its relaxed morality and its accommodation to the social circles in which they move. Secularized Jews want much the same thing, because they see the Church, rightly, as the major obstacle to realization of the liberal dream of a society in which no one believes in anything very strongly, and every individual is free to live his/her own life and do her/his own thing.

I remember a conversation I once had with Leo Pfeffer, a leading proponent of the secularization of American culture.

He was a professor of constitutional law at Long Island University, general counsel of the American Jewish Congress, and perhaps the most influential individual in the shaping of our constitutional law on church-state relations. I asked him if he could not see that including religiously affiliated schools in public aid-to-education programs would increase general support for such legislation. No, he would not hear of it, and proceeded to tell me that when he attended a public school in Brooklyn, pupils were required to sing "Onward Christian Soldiers." That naturally aroused resentment in him that he had not forgotten. In later years he published an article in *The Journal of Church and State* (Spring 1977) under the title "Issues that Divide: The Triumph of Secular Humanism," in which he hailed the beneficent effect of secularization on American religions: "Here [in Catholicism], as in Protestantism and Judaism, American secular humanism is manifesting its potency in altering long-held doctrine and practice and in narrowing the differences that divide Protestants, Catholics, and Jews."

Not all Jewish writers agree with Dr. Pfeffer, of course. Irving Kristol published an article in *Commentary* (August 1991) in which he agreed that "Christianity and Judaism have been infiltrated and profoundly influenced by the spirit of secular humanism." But he urged American Jews to cut themselves loose from secular humanism because it is "gradually losing its credibility" and "is brain dead even as its heart continues to pump energy into all our institutions."

More recently, in a balanced and intelligent article in *First Things* (February 2002), Rabbi David Novak, professor of Jewish Studies at the University of Toronto, reminded religious Christians and Jews that they have more in common than any other two religions have. Despite their ineradicable difference on the Messiah, he argued, they spring from a common stem, share the Ten Commandments, and can form a common front to resist the ongoing and degrading secularization of our common culture.

Let me restate the question. What are the prosecutors of Pius XII aiming at? Is it the realization of Leo Pfeffer's vision of a secular humanist society? Or is it something along the lines of David Novak's civil society, which is pluralist indeed, but in which religion has its recognized place and influence?

"Catch-22"?

April 2002

Decades ago, when I lived and taught in Jersey City, N.J., a newspaper in the neighboring city of Newark published a weekly column under the title, On the Square. The square referred to was Journal Square in the center of Jersey City; the column recounted the political goings-on there, which in those days were renowned, if not in song, at least in story.

One week On the Square published the rumor going round Jersey City that Santa Claus was coming to town. Alarmed at this threat to their livelihood, the political sachems of the city held a confab to discuss what to do about it. Various suggestions were made, none of them particularly helpful. Then up spoke a political realist. "Everybody's got some dirt in his past," he said. "What we've got to do is to look into this guy Claus and see what we can find."

That story often came to my mind in the several months of the campaign against the Catholic Church waged by the *Boston Globe* and its owner, the *New York Times.* I also recalled a couple of lines in Joseph Heller's novel *Catch-22*: "The case against Clevinger was open and shut. The only thing missing was something to charge him with." The *Times* and the *Globe* knew that the case against the Catholic Church was open and shut: it is a major obstacle to the success of the liberalism that they stand for. George F. Will defined it in *Statecraft as Soulcraft:* "The fundamental goal of modern liberalism has been equality, and it has given us government that believes in the moral equality of appetites."

But although the case against the Church was clear, there were not enough people who believed in the moral equality of appetites to make the charge stick and so destroy the credibility of the Church. The missing element that would whip up a storm of moral indignation and a rush to condemn was supplied by digging up the dirt of sexual abuse by priests. That such cases existed had been known since the liberal *National Catho-lic Reporter* made an issue of it in the 1980s. But it became a national scandal because of the carelessness and fecklessness of the Archdiocese of Boston in handling accusations of "child abuse" against some of its priests. (I put the words child abuse in quotation marks because in fact most of the accusations in Boston and throughout the country are of abusing teenage boys, not prepubescent children.) That gave the *Globe* and the *Times* the ammunition they needed.

I do not imply that all or most of the accusations are false. Probably they are not, and the Church seriously needs to do some housecleaning (and surely will do it). But the use the press is making of the facts is also clear: they are being pressed into the service of an agenda. The *Times* does not make priestly sexual misconduct a front-page story week after week, and the *Globe* for even longer, simply because it is news. It is a campaign that is intended to produce results, and they are also clear.

One is to create the impression that homosexual conduct by priests with boys is rife in the Church, and has created a crisis that makes it impossible to take the Church seriously as a moral guide. Ergo, we can stop listening to the Church on such issues as contraception, abortion, pre- and extra-marital sex, divorce and remarriage, and same-sex intercourse. But there *is* no crisis: a news poll taken by ABC found that 6 percent of Catholics and 6 percent of other Americans said there had been a sex-abuse case in their parish or congregation; 94 percent did not say that. Yet we are asked to believe that the Church is in a crisis caused by clerical sex abuse.

There is another but parallel agenda, which we are told will remove or greatly reduce the sexual abuse of minors. That is, a married clergy, the ordination of women, and the accep-tance of homosexuality as an alternative lifestyle. Don't ask me how these fit together, since accepting homosexuality certainly will not remedy the sexual abuse of boys. But these are standard parts of the liberal program. Liberal Catholic reformers of the Church, who can be counted on to agree with that program, are part of the *Times* stable of experts to call upon for comments.

The sin, above all sins, that the press will not forgive is

doing something without letting the press know it. Hence another of the charges against the Church is that it practices secrecy and covers up the sins of the clergy. Covering-up, of course, is something that newspapers never do. I do not recall the *Times* ever printing the fact that it has had to fire one of its highly placed staffers because, despite repeated reprimands, he has not kept his hands off the secretaries, and the newspaper had to settle harassment suits out of court. But that may only prove that such things never happen at the *Times*. We won't know, will we, until the *Times* opens up its files for inspection. In any case, the real fault committed by the church's administrators is not that they did not tell the press, but that they did not remove abusive priests from contact with young people, or, if necessary, get rid of them altogether.

Finally, the top item in the agenda of the press campaign is to force the resignation of Cardinal Bernard Law, the archbishop of Boston. The press brought down a president of the United States, Richard Nixon, by aggressive investigative reporting. It did not bring down President Clinton, but then, it didn't try, nor did it really want to. But think what a demonstration of the power of the press it would be to depose a Catholic cardinal archbishop — and teach the Church who is running this country.

Does this seem fantastic? Go back in history and notice the extent to which the monarchs of Catholic Europe succeeded in controlling the appointment of bishops. In Protestant England, the Crown still appoints the bishops of the national church. It is part of this country's religious freedom that the state neither appoints nor dismisses bishops. But Catholics (and others) may well ask themselves whether we really want to give that power to the lords of the press. As Finley Peter Dunne's Mr. Dooley said, "Being an editor is a hard job but a fascinating one. There's nothing so hard as minding your own business, and an editor never has to do that."

Is There Golf in Heaven?

June 2002

Is there golf in heaven? It is a question that haunts avid golfers. One of them pestered God with it until he finally got an answer. An angel appeared to him one night and said, "I bring you good news and bad news. The good news is that, yes, there is golf in heaven and the course is magnificent. The bad news is that you are teeing off at 9 o'clock tomorrow morning."

In this joke (for it is a joke, dear reader) there is a double revelation, not only about golfers but about all of us. We think of heaven in terms of the life we live here on earth and, however attractive heaven may be made to seem, earthbound as we are, we are in no hurry to go there.

In his autobiography, *Nearer My God,* William Buckley tells of an English lady who asked a Jesuit whether there would be pets in heaven. "Because," she explained, "if I cannot have my dog, Brownie, with me, I shall not be happy in heaven." He, being a Jesuit and an English one at that, was clever enough to give her an answer, which if not true was at least consoling: "In heaven you will of course be happy, and if you cannot be happy without Brownie, you will have Brownie." I myself would have been tempted to say, "Madam, if you ever find yourself in a place where you cannot be happy without a dog, you may be sure that place is not heaven." Which explains, no doubt, why I am not a popular preacher.

Let us continue the discussion with another, and true, story. Both my parents came from the same parish in County Tyrone, Ireland. There was a family named O'Neill in the parish, related to us only in that one of their daughters married one of my uncles. But I made it a point to visit them every time I visited my cousins there. The O'Neills finally dwindled to Dominic O'Neill and his sister Madge. When I called on them the conversation was between Dominic and me because Madge was very hard of hearing. Then, one day I went to see them and found that Dominic was in hospital, so I kept quiet, and let her do the talking. As she talked, I thought to myself, "This old woman has a beautiful soul. Listening to her is like looking into a pool of clear, limpid water. There is no malice in her."

Then she smiled as if she were about to say something naughty, and said, "Sometimes I think how nice it would be to have it all over and finished with, and to be with God." That said it all: heaven is being with God. An automatic response to that today will be, "How boring, being alone with God for all eternity!"

So, another story. An old friend has told me that she was raised by parents of no particular religion, but one clear and cloudless night, when she was taking a walk with her father, he looked up at the star-filled sky and said, "Who can look at that and not believe in God?" What made him say that? I don't know, but my guess is that he realized that the beauty of the sky implied an Absolute Beauty that transcended and explained it.

St. Augustine had similar intuition: "Late have I loved you, O Beauty ever ancient, ever new; late have I loved you! . . . The beautiful things of this world kept me from you . . . [But] you shone upon me; your radiance enveloped me; you put my blindness to flight."

It is hard to understand how anyone who made it to heaven could be bored in the presence of the Absolute Beauty, Absolute Good, and Absolute Truth that is the source of all that is true, good, and beautiful in this world. St. Augustine had it right again when he said, "You have made us for yourself, O God, and our hearts will never be at rest until they rest in You." No matter how many of the good things of this life we get, they do not last, and they fail to satisfy us completely. That is why we get bored with them and with one another. Heaven is where we enjoy an inexhaustible Good, forever.

Nor shall we be alone in heaven, since all those will be there who have sought God with a sincere heart. Even nasty, rotten, and wicked people, if they have truly repented of their sins, done adequate penance for them, and changed their lives will be there. (No, I do not expect that everyone who has ever lived will be in heaven, since I see nothing in Scripture or in common observation that leads to that conclusion.) Those who have persisted until death in doing their own will, instead of God's, will not be with him but in the eternal loneliness that is hell.

Lonely, but not alone. C. S. Lewis has put it well: "We must picture hell as a state where everyone is perpetually concerned about his own dignity and advancement, where everyone has a grievance, and where everyone lives in deadly serious passions of envy, self-importance and resentment." Even the most liberated secularist might prefer heaven to that, especially if he is already living in the highly competitive modern world, where there are only winners and losers, and even winning eventually palls.

The Scandal Racket

September 2002

Whatever can be made a racket will be made a racket. Not by everyone, of course, nor even by most people, but certainly by the smart operators whom we have always with us. For example, according to an editorial in the *New York Daily News*, last year the City of New York paid out a record $557 million dollars to settle civil lawsuits against the city. In contrast, suits against the State of New York are tried in the Court of Claims, where judges are appointed and function without juries. Last year this court awarded $34 million to successful plaintiffs. But the courts that settle cases against the city are composed of elected justices and, says the *News*, are "dominated by self-dealing pols, special-interest groups, and trial lawyers."

And they use juries, which "tend to award huge amounts to plaintiffs, even when the plaintiff was primarily or solely to blame." This, the editorial argues, calls for a reform of tort law, including a recommendation that damage suits against the city be transferred to the Court of Claims.

The situation described here is not confined to New York but exists across the country. Nor does it involve only lawsuits that use governments as milk cows. All institutions that have enough money to be worth suing are targets for suits for damages, unreal or exaggerated as well as real.

I know of at least one case in which Fordham University paid a large sum to an untenured faculty member when it denied him reappointment because he did not perform such routine duties as keeping office hours for students and attending department meetings. He threatened to sue the university for discriminating against him because of his ethnicity; the university's lawyers advised buying him off lest his suit turn into a class-action case. The university administrator who told me this remarked, "We were legally mugged." I daresay there isn't a university in the country in which similar stories could not be told.

The same is true of many other institutions, both public and private. It is not that the charges against these institutions are always or usually false. Rather, it is that there has grown up an industry of bringing suits against institutions which act on the advice of their own lawyers (or the lawyers of their insurance companies) that it is to their long-term interest to settle quietly out of court. This practice is what the press now calls a cover-up, but often enough the institution has been assured that it is financially better off by not fighting the suit in court. I myself would love to see Fordham go to the mat in some of these cases, but then I am considerably less sophisticated in the ways of the law and the courts than the university's lawyers.

The recent scandal of clergy sex-abuse cases reveals how heavily trial lawyers influence the decision-making of bishops. The scandal is commonly referred to as a crisis, but in fact it has largely been made one by the determined muckraking of the *Boston Globe* and its parent company, the *New York Times*. According to the *Times* itself, in mid-June, at least 250 priests had resigned or been suspended in the current year on accusations or admissions of sexual abuse of minors that may have been committed one, two, three, or even four decades ago. That number is about one half of one percent of the country's 46,000 Catholic priests. The number of priests taken out of service may well rise of course, but it will not add up to a crisis that is devastating the Church.

On April 27, 2002, for reasons best known to itself, the *Times* published a report under the headline, "Flush Times for Legal Vanguard in Priest Lawsuits." The most notorious of the attorneys who make big money for themselves and their clients by suing the Catholic Church is Jeffrey R. Anderson, of St. Paul, Minn., of whom the *Times* report says that since the early 1980s he "and half a dozen other lawyers around the country . . . have been suing Catholic dioceses and officials in sexual abuse cases involving priests and children." Mr. Anderson "has represented more than 400 people who say they were abused by priests, and he estimated that he had won more than $60 million in settlements from Catholic dioceses." He would not reveal his own fees, but the report says that "plaintiffs' lawyers typically take a third and sometimes as much as 40 percent of settlements and judgments."

Mr. Anderson, however, would not have us believe that he is driven by the love of money. Rather, he traces his "fury at the church" to his college days in the late 1960s when he became a "rabid antiwar activist." He later focused his anger on the Catholic Church when he learned that his daughter Amy had been molested in childhood "by a therapist who had formerly been a Catholic priest." "Every time I make an effort," he says, "it's for every survivor, and for Amy, too."

Other trial lawyers who prosper by suing the Church have other motives. Roderick MacLeish, Jr., a partner in a prominent Boston firm, explains: "I have very personal reasons for getting into this. I went to an English boarding school when I was 7 or 8. Nothing happened to me but only because I literally fought them off." One may wonder why Mr. MacLeish has not dedicated himself to suing English public schools, or why Mr. Anderson has not focused his fury on therapists, whatever their background.

Mr. Anderson added that he "would welcome the company of other plaintiffs' lawyers. There is money to be made," he says. "I encourage everyone to come in." But he worries that it may attract the kind of plaintiffs' lawyers who will give "this lucrative specialty" a bad name. And he is rightly worried: anything that can become a racket will become a racket.

The (Democratic) Party's Over

December 2002

The time has come for American Catholics to get over our love affair with the Democratic Party. So says John F. Kavanaugh, a Jesuit priest and professor of philosophy at St. Louis University, in a column he contributed to *America* magazine this past October 7. The words I attributed to him above are mine, not his, but they are the clear meaning of what he wrote. He certainly is not advocating a love affair with the Republican Party, but then, it never was "our party," in the way the Democrats were. In fact, Fr. Kavanaugh remains at heart an old-fashioned Franklin Roosevelt-Harry Truman-Hubert Humphrey Democrat, but he is disillusioned with what he sees as the party's abandonment of its tradition.

In his own words, "One thing the Democrats really stand for, however, is abortion—abortion on demand, abortion without restraint, abortion paid for by all of us, abortion for the poor of the earth. I am not a one-issue voter, but they have become a one-issue party."

He could have gone farther. The "one issue" is blossoming into a bouquet of liberal moral nostrums: quick and easy divorce, gay rights, condoms distributed in the schools and, eventually, euthanasia. The Democratic Party today (now in my words, not his) is the party of a well-off, liberal, individualistic, and highly secularized upper-middle-class that strives to win elections by pandering to the real, or at least felt, needs of blacks, Hispanics, Jews, suburban moms, teachers' unions, and other constituencies with grievances.But, he says, the Republicans are little different. What then? He suggests that Catholics who take their religion and its moral teaching seriously should withdraw their registration from both major parties and register as independents. Not many, of course, will do that, but the suggestion is worth thinking about.

It would help if we got over the idea that a vote for a

candidate who can't win is a wasted vote. Not necessarily so. A vote for a sure loser, or a vote not cast at all, can be read as sending a message: none of the major-party candidates satisfies me. One voter sending that message gets no attention from the politicians, but change has to start somewhere. If enough voters register as independents and refuse to vote for pro-choice candidates, attention will be paid. Politics depends on forming coalitions large enough to win elections. It is not necessary to belong to a majority, but only to be a part of a group that a would-be majority cannot do without, and that therefore gets listened to and taken seriously.

Granted, I live in the state of New York, where the choice between the parties is a choice between two evils, separated by a diminishing difference on the issues that mean most to me. The situation may be better in God's country somewhere west of the Appalachians. But the basic lesson remains: to attract the attention of the political movers and shakers, we must show them there are votes to be gained, if attention is paid to our demands. As Professor Robert A. Dahl of Yale remarked in his *Preface to Democratic Theory*, "The making of governmental decisions is not a majestic march of great majorities united upon certain matters of basic policy. It is the steady appeasement of relatively small groups."

It will also help to get over the fear of being accused of "imposing your beliefs on others." What are our opponents doing if not that? It is true that the liberal mind in its innocence does not realize that it is imposing anything on anyone: all it wants is "a woman's right to choose." Anyone who still believes that killing children in the womb is not killing human beings is really not old enough to vote.

The direct and intentional taking of human lives is of its nature a public issue (if the state does not exist to protect human lives, what is it there for?) and is not one to be dismissed with cries of "imposing beliefs." All that is asked for is that the issue be taken for what it is and be admitted to the public forum to be decided by the democratic political process.

It would also help if pro-lifers got over the habit of thinking of that process as an either-or, all-or-nothing contest. If we present the issue as abortion on demand or no abortion at all, there can be no doubt which of the two the American public will support. Politics, however, does not work that way. As Edmund Burke explained two centuries ago, "the decisions of prudence [i.e., political judgment] . . . almost all . . . are determined on the more or less, the earlier or the later, and on a balance of advantage and inconvenience, of good and evil."

We are in for a long, hard fight, where the gains will be slow and at first few, but the only way to make any gains is to get into the fight and stay in it.

Deep Weariness

April 2003

Matthew Arnold was an English poet and a critic of the Victorian age in which he lived. In "Dover Beach," which is probably the best-known of his poems today, he is standing with his wife on the cliff overlooking that beach, and reflects to himself: "The Sea of Faith / Was once, too, at the full, and round earth's shore / Lay like the folds of a bright girdle furled. / But now I only hear / Its melancholy, long, withdrawing roar . . ." Then he turns to his wife and says,

> Ah, love, let us be true
> To one another! for the world, which seems
> To lie before us like a land of dreams,
> So various, so beautiful, so new,
> Hath really neither joy, nor love, nor light,
> Nor certitude, nor peace, nor help for pain;
> And we are here as on a darkling plain
> Swept with confused alarms of struggle and flight,
> Where ignorant armies clash by night.

Arnold once wrote that, since religious faith was dying, we must "turn to poetry to interpret life for us, to console us, to sustain us." But he has also been described as a religious liberal who believed that "men cannot do without Christianity, but cannot do with it as it is," anticipating Garry Wills by more than a century. In another poem, "Obermann Once More," Arnold says of the ancient pre-Christian society,

> On that hard pagan world disgust
> And secret loathing fell.
> Deep weariness and sated lust
> Made human life a hell.

Arnold wrote those lines in a despairing mood of regret for the inevitable death of Christianity. For my part, I see in them a ray of hope for its revival. I do not see how the liberal, secularist, and individualistic society that now sets the goals of life for us and our rising generation, can long endure without provoking revulsion and regret.

Christopher Caldwell described our current Western culture well in an article in the *New Republic* (April 1999): "In a society organized around a succession of acquisitions and thrills, questions of lifestyle determine one's identity, one's rank in society, one's allegiances, one's loves and hates. It's not a matter of monolithic, time-honored religion versus itty-bitty, flighty lifestyle. It's religion — marginal vestige, subculture, private matter — versus lifestyle — the engine, the symbol, the central organizing principle of the most powerful nation in the history of mankind."

He goes on to explain what is at stake in the decision to abort a child. It is "a vastly expanded roster of life choices: education, travel, career advancement, class advancement, money, fine dining, entertainment, and sports, plus a recreational-sex career that can run at full throttle (if that is what you want) for thirty years or more." Such a range of choices will always attract a large part of the population, but can it be the engine, the symbol, and the organizing principle of a whole society that intends to last?

Statistics on population decline give reason for doubt. The *Times Literary Supplement* (London) on February 8, 2003, included a review of a report published by United Nations Publications (New York) under the title, *State of the World Population 2002*. The outlook for Europe is not promising (and the United States is not far behind). "European populations," says the review, "are no longer reproducing themselves. . . . By 2050, the European population is predicted to be down to 600 million, from 725 million today." To achieve population stability, i.e., replacement of the present population but without increasing it, Europe would need an average birthrate of 2.1 children per woman (and to get that, the three-child family would have to be accepted as normal). In fact, the average European birth rate is estimated at 1.34. But the replacement rate is unlikely to be achieved. "The reason is that modern conventions for family life are built around the now firm idea, and economic necessity, of both parents working and earning," which "is not easily compatible with more than two children."

The review of this report states that population decline leads to economic decline. "An industrial or post-industrial economy *is* its population. When populations grow, economies grow, when they stagnate, economies stagnate, when they decline, economies decline. . . . It is population that creates demand and pressure in a modern economy; when it starts to run out of people, it runs out of steam." Then people "see themselves as living in an environment of decline," which makes them reluctant to bring children into such a world.

"What happens if Europe falls into economic decline?" That is a secular question that is well worth thinking about. But it is my concern here inasmuch as it affects the spiritual question that I raised earlier: can the range of choices that make abortion so apparently necessary sustain Western society? Is the availability of those choices what makes life worth living? Or does it produce a deep weariness and a profound emptiness that kills society's soul, and eventually weakens it culturally, economically, politically, and even militarily? Remember, the Roman Empire collapsed when it could no longer raise troops from within itself to resist barbarian invasions, and had to recruit some barbarians to fight off other barbarians.

Writers on both left and right have criticized contemporary liberalism for conceiving of man as a bundle of appetites clamoring for satisfaction. For people of that description, the good society is one that satisfies their appetites with an impartial hand. It now behooves the member of the Catholic Church and, I would add, of all religious bodies that believe in God the Creator and accept his commandments, to force the moral issues that can no longer be excluded from politics.

For a change, we might reverse the attack and press the secularists on what they have to offer. Is it only that vast roster of life choices that Christopher Caldwell says are the engine, the symbol, and the organizing principle of the most powerful nation in the history of mankind? How many people will get those choices and, if they get them, will they find that they satisfy their deepest desires? Just how much does this world have to offer? As Pascal said in the seventeenth century, if the human condition were really happy, we would not have to divert ourselves so much to keep from thinking about it.

But there will always be some people who think about it, and they are the ones we should be talking to.

The Real Crisis

August 2003

We have heard so much in the past year and a half about the crisis caused by the clergy sex-abuse scandal that we forget that it is but one of the effects of a crisis that went before it and had widespread consequences that are still with us. Another of those effects is the decline in vocations to the priesthood and the religious orders of men and women.

"Everyone knows" today that this vocation crisis is the result of the refusal of reactionary elements in Rome and "the hierarchy" to permit a married clergy, the ordination of women, and acceptance of homosexuality. Another necessary reform is that the hierarchy should listen to the laity and allow them to solve their moral problems, free from restrictions imposed by a rigid structure of authority.

Well, anyhow, the enlightened thinkers among us know these things. Strangely, they do not seem to know, or to care, that a similar crisis of vocations exists among Protestants and Jews. The Jewish situation is described in an article in the May 2003 issue of *Commentary*, a highly regarded monthly journal published by the American Jewish Committee. Entitled "The Rabbi Crisis," the article was written by Jack Wertheimer, provost and professor of American Jewish history at the Jewish Theological Seminary in New York.

According to Professor Wertheimer, after a period of decline in the number and size of synagogue congregations, since the late 1980s the demand for rabbis has increased, but the supply has not. In short, there is a shortage of rabbis serving congregations. He does not attribute it to the requirement of celibacy, for there is no such requirement in Judaism. Nor does he explain it by the attraction of high-paying jobs for young men who might otherwise become rabbis. On the contrary, he says, "In keeping with the rising demands, compensation [for rabbis] has reached impressive levels."

Yet "ever-growing numbers of rabbis" are leaving their congregations to serve as teachers, administrators, or chaplains in a variety of Jewish institutions, even at a "lower remuneration than the pulpit rabbinate." Other compensations attract them, "including more reasonable job requirements, fewer 'bosses,' and a clearer chain of command." Finally, while "all rabbinical schools except those within the orbit of Orthodoxy now ordain women . . ., the supply side [for rabbis] looks very poor."

One reason for this, says Wertheimer, "was the society-wide assault on authority," which many rabbis gave in to. They "refashioned themselves, trading in their suits for leisure wear, abandoning the title 'Rabbi Cohen' for 'Rabbi Bob,'" relinquishing "their roles as authorities in matters of Jewish religious law," and making [in the words of Daniel Jeremy Silver] "a virtue of being non-judgmental." This may have made them more popular, but it has tended to undermine the authority and respect that rabbis once had.

Since in Judaism there is no central authority, power rests with congregational boards in the synagogues. "Increasingly," according to Wertheimer, "congregational boards are drawing upon business models" to judge the success of their rabbis. This seems to say that it is not what the rabbi preaches that counts, but how many people he draws to synagogue services. "With the rabbi relegated to the role of manager, and success increasingly measured in quantitative terms, the deeper, religious purposes of the synagogue tend to fall by the wayside." But this attitude ignores "what the rabbis themselves most value — serving as teachers of the religious tradition" — and values "what they least wish to do," which "virtually guarantees low rates of job satisfaction and retention."

Furthermore, "the decades-long erosion of authority, and of authority figures, in American culture at large has translated into an all-out assault upon 'hierarchy' within the synagogue . . . Feminists have fueled this depreciation of 'hierarchical' models of leadership, [and] quite a few seem to agree that the very exercise of religious authority borders on the psychopathological."

Wertheimer disagrees with them. "Thanks to the campaign against 'hierarchy,' rabbis have been stripped, or have stripped

themselves, of their traditional prerogatives in the very area —
religious principle — where those prerogatives matter most . . .
In this new Judaism, the role of the rabbi is to be a 'care-giver,'
a hand-holder, a counselor."

Heaven forfend that such things should happen in Our
Holy Mother, the Catholic Church. But as we look back over
the past forty years, we may feel that Wertheimer's views are
worth reflecting upon. At a time when loud demands are being voiced that bishops do a better job of supervising what
goes on in parishes, we might venture a suggestion that they
pay attention to what is and what is not being taught in the
pulpits.

The Primacy of Choice

February 2004

In the kingdom of the blind the one-eyed man is king, according to an old saying. In the kingdom of choice in which we now live in this land of the free, everyone is a king or a queen. Or even both together, for bisexuals have rights, too, you know.

Yet there are basic aspects of our very being about which we had no choice, and they put real limits on the rest of our lives. We did not choose to be conceived. We did not choose to be born. We did not choose to be boys or girls. We did not choose our parents or the whole genetic heritage they passed on to us. We did not choose the color of our skins or our eyes or our hair. If we have significant musical, or intellectual, or athletic talents, we did not choose them for ourselves, nor did we choose the lack of them.

I'd love to tell you that I tried out to be a pitcher for the New York Yankees, but all I had on the ball was blinding speed and a sharp-breaking curve, and that was not enough. The truth is, I had nothing on the ball, and there was nothing I could do about that. Like everyone else, I have had to make the most of what I've got, and there is no use saying that it's just not fair.

The modern mind finds that hard to accept. The scientific search for ways to control nature and extend the range of choice goes on relentlessly. I don't complain about that, since the fact that I am alive today and well enough to write this column is a triumph of modern medicine. But we are reaching the stage where the dream of changing human nature and remaking it seems realizable. I heard recently that the genetic engineers expect to be able to work on a newly fertilized human ovum and change its chromosome so that the girl-child just conceived will be a blond-haired boy with blue eyes. I don't know if that is true, but if the genetic engineers succeed, it will be a social disaster, in which women will probably end up holding the short end of the stick.

More to the immediate point, the ability to change the sex and the appearance of children at conception will certainly increase the power of human beings to choose. But the choice will not have been made by the children subject to it. The decision may be given to their mothers as part of the famous "woman's right to choose." Or that right may be expanded to give the child's father a look-in. In the not very long run, however, it will become a political issue because of the influence it will have on the future of society. In this country, the U.S. Supreme Court may find a "compelling state interest" in maintaining an adequate balance of the sexes.

But the political battle will go on, as it has on the issues of abortion, sodomy, and gay marriage. There will be much trumpeting of the society's need for the absolute freedom of scientific research. And of the primacy of individual choice. And of the view that moral judgments are only expressions of individual preferences and are not judgments about objective good and evil. The media will weigh in with denunciations of the Church for imposing on Catholics in public office its moral preferences on matters of public policy.

It is important to note that what ultimately matters is not only what we do but how we understand what we are doing and want to do. Contraception, for example, is now widely accepted because it solves problems. But the acceptance very soon changed our understanding of what sex is, what it is for, and how we may conduct sexual relations.

It is no accident that turning contraception into a constitutional right was followed by a successful demand for abortion, then for sodomy, and by a further demand for gay marriage. It is no answer to say, "My husband and I would not dream of doing those horrible and disgusting things." I don't doubt that, but I notice that some Catholics who sincerely say that nonetheless refuse to condemn homosexual acts as immoral because that would be imposing their beliefs on others, and besides, "they can't help it."

We live in a society in which it is taken for granted that when you send your daughter to college she will be equipped with diaphragms and condoms. If she gets pregnant, she must have an abortion, lest her life be ruined. If she marries, and the marriage "doesn't work," she will get a divorce; if she is still a Catholic, she will seek an annulment. If she doesn't get one, she will remarry anyhow. If she is not attractive enough to find another husband, and turns to lesbianism in the quest for love, we will understand. If all of this seems prejudicial to daughters, double it for sons.

The only point I am trying to make is that the primacy of choice is wrecking our sexual morality, but not only that. At a deeper level, it is destroying our ability to have a social morality that goes beyond sexual conduct to question the right of any society to establish and maintain social standards on any other than utilitarian grounds. And that just might lead us, as our culture disintegrates around us, to question the primacy of individual choice.

Catholic Individualism

April 2004

Liberalism as we know it has become a radical individualism that permeates our culture. As Robert Bellah once remarked, political discourse in this country is carried on between conservative liberals, who believe only in the free market, and liberal liberals, who believe only in individual rights.

That is the liberalism, on both sides of the aisle, that the Catholic Church has consistently rejected. In his encyclical *Populorum Progressio*, Pope Paul VI rejected what we too often call conservatism as "unchecked liberalism," and described it as a system "which considers profit as the key motive for economic progress, competition as the supreme law of economics, and private ownership of the means of production as an absolute right that has no limits and carries no corresponding social obligation." Today's liberalism is the most recent development of what Pope Pius IX had in mind when, in his famous Syllabus of Errors, he condemned the proposition that "the Roman Pontiff should reconcile himself to and come to terms with liberalism."

Yet there is and always has been a Catholic individualism. Cardinal Ratzinger has spoken of "God's unconditional respect for the freedom of his creature." Pope John Paul II has explained that freedom is not simply the lack of restraint of man's appetites, but rather the ability of the human will to make self-determined choices: "All of God's action in human history respects the free will of the human 'I.'"

In *Populorum Progressio* Paul VI had already stated that freedom entails a responsibility of the highest order:

> In the design of God every man is called upon to develop and fulfill himself, for every life is a vocation. . . . Endowed with intelligence and freedom, he is responsible for his fulfillment as he is for his salvation. He is aided, or sometimes impeded, by those who educate him and those with whom he lives, but each

one remains, whatever be these influences affecting him, the principal agent of his own success or failure. By the unaided effort of his own intelligence and his will, each man can grow in humanity, can enhance his personal worth, can become more a person.

Then Pope Paul added: "However, this self-fulfillment is not something optional. . . . [Human] fulfillment is, as it were, a summary of our duties." Duty is prior to, and commands and guides free choice. Human nature is a very rich nature that offers us a wide range of opportunities, careers and ways of living, all of them legitimate, if they are contained within a framework of moral obligation set by the will of God as revealed to us by our nature and by his special revelation of his will for us.

The relationship between God and men revealed in the Bible is a history of creation, sin, punishment, repentance, forgiveness, and salvation. In the earlier books of the Bible, the relationship was principally between God and his often erring and rebellious people. The people of Israel sinned and were punished as a people.

But in the sixth century B.C., the prophet Ezekiel, speaking for God, declared that the sins of the fathers were not visited upon their sons. (The consequences of parents' sins obviously do descend upon their children, but not their guilt.) "The child," said Ezekiel, "shall not share the burden of the parent's guilt nor shall a parent share the burden of a child's guilt; the righteousness of the righteous shall be accounted to him alone, and the wickedness of the wicked shall be accounted to him alone" (18:20). In the New Testament we read: "It is appointed for men to die once, and after that comes judgment" (Heb. 9:27).

That is a biblical and Christian individualism. But it is not a denial of the implications of our common nature for our life in society. One of the most obvious examples of our nature as social beings is the reality of two sexes, which are designed by nature to join in marriage and to raise children. Perhaps the most important obligation of every generation is to beget and raise its own next generation. That is a project which all of us, married or not, should aid and promote for the common good of mankind.

An example of an opposite and radically individualist view is furnished by the late Supreme Court Justice Harry Blackmun in the case of *Bowers v. Hardwick* (1984):

> We protect those rights [of privacy] not because they contribute, in some direct and material way, to the general public welfare, but because they form so central a part of an individual's life. We protect the decision whether to marry precisely because marriage is an association that promotes a way of life, . . . And so we protect the decision whether to have a child because parenthood alters so dramatically an individual's self-definition, . . . And we protect the family because it contributes so powerfully to the happiness of individuals, not because of a preference for stereotypical households.

With these and other words in his opinion, Blackmun reduces human rights to individual desires, and human society to a collection of self-centered individuals seeking personal happiness. That is a liberal individualism radically different from the Catholic one.

The Linchpin of Sexuality

June 2004

Dr. Leon Kass, the University of Chicago professor who chairs President Bush's Council on Bioethics, has said in the *New Republic* (June 2, 1997), "Thanks to the sexual revolution, we are able to deny in practice, and increasingly in thought, the inherent procreative teleology of sexuality itself."

The key phrase in that statement is "in thought." What we do certainly is important, but our understanding of what we are doing is even more basic. That is why the Catholic Church has insisted more stringently on orthodoxy (right belief) than on orthopraxis (right conduct). Sin is evil, but not understanding that it is sin is a social disaster.

In contemporary Western societies, the Church stands almost alone in condemning contraception as against nature and therefore sinful. Many persons disagree with her on contraception, but not on other sexual acts that the Church condemns (e.g., sodomy) because they do not see the unifying thread of thought that runs through all of Catholic sexual moral teaching.

In Catholic thought, we live in a universe created by God, and man is a creature made in God's image and likeness, from which all his obligations and rights flow. There is only one human race, despite our habit of dividing it into five races. The one human race, however, is divided into two irreducibly distinct sexes that are designed by nature to complement each other in begetting new human lives. This is Dr. Kass's "inherent procreative teleology of sexuality."

To deny that this teleology is normative is implicitly to accept as morally permissible not only contraception but also a long series of other acts. The implications of that denial are being made more explicit every day. The sexual revolution springs from the change in thinking that makes those implications socially acceptable. Attempts to control the consequences of the change by utilitarian or proportionalist moral reasoning have visibly failed. Multitudes of people today, including practicing Catholics, simply do not see what is wrong with the actions that the Church forbids. They often do not even know that the Church forbids them, because the clergy have not told them.

Yet the Church has a clear and coherent doctrine on sexual morality. Sexuality is inherently procreative. Yes, sexual intercourse is and ought to be an act of love that binds man and wife together. But the act of love is defined by the ordering to procreation that is built into it by nature and therefore by God. So the Church insists that the integrity of the act must always be preserved.

It follows that it must be performed with the organs of reproduction, and that it may not be sterilized before, during, or after its performance. Homosexual perversions of the act, and substitutes for it such as masturbation and pornography, are likewise barred. Procreation, when it occurs, must be the result of the natural sexual act, not of artificial insemination. The persons who engage in the act must therefore be of opposite sex and married to each other. If conception results, the living human being that is conceived may not be aborted. Sexuality is inherently life giving, which is a physical and moral reality that must be respected.

The relationship of sexuality to life extends naturally to the prohibition not only of murder, but of suicide and euthanasia as well. Our lives are not merely our own. They belong to God and, while they do not belong to the state, they are fundamental to the existence and well-being of civil society, which the state has the duty of protecting even, if necessary, against our wishes. Or are the cops violating an individual's civil rights when they grab him before he jumps off the bridge?

On all of these matters, the teaching of the Church is not unintelligible, but perfectly clear and rational, and it hangs together very well. But if we pull out the linchpin, "the inherent procreative teleology of sexuality," the structure of traditional sexual morality falls apart. As R. Albert Mohler, president of a Southern Baptist seminary, has said (*First Things*, December 1998), "The Pill allowed a near-total abandonment of Christian sexual morality in the larger culture. Once the sex act was severed from the likelihood of childbearing, the traditional structure of sexual morality collapsed."

Dr. Mohler would allow contraception within the bounds of marriage. But accepting contraception has an effect on the way in which we conceptualize sex and the sex act, and that cannot be ignored. Even if confined to marital intercourse, contraception contributes mentally to our ambiguity about homosexual relations, our high rates of abortion and divorce, and the distribution of condoms to schoolboys and morning-after pills to schoolgirls, among other results of the sexual revolution.

Modern Superstition

August 2004

Some fifty years ago, a Syracuse, N.Y., newspaper reported that a "Weeping Madonna" — a statue of the Blessed Virgin that wept tears — was drawing crowds of visitors to a house in that city. The newspaper sent a reporter to stand outside the house and ask people as they came out what they thought of this marvel. A Catholic priest said, "We don't know how to explain this phenomenon." A Unitarian minister said, "There must be some natural explanation."

How did he know that? Well, he didn't really *know* it, but spoke out of a worldview. That is, he began with an understanding of the universe as a closed system of matter, in which everything that happens can and must be explained from within the system, and not attributed to any cause that transcends the system. Hence, "there must be some natural explanation."

Now, whether the weeping Madonna is to be explained naturally or supernaturally is irrelevant here. My point is that a lot of modern and postmodern thought assumes certain presuppositions without acknowledging them. Or, to be fair, without knowing that it is doing so. The self-confident rationalism of the Enlightenment, which is now followed by post-modern intellectual despair, is an example.

I remember when I was a college student, many decades ago, having a summer job at the Lake Placid Club in the Adirondack Mountains. Most of my fellow workers were students at Cornell or Syracuse Universities. One day, as two of them walked by me, one was saying, "The universe is ultimately purposeless." Young though I was, I immediately recognized that he was quoting something a professor had said in the classroom. Possibly it was the famous Carl Becker of Cornell, who regarded man as "little more than a chance deposit on the surface of the world, carelessly thrown up between two ice ages by the same forces that rust iron and ripen corn."

Once people rejected God the Creator, they were left with a self-explanatory universe, open to investigation by modern science, but purposeless and therefore meaningless. We are here, we were born, we live, we shall die, and there is nothing beyond that. We may indeed choose the values by which we will live but, as Leo Strauss remarked, we cannot really believe in them because we know that we created them.

Why, then, do people cling to this view of the world? One reason is that it leaves them free of any alleged truth that imposes certain presuppositions on them. "I am free to make up my own universe, my own values, my own moral code, and thereby to satisfy my dominant desires."

Another reason is that "credulous belief" in scientific reasoning which Thomas Spragens has called "the principal superstition of modernity." David Lindley, in his book *The End of Physics* has explained: "We give the name of science to those areas of intellectual inquiry that yield to mathematical analysis. . . . And that is why mathematics is the appropriate language. . . . The puzzle becomes a tautology . . . because we reserve the name 'science' for anything mathematics can handle. If it is not mathematical to some degree at least, it isn't really science."

And to many people it isn't real at all. Lindley does not agree, and says, "Art appreciation, for example, requires a genuine effort of intellect, but we do not suppose that the degree to which a painting touches our emotions can be organized into a set of measurements and rules."

Yet once we have come to believe that we can take as true only what has been proved by rigid mathematical reasoning, we have set a gulf between what is true and what is good or beautiful. The latter are seen as emotional responses that may satisfy us but must not be imposed on other people who do not feel them.

As Thomas Hobbes said some centuries ago, "'Good' and 'evil' are names that signify our appetites and aversions," which vary from person to person, and from one time and place to another. Hobbes is often thought of as a proto-Fascist, but he is arguably a forerunner of contemporary liberalism, whose idea of good and evil can be found in university faculties and on the editorial boards of newspapers.

It seems to me, however, that one cannot study medicine without coming to see that the human body is an organism, consisting of a variety of organs that are organized to produce and protect the life, health, growth, and development of the whole body. These, therefore, are not merely preferences that we feel but, on the contrary, constitute the natural, built-in good of the body, antecedent to any choice of ours.

We can enjoy eating and drinking, but only because our organs are made for nutrition and hydration. We can enjoy smoking tobacco and marijuana, but only because we have lungs to take in air and supply the body with oxygen. These are realities that can be recognized, and are not presuppositions that mad fanatics impose on others who do not share them.

Who Says So?

October 2004

"The culture is changing" is a current liberal mantra. It is true that cultures change, more or less rapidly or slowly. But this mantra means that our culture is changing rapidly — and there is nothing we can do about it.

One prominent example is the way in which we are to speak of men and women. The personal pronouns he and she are still in use, but very much under new rules. If "he" refers to a male person, "he" is appropriate and acceptable. But if it refers to a kind or class of persons, it must be "he or she," because "he" excludes "she" and assumes that a woman cannot be in that class. And that is an unjust exclusion of the whole female sex. But this assumption rests on the premise that "man" and "he" everywhere and always mean "male."

This premise reveals a profound misunderstanding of the English language, in which the basic and primary meaning of "man" is "human being," and the appropriate pronoun is "he." A secondary meaning of "man" is human being of the male sex. In the alternative secondary meaning, "woman" designates a female human being. Wo-man=a female man, as the first syllable indicates. It is an old English word one of whose earliest forms was "wifman," obviously related to "wife" and the German *Weib*, i.e., female.

Denying this and insisting on what is called "inclusive language" leads to a wooden, awkward, and clumsy manner of speaking English. It makes one think of Henry Higgins' first words about Eliza: "By right she should be taken out and hung for the cold-blooded murder of the English tongue." Carried to its logical extreme, it would lead to such translations of the gospel as "If anyone would come after me, let him or her deny himself or herself, take up his or her cross, and come follow me."

There are various dodges for avoiding the wrath of the feminists (who are males as well as females). One is to use the plural rather than the singular, so that we can say "they" and "their" rather than "he or she," as in "Every American has a right to their own opinion." Another is to turn the singular pronoun into "s/he," as one of my graduate students used to do in her written papers (but I never learned how she pronounced that). The faculty statutes of a university that I once knew never used the third-person pronouns "he" and "she" at all. They were uniformly replaced by "the individual." To be a consistent ideologue, it seems, requires a lack of any sense of the ridiculous.

Despite its absurdity, inclusive language is creeping into certain institutions, most notably the academy, the Church, and the law. It turns up in the opinions of certain justices of the U.S. Supreme Court. For instance, Justice John Paul Stevens uses "she" when the reference is to a person of either sex; in an assisted-suicide case, he spoke of "the person's interest in ending her life." We now find this sort of thing in the Catholic liturgy, in such lines as "One does not live on bread alone," a new translation whose only purpose is to avoid the word "man."

I recently sat in on a conversation among some academics younger than myself. They were discussing problems they encountered in getting their scholarly books published by major university presses. Gaining tenure and promotion, they said, depended on publication by these presses, which in turn required them to write in inclusive language. But the young professors tamely accepted this, saying "The culture is changing."

I don't blame them, because their careers are at stake. But they are wrong in not seeing that the culture is not going through a "natural" and unplanned change. Instead, it is undergoing a concerted effort to change the culture by changing the way we speak. It is no accident that Mrs. has been replaced by Ms. Mrs. is alleged to demean a woman by suggesting that her place and importance in society is determined by her position as a man's wife, rather than by her job and the career in which the job is a step upwards.

One might think that being a wife and the mother in a family is more important to society's health and welfare than being an account executive in an advertising firm. As we reckon success in our contemporary society, however, it is not so. Yet a look at our rising number of divorces, our abortions, youthful delinquents, and other results of family breakdown might lead us to entertain doubts about the reigning liberal concept of equality.

One thing we might do, however, when we are told that our language is changing because "the culture is changing," is to ask, "Who says so?" And, of course, why do we have to listen to him, or her, or them?

In a society where opinion is constantly manipulated by pressure groups that have enough power and influence to determine what is "politically correct," too many of us fail to ask, "Who says so, and why should we listen?" Cultural change is not always something that just happens. It is often shaped and imposed by those who want to bring about a certain change in our culture, and is accepted by those who don't care enough to object.

The Faith of Liberals

January 2005

The Republican triumph in last year's national election was met by a wave of distraught emotion in the media and the academy. It was widely denounced as a victory of "bigoted Christian rednecks." In the *New York Times* Maureen Dowd went into a hissy fit, and Garry Wills mourned the end of the Enlightenment.

The calmest and most restrained response from the liberal side that I have seen is a statement by Robert Reich, who was a member of President Clinton's cabinet. He said: "The true battle will be between modern civilization and anti-modernists; between those who believe in the primacy of the individual and those who believe that human beings owe their allegiance and identity to a higher authority; between those who give priority to life in this world and those who believe that life in this world is mere preparation for an existence beyond life; between those who believe in science, reason, and logic and those who believe that truth is revealed through Scripture and religious dogma."

In Mr. Reich's world, it seems, there are only science, which alone really knows, and dogma, which does not know but simply imposes its beliefs. But the modernist mode of thought has its own problems. Alan Ryan, the warden of New College in Oxford University, revealed one of them when he said, "What decides the moral argument in the case of abortion is the wickedness of making other people's deepest and most difficult decisions for them and enforcing them by law." It follows, then, does it not, that there is a norm that transcends individuals and binds all of us by telling us that it is wicked not to leave the abortion decision to the individual?

Mr. Reich believes in "science, reason, and logic." But what is the criterion of these intellectual activities? In a recent column on a similar subject, I quoted the physicist David Lindley, who helps to explain how "science" has become tantamount to truth. "There is a temptingly simple explanation," he writes in *The End of Physics*, "for the fact that science is mathematical in nature: it is because we give the name of science to those areas of intellectual inquiry that yield to mathematical analysis. . . . We reserve the name 'science' for anything that mathematics can handle. If it's not mathematical, to some degree at least, it isn't really science."

The liberal mind then leaps to the conclusion that it isn't real at all.

That explains why liberals can be so intolerant without knowing that they are intolerant. As the late Christopher Lasch put it: "What makes liberalism such a seductive but also such a pernicious ideology is its refusal to recognize itself as an ideology. It insists on its own neutrality, claiming to represent nothing more than a set of procedures. Its superiority allegedly lies in its indifference to ideology. But of course liberalism, too, implies a 'philosophical outlook,' a 'conception of human nature,' and a set of assumptions about 'the meaning of life.'"

The basic assumption behind this individualistic liberalism is the primacy of the individual, all other elements of social life being conventions agreed upon to make social life among individuals possible, as Thomas Hobbes proclaimed more than three centuries ago. These conventions become what George F. Will has called liberalism's belief in "the moral equality of appetites" (which leads to the now prevalent liberal piety that regards asserting a common moral code on such matters as marriage, the family, and abortion as somehow wicked and immoral).

Catholics, and especially Catholic educators, have not been immune to this kind of thinking. As Archbishop John J. Myers of Newark has remarked, "Catholics in America [in the second half of the twentieth century] entered and embraced a culture that was radically different from the vaguely Protestant and mildly anti-Catholic culture of our first 200 years. To say that we were not ready for this encounter is an understatement."

One result of our acceptance of contemporary culture is

that we have unreflectingly accepted its basic belief that science knows, while moral judgments are expressions of personal or group preferences — those "values" that must not be permitted to affect public policy and law. In modernity's dominant myth reason is totally dispassionate and uninfluenced by emotion or religious belief. This may work well enough in dealing with those aspects of reality that can be handled by mathematical analysis. But it denies any intellectual knowledge of the good. Thus, the goal of the science of medicine is to preserve life and health, but only if the patient wants them. If he does not, Dr. Kevorkian may be called upon to help the patient commit suicide. The patient's good (like everyone else's good) is what he wants, not the objective and real good of life.

Welcome to the brave new world predicted decades ago by Aldous Huxley and C. S. Lewis, a world that we make out of the materials furnished by a meaningless universe, beyond which there is no real world and no God — except us, of course.

Political Thinking

There are people who talk incessantly about politics but don't know how to think about it. For them, political issues are matters of principle — right against wrong, good versus evil — and the answer to every question is yes or no, either or, all or nothing. Anything less than that is a betrayal of principle, not to be endured.

Edmund Burke, an English parliamentarian who died in 1797, was a severe critic of the French Revolution and its abstract ideology that derived its political theory from the natural and imprescriptible "rights of man." "For you know," he wrote to a friend, "that the decisions of prudence . . . almost all . . . are determined on the more or the less, the earlier or the later, and a balance of advantage and inconvenience, of good, and evil." There are some things, he believed, that cannot morally be done, but even then, whether criminal law should or even can prohibit them in all circumstances is not always clear.

St. Thomas Aquinas, who died in 1274, wrote in his *Summa Theologica*, "Human law is enacted on behalf of the mass of men, the majority of whom are far from perfect in virtue. For this reason human law does not prohibit every vice from which virtuous men abstain; but only the graver vices from which the majority can abstain; and particularly those vices which are damaging of others, and which, if they are not prohibited, would make it impossible for human society to endure: as murder, theft, and suchlike, which are prohibited by human law." Or, to quote Burke once again, "It is no inconsiderable part of wisdom to know how much of an evil ought to be tolerated."

I am *not* suggesting that abortion is not tantamount to murder and should therefore be tolerated. But the fact is that it is not only tolerated but stubbornly protected by the Supreme Court, which has taken the matter out of the hands of the citizens. Yet abortion is currently a bitterly contested issue and will continue to be one.

I have no doubt that the deliberate and intended killing of a human child in the womb is always a serious moral wrong and a grave social evil. But I wonder about the wisdom of insisting that nothing less than a constitutional amendment banning it everywhere and always is a wise goal in our present circumstances. To take that position is to give up any chance of limiting abortion by law. The votes are simply not there to achieve that goal, and to insist that nothing less will do is to achieve nothing at all.

Nor do I think that totally reversing *Roe v. Wade* by appointing new and saner justices to the Supreme Court is likely to happen soon. I have lost my respect for the court, but even better members of it, while they may modify that decision, cannot be expected simply to reverse it. Even if that decision were reversed, it would not forbid abortion but would transfer the regulation of abortion from the judicial to the political process. Even that, however, would be an achievement well worth working for, as the fury with which liberals oppose it demonstrates.

The court's effort to take the abortion issue out of politics by declaring it to be a constitutional right has clearly failed. Abortion remains and should remain a political issue. But *Roe v. Wade* has become a precedent deeply fixed in the court's jurisprudence, and reversing it is going to take a long time and require a step-by-step series of decisions that make exceptions to the sweeping dictate of the original decision and the decisions that have followed it. The beginning of that process is the reasonable result to hope for of President Bush's recent nomination of Judge John Roberts to the Supreme Court.

Under the Constitution, Congress has the power to remove abortion from the jurisdiction of the federal courts. But it won't do that, because politicians prefer to leave the "hot potatoes" issues to the federal judges, who do not have to stand for re-election. Yet we also live in this pressure-group democracy, and those who are willing to ignore the screams of the liberal media can influence results.

They will not do that, however, if they ask for too much too soon. It is essential, therefore, to consider not only what we should strive for but how much we can achieve in the circumstances that exist here and now.

I remember, on visits to Ireland, hearing the remark that the curse of Irish politics is that compromise is considered to be a dirty word. I also remember hearing that you don't have to be Irish to be thick — but it helps. Let me add that the Code of Canon Law of the Catholic Church states as a principle that *nemo tenetur ad impossibile* (no one is bound to do the impossible). We are bound to do what we can in the circumstances that currently exist.

Those circumstances require a reasonable estimate of the extent to which a law banning or regulating abortion can be enforced. Otherwise we shall be inviting the sad results of the Eighteenth Amendment, that attempted to ban the sale of alcoholic drinks in this country. Suppose that, instead of trying to outlaw abortion outright, the law required that all abortion be performed in hospitals, with the agreement of doctors other than the abortionist as to the medical necessity of this abortion. Such a law, if enforced, would put the abortion clinics out of business.

I am not recommending that law or any other law as "the" solution to the current scandal of the mass killing of infants in the womb. Nor am I urging citizens to vote for "moderates" who are willing to make some concessions that will save as much as can be saved of abortion on demand. But I do recommend that we stop demanding what we know we cannot get, and concentrate on reform of abortion law. That will also require loud and continued criticism of the U.S. Supreme Court because, as Finley Peter Dunne's Mr. Dooley famously remarked, "The Supreme Court follows the election returns." We live in a moment when we may be able to observe the truth of that comment, if we work at it.

The Basis of Society

March 2006

The most important thing that any generation has to do is to raise its own next generation. Raising it includes far more than giving birth to the children who will be the new generation. Raising them, of course, requires the contributions of hundreds and thousands of people whom the newly born babies may never see. But the generations already here have created the moral and cultural atmosphere in which the little boys and girls will grow up and begin to live their lives.

Children are given birth to by women, who far too often have to raise them without the aid of the children's fathers. That these unfortunate children sometimes grow up satisfactorily is a credit to their mothers, but it is no proof that the absence of their father is of no or minor importance to the upbringing of the children.

Marriage, contrary to what adolescents believe today, is more than an agreement between two people to live together, sharing bed and board. For one thing, it is between two people, one male and one female, who are designed by nature to be partners in procreation. They are therefore founders of a family, which Leo XIII, in *Rerum Novarum*, called a small community but a true one. It comes into being by the choice of man and wife but it then has a reality beyond their consent.

Our contemporary culture, especially in the English-speaking world, is shot through with a radical individualism. We therefore find it hard to see reality in anything but individual persons and things. We take individuals as real, all else being mental constructs that we frame in our minds. And, in the minds of multitudes of contemporary youths, the young man and woman who marry are real, but their marriage exists only in their minds and in the letter of the law that regulates marriage. It can be revoked by choice as it was begun by choice.

Hence in political thought the early modern mind framed

the contract theory of the state. According to the Englishman, Thomas Hobbes, man is by nature an enemy to man (a result of competition for this world's goods). But lest we all perish in a war of each against all, we agree to surrender our freedom to a government that can protect us from one another by maintaining an order that can give us a satisfactory degree of peace and enjoyment. A more popular version of the contract theory was taught by another Englishman, John Locke, who had a considerable influence on America's Founding Fathers. In France, Jean-Jacques Rousseau taught that the man who first staked out a plot of ground and said, "This is mine," and found others silly enough to believe him, was the true founder of civil society. In all such political theories, if citizens are guided by enlightened self-interest, they will establish the order that best serves both peace and liberty.

The question that is increasingly before us today is whether social goals can be served by enlightened self-interest alone. It is not enough to say that all human beings have rights. But is the protection of individual rights enough? Or is human nature so framed that it cannot develop itself and achieve its goals except in and through a community in which we share a common life? And is a common life only the peaceful pursuit of individual desires? Or, on the contrary, are the goals of society goods that are commonly recognized and socially pursued?

Someone once told me of a couple he knew who took their ten-year-old daughter to a movie. It turned out to be the story of a man who divorced his wife and married a younger woman. On the way home in their car, the parents denounced the movie, but their daughter said: "They just wanted to be happy." We cannot blame a young girl for believing that happiness is the supreme goal of life, and marriage is the high road to it. But that in fact leads to a society in which people switch marriages in order to gain a happiness that is nowhere guaranteed. Society is not a collection of individuals contracting with each other to provide the necessary conditions for pursuing individual goals. It is a community of communities that contribute in various ways to the overall common good, in which the proper raising of children stands high.

The *New Yorker* once published a satiric comment on this

radical individualism. It was a cartoon that depicted two boys walking on a street that resembled New York's Park Avenue. One of them was saying, "My mom got a new boyfriend, and my dad got a new girlfriend. All I got was a new therapist." So much for just wanting to be happy. Marriage, properly understood, founds a community, a small one, but a real one that does not leave man and wife as independent as they were before. To exist and function, it must have a structure of authority. Hence, as St. Paul, in the Letter to the Ephesians, advises married couples: "Husbands and wives, give way to one another. Wives, obey your husbands [which, being translated, means, Know when to keep quiet]; Husbands, love your wives [which means, Remember, she is not your property, or your servant, but your partner]."

The goals of social life, then, are social goods that can be won only by participating with other persons in common efforts of thought, words, and action. "It is not good for man to be alone," says the Bible, and Aristotle defines man as a political being, i.e., one designed by nature to live in a polis, the most perfect form of society recognized by Greek philosophy. Or, as Aquinas put it, man is a social and political being, who cannot fulfill his nature and himself except in community with others pursuing common goals recognized as truly good.

The foundation of this social pyramid is the family, consisting of father, mother, and children. If it is deficient and weak, so will the society built upon it be. It might help if our young people stopped just wanting to be happy, and began to think of marriage as a vocation to raise a family, in which father and mother have distinct and complementary functions. It might also help if parents, priests, and lawyers stopped solving people's problems for them by making divorces and annulments the common and accepted way out of problems of married life. Ultimately, the husbands and wives (or some of them, for there are sometimes innocent parties) are the problems, which can be resolved only by a moral conversion. In the long run, I believe, that requires a sincere religious conversion.

Laughing at the Court

August 2006

I am not a lawyer, nor do I pretend to write as a lawyer. But I have a laugh from time to time as I read opinions of the U.S. Supreme Court. Here are a few of them.

The case of *Zablocki v. Redhail* was decided by the court in 1978. Redhail was a high school student who had begotten a child with a young woman, but did not want to marry her. He was ordered by a court to pay her for the support of the child, but being unemployed and indigent, he did not do so.

Redhail then made another young woman pregnant, and they wanted to marry. Redhail applied to Zablocki, a county clerk, for a marriage license, but was refused because Wisconsin law forbade granting a marriage license to a person who was under court order to pay child support and was failing to pay it. The case was finally brought up to the U.S. Supreme Court. Justice Thurgood Marshall wrote the opinion of the court, which declared the Wisconsin law unconstitutional because it deprived Redhail of a right that was implicit in the Due Process Clause of the Fourteenth Amendment which says: "nor shall any State deprive any person of life, liberty, or property without due process of law."

But where in that clause did the court find a freedom to marry that was independent of state regulation? Justice Marshall offered several grounds for finding the Wisconsin law unconstitutional. One of them was: "The woman whom appellee [Redhail] desired to marry had a fundamental right to seek an abortion, see Roe *v.* Wade. . . . Surely a decision to marry and raise the child in a traditional family setting must receive equivalent protection."

Underlying this argument are the assumptions that abortion and marriage stand on equal constitutional grounds, and that young Redhail was capable of furnishing the child with "a traditional family setting." At this point one is surely permitted a laugh, or at least an amused smile.

Since the court handed down its decision in *Roe v. Wade* (1973), in which it affirmed a constitutional right to abort, the liberal press and media have assumed that this decision reflects American public opinion. But in fact a sizable number of states and local governments passed laws and ordinances designed to limit its effects. The court routinely struck them down.

In *Planned Parenthood v. Casey* (1992) three justices (Souter, Kennedy, and O'Connor) voted with the majority, but submitted an additional opinion of their own that suggested that one of the functions of the Supreme Court is to save the American people from themselves by taking certain issues out of politics, mainly issues that were so dangerously divisive that they threatened to tear the nation apart, and should therefore be left to the Supreme Court to resolve. Whatever one may think of that proposition, one cannot but laugh at the idea that it would take the abortion issue out of politics, any more than that the Supreme Court's *Dred Scott* decision prevented the Civil War.

The process that began shifting moral issues from legislatures to courts did not begin, however, with *Roe v. Wade* but with an earlier case involving a Connecticut law forbidding the sale and use of contraceptives. The removal of this issue from legislatures to courts began in 1965 with an opinion of the Supreme Court, written by Justice William O. Douglas, in the case of *Griswold v. Connecticut*.

Planned Parenthood had a clinic in New Haven that gave "information, instruction, and medical advice" on the use of contraceptives, in violation of a state law, for which Griswold, the clinic's executive director, was indicted and found guilty. Planned Parenthood had some trouble in finding a prosecutor willing to prosecute, since by this time contraception was a widespread practice and politicians were not looking for trouble. But one was eventually found, and the case made its way to the U.S. Supreme Court.

Justice Douglas wrote the opinion of the court. He began by admitting (as the court had often done), "We do not sit as a super-legislature to determine the wisdom, need, and propriety of laws that touch economic problems, business affairs, or social conditions." But the law now before them was essentially different because it "operates directly on an intimate relation of husband and wife and their physician's role in one aspect of that relation."

There remained, however, a problem, which Douglas admitted: "The association of people is not mentioned in the Constitution nor in the Bill of Rights [the first eight amendments added to the Constitution]." He handled this problem by citing a number of cases in which the court had found violations of the Constitution even though they violated no text found in the Constitution, and concluded with these now famous words: "The foregoing cases suggest that specific guarantees in the Bill of Rights have penumbras, formed by emanations from those guarantees that help give them life and substance. . . . Various guarantees create zones of privacy [that are constitutionally immune from state intrusion]."

The court, of course, would be the organ of government that decides cases that it can find in these zones. It has done so, for instance, in finding laws banning abortion and homosexual acts unconstitutional as violations of "privacy" that are not mentioned in the Constitution's text. The court has found laws banning assisted suicide to be constitutional, but some justices, in their concurring opinions, suggested that they might find laws permitting assisted suicide constitutional if they were worded differently. The court has yet to decide whether same-sex marriage is a constitutional right, or whether a state may deny an adoption agency the power to refuse to let homosexual couples adopt children in their care. But such cases are, or may be, in the offing.

To return to the *Griswold* case, Justice Hugo L. Black dissented vigorously, not because he agreed with the Connecticut law, but because he rejected the court's argument for finding it unconstitutional. "The Court," he said, "talks about a constitutional 'right of privacy' as though there is some constitutional provision or provisions forbidding any law ever to be passed which might abridge the 'privacy' of individuals. But there is not." "Privacy," he added in another line, "is a broad, abstract and ambiguous concept" not fit for "some constitutional provision." Its use in a judicial decision is in effect "to claim for this Court and the federal judiciary power to invalidate any legislative act the judges find irrational, unreasonable or offensive." As for recurring to the Ninth Amendment for the same purpose, as some of the justices had done, he added, it "would make of this Court's members a day-to-day constitutional convention."

There is nothing laughable in that (unless one is a liberal activist who wants the court to impose his agenda on us). To make that point, let us quote some words from Justice Kennedy's opinion in *John Geddes Lawrence v. Texas* (2003). The case concerned the validity of a Texas law that criminalized sexual intercourse between persons of the same sex. The court found the law unconstitutional as violating the Due Process Clause of the Fourteenth Amendment.

In his opinion Justice Kennedy laid it down that the effective norm of due process in cases like this was prevailing public opinion: "we think that our laws and traditions in the past half century [i.e., the era of the sexual revolution] are of most relevance here." Then, quoting his own concurring opinion in an earlier case, he says: "[H]istory and tradition are the starting point but not in all cases the ending point of the substantive process inquiry." Kennedy concluded the opinion of the Court with this statement:

> Had those who ratified the Due Process Clauses . . . known the components of liberty in its manifold possibilities, they might have been more specific. They did not presume to have this insight. They knew times can blind us to certain truths and later generations can see that laws once thought necessary and proper can in fact serve only to oppress. . . . As the Constitution endures, persons in every generation can invoke its principles in their own search for greater freedom.

A reader of those propositions may gasp in admiration of the sheer cool nerve of their author and his fellow justices who agreed with him. But a better response would be a loud guffaw.

What's Your Worldview?

October 2006

Wh[^]hat's your worldview?

There is a multitude of people who, if you asked them that question, would reply with a blank look and an exclamation of "Huh?" Yet everyone *has* a worldview — some understanding, however vague, of the nature of reality. Whether or not they consciously think of it, it underlies the decisions they make, because it furnishes the range of choices they see the world offering them, and the chance they have of obtaining what they have chosen. Their worldview sets both the goals and the limits of their concept of success.

In many people's worldview, the universe is merely a vast multitude of material things and the relations among them; everything that happens in this system must find its explanation *within* the system, simply because there is nothing at all outside it. There is no need, in this worldview, to call upon God and his revelation in order to explain the mysteries of the universe. Science will progressively do that for us. This view of the world and of our understanding is called Scientism. Not all scientists hold it, but those who do, regard it as taking the place in the Western mind that formerly was held by revealed religion.

Pope Benedict XVI addressed the question of the relation between religious faith and reason in a talk he gave to an audience of scientists in the University of Regensburg, in Germany, where he himself had been a professor. It is important to note that Benedict was not speaking to the universal Church on a question of doctrine, but as an academic speaking to an academic audience on an important issue. That kind of address usually remains unnoticed outside academic circles, but when delivered by a pope, it falls into the hands of journalists and maniacs.

If a worldview is basic, then belief in God as Creator and Sustainer of the universe is a worldview that makes a vast difference in our lives, both individual and social. It cannot be dismissed from discussion on the grounds that scientific reasoning has been arbitrarily declared the only acceptable method. First, then, Benedict wants to deal with a certain conflict between worldviews on the question of God and religion.

The two worldviews he contrasted—in the part of his lecture that was to have global repercussions—were those of Christians and Muslims. In Christianity, he said, compelling people by force to adopt a religious faith is seen as "contrary to God's nature." (According to *The Catechism of the Catholic Church* [no. 160], "The act of faith is of its very nature a free act.") But in the Muslim worldview, "God is absolutely transcendent. His will is not bound up with any of our categories, even that of rationality." A French Islamist has pointed out that a medieval Muslim philosopher "went so far as to state that God is not bound even by his own word. . . . Were it God's will, we would even be bound to practice idolatry." Now, there is (so far as I know), no central authority in Islam that can determine what is binding "Muslim teaching." But what the media have reported in the present decade on the Muslim penchant to resort to violence as a way of settling disputed questions seems to throw some light on what the pope said in Regensburg about the Muslim belief in God as a Supreme Will not bound by reason.

From this contrast, the pope moved on to make a broader point about what he called "the profound harmony between what is Greek in the best sense of the word [that is to say, philosophical reason] and the biblical understanding of faith in God." St. John the Evangelist began his gospel with the words, "In the beginning was the Logos." "Logos," Benedict explained, "means both reason and word, a reason which is creative and capable of self-communication, precisely as reason. John thus spoke the final word in the biblical concept of God. . . . The encounter between the biblical message and Greek thought did not happen by chance."

But the pope went on to point out that this thesis—that critically purified Greek thought formed an integral part of

Christian faith—has been under attack for centuries, within Christianity itself. There has been a longstanding attempt to "de-Hellenize" the faith, to purge it of its Greek heritage. This effort, said the Pope, "has more and more dominated theological discussion since the beginning of the modern age."

The first stage of this process was the Reformation in the sixteenth century, with its principle of *sola scriptura*, i.e., Scripture alone is the rule of faith. This liberated faith from Greek philosophy in the hope that faith could, thereby, become more fully itself. The second stage was a new focus on the humanity of Jesus, a theological move that "was said to have put an end to worship in favor of morality [and] a humanitarian moral message." This second stage was evident in the liberal theology of the nineteenth and twentieth centuries, and was, the pope noted, "highly influential in Catholic theology too."

Benedict continued: "The modern self-limitation of reason [has been] further radicalized by the impact of the natural sciences. This modern concept of reason is based . . . on a synthesis between Platonism (Cartesianism) and empiricism, a synthesis confirmed by the success of technology." The "Platonic" element is the mathematical structure of matter, which makes it possible for us to understand and use it. We can exploit nature and, through experimentation, make it serve our purposes.

Two principles follow from the above: First, "only the kind of certainty resulting from the interplay of mathematical and empirical elements can be considered scientific. Anything that would claim to be scientific must be measured against this criterion . . . [and second,] by its very nature this method excludes the question of God as being unscientific."

It is precisely this truncated idea of reason—a very harmful consequence of the worldview of scientism—that the pope was calling into question. He stated emphatically that he is not trying to deny or reverse the achievements of modernity. I agree: If, at my advanced age (please don't ask what it is), I am *compos mentis* and in reasonably good health, it is due to the advances in medicine during my lifetime. But if scientific reasoning is the only acceptable kind of reasoning, how many of the convictions on which we base our lives and our culture have we achieved by flawless logic? No society can sustain its culture on that basis. But, as Pope Benedict said in his conclusion, the room is open for discussion of our differences, great though they are. That is not a declaration of war on Islam, on science, or on anything else; it is merely an act of gratitude for the gift of reason with which our Creator endowed us, and a declaration of our continued willingness to use this gift for its proper purpose.

Rot in the Soul

February 2007

Some decades ago, I spent a few summer weeks in a Jesuit community outside Paris. One Sunday, a Jesuit lay brother invited me to go with him to a ceremony in the basilica on Montmartre. After the ceremony we all processed out to the brow of the hill, where the archbishop of Paris blessed the city. Then we walked back.

On the way we passed a group of elderly gentlemen who waved their left fists in the air and sang a song that I presumed was not a hymn, because they had set up a banner that identified them as the French League of Free Thought with their motto: "*Ni Dieu ni Maître.*" That slogan, "No God, no Master," expresses the spirit of the Third Republic of France, and of secularist liberalism in other countries as well.

A former member of President Clinton's cabinet once proclaimed that the cultural and political clash in this country is between "those who believe in science, reason, and logic, and those who believe that truth is revealed through Scripture and religion." (Makes you wonder what part of this country he was born and raised in, and why you have to be an atheist if you want to be a scientist.)

One result of this trend has been remarked upon for some time now by a number of observers. Roberto Mangabeira Unger, for example, has said, "Disintegration is the defining experience of modernism." Similarly, Carroll Kearley: "Modernity sees happiness as the fulfillment of an endless succession of indiscriminate desires." As E. Z. Sheppard has commented, "We live in an America where the seven deadly sins are taken about as seriously as the Seven Dwarfs."

These remarks were hardly new. More than two thousand years ago, Aristotle had said: "It is the nature of desire to be infinite, and the mass of men live for the satisfaction of desire." Aristotle certainly did not believe in the equality of desires, nor have all varieties of liberals believed in it. But as modernity has progressed in the past several centuries, it has become an ever-broadening defense of individual freedom to satisfy desires.

In the late fourteenth century a Franciscan logician, William of Ockham, propagated the idea that only individual things and persons exist and are real. Therefore relations among them are not real but are mental constructs that we create and impose on them on the basis of resemblances. So also are general ideas like the natures of oaks, horses, and men. As the last line in Umberto Eco's novel *The Name of the Rose* puts it, "*Stat rosa pristina nomine; nomina nuda tenemus.*" ("The nature of a rose consists in its name; we have nothing but names.") This philosophy is called nominalism, from the Latin *nomen*, i.e., name.

If we have nothing but names, then marriage, the family, the tribe or clan, the nation, the state, and federal unions of states are purely human creations based on human decisions, not on human nature and its natural needs. It follows that human institutions are based on our desires, not on our nature as social beings. Since permitting the satisfaction of all desires leads to anarchy, we agree to limit desires but only to the extent necessary to prevent the "war of each against all" that is the basis of Thomas Hobbes' political philosophy. Except for that necessary limitation, individual liberty trumps alleged social needs.

That this attitude is widespread today is shown by a common response to the demand for legalizing gay marriage: "It won't affect *my* marriage," as though marriage were only an individual choice without social importance. That attitude merits repeating a comment made by the famous German writer Goethe: "Everything that liberates the spirit without corresponding growth in self-mastery is pernicious."

An opposite view was expressed by the equally famous Scottish philosopher David Hume: "Reason is, and ought only to be, the slave of the passions that we have." Which is to say that we have to use our intelligence to find means to satisfy our felt desires. The triumphs of reason in today's Western world are in technology, not in recognition of what is truly food for human beings.

In a brilliant essay in the book, *Liberalism and the Good*,

Kenneth L. Schmitz traces the effects of nominalism on scientific, social, and political thought. In my own clumsy and possibly inaccurate summary, the result of nominalism and its modern successors has been a radical individualization of the human mind and will. According to Schmitz, "What holds for all the variant positions [in the development of the liberal tradition] is that the individual human will is the impetus moving us prior to all else and the ground of all value." This is the rot in today's liberal soul. Nothing has value or is good in itself, but only for those who have a desire for it.

The problem for politics then is to keep conflicting individual desires within limits that allow us to live together in a sufficient degree of peace. But can politics alone solve this problem? President George Washington thought not when he said in his Farewell Address, "Of all the dispositions and habits which lead to political prosperity, religion and morality are indispensable supports."

The Hearts of the Faithful

June 2007

The face of the earth has changed over the centuries and is changing more radically in the twentieth and twenty-first centuries. The world is getting smaller as rapid travel over long distances has become common. Our economies are becoming, through globalization, a world economy. Racial differences predictably will gradually disappear as persons of different races marry one another and blend into a single human race. At the same time we have become more and more skilled at killing one another in large numbers, and more prone to resolve political and cultural differences by resorting to large-scale violence. Compared to us, earlier ages were pikers.

That raises the question whether we can expect the human race to renounce the use of force and violence when the stakes are, or are thought to be, high enough. Religion has not succeeded, but atheists and agnostics cannot rejoice in that. In the Middle Ages, the Church did try to mitigate the use of force. For instance, in the year 1215, the Fourth Lateran Council condemned the crossbow as a weapon too inhumane to use, but much good that did in restraining warriors engaged in contests where life and death were at stake. Today we have atomic bombs, not to mention a host of other weapons more deadly than earlier ages even imagined.

Reflecting on that is enough to make one believe in original sin. The modern mind, of course, will not hear of that. However, it might agree that there is something seriously wrong with us. But can it come to see that reason alone cannot cure our malady? The cultural elite among us claim that enlightened self-interest could, and will if we let it, convince us that willingness to reason and to compromise with our adversaries will lead us to a lasting peace.

But what do we know about human beings that would

lead us to believe that? I remember that, toward the end of World War II, when it was clear that we and our allies had won it, I attended a talk by a U.S. senator. He told us that when a school has had a championship team in some sport, it will lose some of its best players when they graduate. We, the winners of the war, he said, must keep our winning team together after the war. When I heard that, I thought, "Keep the U.S., Britain, France, and the Soviet Union together? What planet is the man living on?"

I am not opposed to the United Nations; it is at least an effort, but it will not succeed if it has to rely upon enlightened self-interest. As the late Cardinal John Wright once wrote, "The wrath of the stupid has laid waste the earth quite as often as the craft of the bright." (Even the craft of the bright has not been all that successful.) We cannot rely on reason alone to tame our selfish passions. (As Henry Kissinger has remarked, power is the ultimate aphrodisiac.) Our problem is basically a moral one rather than an intellectual one. A sane philosophy will help us to deal with our passions, but it will not be enough. We cannot think ourselves out of the radical individualism and utilitarianism that afflict us in the liberal democracies. We need a deep change of heart. Nor will any merely political system do it for us.

Even God won't do it for us. But we cannot do it without his help. Or, to put it in other and perhaps more widely acceptable terms, our problem will not have any solution without the help of a higher power that will change our hearts even more than our minds. Here, I suggest, we need to believe in a transcendent norm of morality—not of our creation but which depends upon a power greater than ourselves—that will aid us if we ask for help and guidance, not for the solution to all our problems. Yes, ACLU, I am talking about God, not suggesting an established religion, but rather for the conversion of many hearts in our people.

I am not looking forward to a mass conversion of humanity. There seems to be a psychological law of gravity that pulls us down into the satisfaction of our desires, which we may extend to those whom we love, but only so far. Jesus told us to love even our enemies. St. Thomas Aquinas explained that love is willing what is good for someone, which includes ourselves (there is a legitimate and praiseworthy love of ourselves) and love of those whom we may have to defeat but without hating them and seeking to destroy them.

How do we go about this conversion of our fellow men? It will never be fully accomplished in this world: the Garden of Eden is gone and Heaven is not yet. But we can begin with an old hymn: "Come, Holy Spirit, fill the hearts of your faithful and enkindle in them the fire of your divine love. Send forth your spirit, O Lord, and they shall be created and you will renew the face of the earth." This is not asking God to solve our problem for us, but to change human hearts by enkindling them with his love, and so to change the face of the earth.

Women's Hearts

August 2007

Women have a gift for getting the hearts of men and children wrapped around them. It is the gift of loving and caring without thinking of themselves. I recently had a phone conversation with a woman friend who told me that one of her sisters had had a cancerous breast removed. But, she said, her sister's major concern was that if the cancer spread she would not be able to take care of her sick husband. I suspect one has to have a woman's heart to care like that.

Women are the caring sex, and they don't have to be forced to care. In fact, you can't stop them; it is a trait that goes with being women. Everywhere and always? No, silly. Women can be selfish, or very limited in their affections. Some of them love their own families but few other people besides. But there is no denying that, when seeing suffering or the need of others for help, they find it harder than men do to pass them by.

By giving care and love as freely as they do, women reveal a precious gift to the human race. I say gift rather than a talent. By talents I mean abilities that women, like men, can use to their own advantage and advancement as well as for others.

When a little girl lying in her cradle finally gets her eyes in focus and sees that when she smiles daddy smiles back, she has discovered a talent that she can (and will) use throughout her life. Some girls never get beyond that, but most women also develop a feminine desire to help and console.

When I was a little boy, I knew that women would always help me if I asked them (to tie my shoe laces, for example). Men might help me, or they might wave me away, or even yell at me to go away and stop bothering them.

There are people who seem to be incapable of understanding that generalizations (statements that are generally true but admit of exceptions) can be valid. If one says, as I am saying, that women are generally more caring than men, these people hasten to tell you that their fathers really loved them. I don't doubt that, but I am glad that my mother was a woman.

I am not implying that all women should renounce careers in order to stay at home and raise children. The Catholic Church has always praised virginity and celibacy, without condemning marriage, and has canonized women who never married or did not remarry when their husbands died. But I disagree deeply with the late Betty Friedan, who denounced regarding women as "baby-making machines." After all, no babies, no human race, and no expanding economy.

We need wives and mothers more than we need female CEOs, not because career women are a threat to society but because without the wives and mothers society dies, not only physically but culturally. The saying "The mission of women is to civilize men" should be listened to.

If I recall correctly, after the census of 2000, the Federal Bureau of the Census reported that if the then-prevailing birth rate remained as low as it was, we could expect that by the census of 2080 the population of the United States will have begun to decline, and the decline will not be offset by immigration.

There is no use in pretending that 2080 is so far away that we need not be concerned now about population decline then. Many children born now will still be alive 72 years from now. They, and their children and grandchildren, will be the products of two-child families, which will be the reason for the shrinkage of the overall population. Some governments in Europe, Sweden, and France for instance, are already offering subsidies to women for having more children — to little avail.

The situation I am speaking about is a complicated one, and I am not pretending to resolve all its problems. But I think we should recognize that the ideology that calls itself feminism should properly be called masculinism. The slogan, "Anything boys can do, girls can do" might win the approval of the U.S. Supreme Court, but even that august body is not likely to agree that anything girls can do, boys can do. Only girls can do it, because only they have mankind's most precious gift: womanhood.

Believing Anything

December 2007

The universe, we are asked to believe, came from nowhere and from no previously existing materials, and was propelled into being by no existing forces. The Big Bang theory, of course, postulates previously existing material and an explosive force that makes it expand, but it no more explains them than the preceding sentence does.

The universe, we are assured, has reached its present form by a process of random variation, controlled by no directing force. We ourselves are but whims of chance.

One is reminded of a story told about the Duke of Wellington, who was invited to a royal reception after his great victory at Waterloo. He attended it clad in his uniform, with all his medals on his chest. A man approached him and said, "Mr. Smith, I believe?" "Sir," replied the duke, "if you believe that, you can believe anything."

I can't vouch for the truth of that story, but it illuminates my attitude toward the atheistic theory that the universe is self-existing and self-explaining. That is an explanation, however, that does not explain but is believed, not because of its inherent truth but because it gets rid of belief in a Creator God.

But can random variation explain all the changes that are required to produce the present world of living beings? As Aristotle said, what happens by chance happens rarely and cannot be foreseen.

Those who believe that random variation is sufficient do not, of course, think that its results ever have been or are foreseeable but only that, given enough time (with lots of zeroes thrown in) random changes have been enough to explain the living world that we now know. We ourselves, like all the other higher animals, are the random results of random variations.

I am not questioning the evolution of species, but asking why it is considered necessary to reduce it to random variations that lead, always by chance, to new species of beings endowed with higher and higher abilities.

For many believers in what we may call scientism, the reason for their belief is that it leaves our understanding of the universe and, in particular, of our world within it, to science rather than to philosophy or divine revelation.

For such thinkers, evolution refutes religion because it does not need God. It has happened without any prior cause, is happening, and presumably will continue to happen into an indefinite future. But don't ask why, because the why question is not answerable by a scientific method that recognizes no mind behind the evolutionary development of life.

Evolution so understood will be slow and unintended by any mind, but will produce life and by a long series of accidents move it to higher levels.

The higher forms, however, will not be intended by lower forms that do not have the ability to produce them. The higher forms may emerge by random variations or, more likely in the human race, through deliberate elimination of its "inferior" elements.

Hitler's Nazism comes immediately to mind, as an effort to purify a national bloodstream by a dictator and a party unhampered by a religious conscience. But do we know that none of the million abortions performed in this country every year are inspired by doctors telling pregnant women that the infants in their wombs are afflicted by physical or mental defects?

Or, particularly in atheistic social circles, in which the highest intelligence belongs to our minds, is evolution too dangerous a project to be left in human hands?

The Idea of the Good

January, 2008

I have now lived through more than forty years of adolescent rebellion, from 1960 on. A writer in the Jewish monthly *Commentary* has described it as a "culture-wide revolt against authority." And so it was and is, but I am principally concerned about it as it has affected the Catholic Church, its clergy, religious orders of men and women, and those parts of the laity called "pick and choose Catholics."

They commonly call themselves liberals and share certain attitudes. One is that the Church is out of date and needs to catch up with the contemporary culture, because it is the culture in which the members of the Church have to live.

One might think that before jumping into that culture, it would be wise to take a hard look at it and its consequences. But remember, we are speaking of adolescents (who can be of any age, so long as the culture satisfies their felt needs, never mind its other consequences).

For example, the invention of the atomic bomb put an end to the Second World War and made the world safe for democracy. Today we live in fear of certain Islamic countries getting the bomb.

The invention of effective contraceptives has solved the problem of birth control, but it has also created "safe sex" and is the root of the "sexual revolution" which, according to an article I once read in the *New York Times*, now starts in middle school.

It has also raised this question: If it is possible to sterilize the sexual act while performing it, why is it necessary to use complementary organs of procreation? I remember hearing a university professor tell an audience, "I achieve my personal identity through oral and anal sex." Then, if that is true, why may not persons of the same sex marry each other?

Another result of the sexual revolution is the oft-recited assertion that half of the marriages in this country break up, which implies that Great Britain is surpassing America as the Land of the Free. But does that really help Britain?

Deeper than the sexual revolution is the intellectual one, which tells us that moral judgments are merely subjective and beyond proof as right or wrong. To gain knowledge of the real world we must turn to science. Yet as Thomas Spragens of Duke University has remarked, "A credulous interpretation of scientific reasoning is the principal superstition of modernity." Scientific reason has been remarkably successful in understanding the material universe, but moral judgment is beyond its grasp; hence science can furnish us with no grounds for making or deneying moral judgments. To put it in other words, science can tell us what can be done, but not whether or not it morally ought to be done. Science is not a philosophy or a theology.

Roger Kimball, in an article in the October 8, 2007, issue of *National Review*, discussed the difficulty of rescuing the universities from what he calls their domination by a "left-wing monoculture" in their faculties and administrators, and a consequent "reign of political correctness." He admits that overcoming this mindset will be difficult and slow, but adds that success will depend on "possessing an alternative vision of the good."

That is in fact the essential point. Moral judgments are judgments about good and evil. That they are taught by churches and other religious bodies is not a reason for ejecting them from public discourse and policy-making. Or are "Thou shalt not kill, thou shalt not steal, and thou shalt not bear false witness against thy neighbor" to be left outside the voting booth? Is it really necessary for a citizen to check the conscience at the door when he enters the public forum?

Kimball adds: "Some observers believe that the universe cannot really be reformed until the current generation—the Sixties generation— retires from faculties." But that, he admits, will take two decades and, in any event, "deep and lasting change in the culture at large." I agree with him that such a change is essential, and that success "depends upon possessing an alternative vision of the good."

That is essential, not only in our universities but in our whole society and its success-oriented culture, with its quest for pleasure and flight from pain.

The process of curing our cultural ills cannot be left to the intellectual elites who defend it in the name of liberty. Let us therefore never let them talk down to us, but challenge them on questions of human good. And if they quote the First Amendment on the establishment of religion, make them take out their pocket copies of the Constitution and read the text of the First Amendment. It says less than they think it does. As for us, our part is to speak up and keep on speaking until the modern mind opens its eyes to what it has done.

Something New and Different

March 2008

There has recently been a wave of articles and books written by people who claim that there is no God. Their theory is that the beginning of life and the subsequent evolution of living species can be attributed to random variations in matter and "the survival of the fittest." That is said to do away with the need of God the Creator. But it leaves us with gods: our own brilliant minds. They can tell us all that we need to know about the material universe, which is the only universe there is. Implicit in this theory is a further one: There is no God, but there are gods, namely those of us who can change human beings into new, disease-free, and possibly superior species. Those who accomplish these results will be the true gods of mankind.

This kind of thinking is not new. We can find it in the writings of British authors such as Aldous Huxley and C. S. Lewis (who were horrified by it and warned against it). But recently I have read news reports about scientists who are trying to combine human genetic material with the material of other species.

They may only be trying to create new bodies that can be used to furnish spare parts for sick or wounded human beings or information that will help to cure diseases. But they may be dreaming of improving the human species itself, by blending it with certain aspects of what are in all other respects inferior species. I don't know if anyone is contemplating that; if there is, he is playing God. That is a dream which could occur to an atheist.

For to such a mind, there is no reality outside of or above the material universe. Life, of any kind, is a product of changes in matter, as certain chemicals happen to combine in lifeless materials and become human beings. But if such beings can result from accidental and unintended changes in matter, surely minds endowed with human intelligence can understand and intend them. If that is so, it will be argued that preventing the effort is stifling science and standing in the way of progess.

But can we improve human nature by combining it with elements taken from other species? Well, why not? Darwinian evolution tells us that the emergence of human life was the result of endless and unintended changes in matter. If that is so, why can't we help it along? And why should we be hampered by clinging to an Aristotelian conception of the nature of man? Science, as I was once told, deals with facts, not with values. So, if science can produce descendants of the present human race, who are different from and possibly superior to any persons we now have, will they not be an aristocracy that will do a better job than any persons we now have?

But that question raises a deeper one: where do we find the norms by which we can judge whether the new human (or post-human) race is really an improvement? Or do we settle for the same humanity that we now have, but with better health, clearer minds, and longer lives? I recall reading this statement made by an evolutionist: "The universe is contingent; it could all have turned out differently." If that is so, that the highest level of evolved beings is the result of a series of accidents, then we cannot rely on it to produce a new and better race, and it is up to us to achieve that goal. Then where do we find the definition of that goal and the norms for arriving at it? And which persons will decide on the goals we are to strive for and the norms for achieving them?

Now, all of this may sound like science fiction — and so it is. But in an age in which the demands of scientific researchers are considered to trump moral objections because the objections will interfere with the future welfare of mankind, it is well to remember that science does not have all the answers. We have to turn to other grounds for moral judgment such as history, literature, philosophy, and — dare I say it? — religion.

The Rock of Culture

May 2008

The problem facing the Catholic Church today, at least in this country and in what we call the Western world, is not keeping Catholics in the Church. Rather, it is persuading them to believe what the Church teaches. I am thinking of an essay that I read a few years ago, written by a university professor who had converted to Catholicism. He later wrote that in this country most Catholics and Jews are really Protestants. He did not deny that Protestants are Christians; nor do I. What he had in mind was the Protestant principle of private judgment: what a Protestant believes is not what his church teaches, but what the individual member of the church accepts as his belief.

Most Protestants, I assume, accept the Bible as the revealed word of God. But the interpretation of that word belongs ultimately to the individual believer. Now, I am not about to enter into an argument about the validity of that principle, but am only stating that it is not a valid principle for members of the Catholic Church. I know, as I learned when studying theology, that the Church teaches on several levels, not all of which are binding articles of faith. But what the defined articles of faith are is for the papacy to determine. Contrary opinions — no matter how many liberal theologians teach them, or how many distinguished Catholic universities they are taught in — are not decisive.

Avery Cardinal Dulles published an article on this point in the May 2008 issue of *First Things*, under the title, "The Freedom of Theology." In it he says: "The service of theology to the magisterium [the teaching power of the Church] can, on occasion, involve criticism. Scholarly investigation may indicate that some reformable teaching of the Church needs to be modified or that the traditional concepts and terms that are used for the communication of the faith are misleading when repeated today. If so, theologians have the right and even the duty to make their views known."

But no theologian has the right, let alone the duty, to contradict the clear teaching of the Church. He may state reasons why he thinks the Church could modify it and may propose reasons why it could be done without denying the Church's authority. Cardinal Dulles goes on to say: "Just as the theologian may sometimes be entitled to raise questions and present doubts about current official teaching, so the magisterium has the right to keep dissent from impairing the unity of the Church and the integrity of the faith. The hierarchy has an inalienable responsibility to see to it that the Christian faith is transmitted without diminution or distortion."

The cardinal does not say it, but it seems clear that he does not accept John Stuart Mill's argument — in his famous essay *On Liberty* — that when all opinions may be freely expressed, the sounder and better ones emerge and are accepted. The history of the past 500 years in Christian theology should be enough to raise doubts about that. Besides, in church circles it assumes that all the participants to the debates are pure-minded searchers for the truth rather than worried persons trying to "keep people in the Church."

There are Christians, both inside and outside the Catholic Church, for whom some Catholic teachings are too difficult to live by and therefore can be dismissed as not necessary to obey. It is difficult to engage in discussion with such persons, because their objections are not primarily intellectual. Yet the questions they raise will not go away. The invention of effective contraceptive devices is leading not only to eventual population decline but to the phenomenon of Safe Sex and its deleterious effects on sexual morality and on that basic institution of society, the family. Half the marriages in this country "break up." This behavior is now taken as normative in a society in which liberalism has degenerated into a radical individualism: if people are not happy in their marriage, they have the right to divorce and try another marriage.

The growing number of two-child families has had the side-effect of a drop in vocations to the priesthood and the religious orders of women. Among other aspects of modernity is the growth of the belief that higher education for women must lead to careerism, the assumption that the purpose of their higher education is not, as was once believed, the broadening and enriching of women's minds so much as a preparation for a job and a career. But it may be that society has a greater need of wives and mothers than of female executives. The prejudices of our individualism, however, prevent us from entertaining that idea.

Our culture, like every culture in history, faces problems that require solutions. But technology, a rigid egalitarianism, and loss of respect for moral authority are an impediment to solving them. Ultimately, we will need to re-establish our lives on the foundations of a morality we can trust. The moral authority of the Catholic Church has served in this capacity in the past, and can do so again.

"You are Peter and on this Rock I will build my Church."

The Spiritual Solution

July 2008

Hi, I'm Joe Average. Let me tell you my problems. My wife and I need contraception. My daughter needs an abortion. My son needs a divorce. My other son is homosexual and needs a same-sex lover. My mother is dying in pain and needs to be put out of her misery. Those are my problems; now don't tell me I can't solve them.

A French writer once remarked that an American believes that if there is a problem there must be a solution. There is something in that. We are optimistic problem-solvers, quick to resent any criticism that interferes with science and blocks the improvement of the human condition.

Changes, however, may indeed solve some problems while creating new ones. Contraception gives us birth control and has created the sexual revolution.

I am also thinking of Thomas Paine's book *The Rights of Man* (published between the American and French revolutions), in which Paine prophesied that replacing monarchies with republican governments would prevent wars and lower taxes. Is that not something to wonder at? Were the bloodbaths of the twentieth century due to the absence of democracy? Was not Adolf Hitler elected in the German Weimar Republic? Or are there flaws in human nature that mere forms of government cannot cure?

Can advances in medical and psychological science cure those flaws? I don't ask those questions in order to deprecate science; I am too much in debt to both of the sciences that I have just mentioned to want to do that.

But, to quote once again what Professor Thomas Spragens of Duke University says in *The Irony of Liberal Reason*, "A credulous interpretation of scientific reason is the principal superstition of modernity."

I have recently come across a review of a book entitled

Original Sin. The review states that the belief that our nature is flawed and cannot be cured by science or philosophy alone is creeping into some modern minds. If this is so, it suggests that the root cause of the disorder in human lives is the disorder in twisted and excessive desires that do not coincide with our natural human good.

The standard listing of these twisted desires is pride, greed, lust, anger, envy, gluttony, and sloth. A more recent list is simply money, sex, and power. Henry Kissinger has called power the ultimate aphrodisiac, and the history of the twentieth century bears him out. (To illustrate that point, I remember reading a report on a meeting Winston Churchill, Harry Truman, and Joseph Stalin had after the Second World War. Truman suggested asking the pope to mediate among them when their policies clashed. Stalin replied by asking "How many divisions does the pope have?")

The satisfaction of these desires, especially when they become drives, leads to the exploitive treatment of the minds, bodies, and emotions of ourselves and other persons. The ways of doing this are almost numberless and are described in a vast variety of publications and other means of communication.

What to do about this? There is no simple answer. But we may doubt that "enlightened self-interest" is an adequate answer. I suggest that any answer must be spiritual, not merely material, political, or philosophical. It must be spiritual and aim at persuading us to change our sinful desires and surrender to God. And that will be no easy task.

Nor will it be a task that fully and finally achieves its goal. For one thing, it must be redone with each new generation. Moreover, it will always require dedicated persons who will carry on the task: parents, relatives, teachers, clergy, and spiritual institutions.

And it must rely on the continuing help of God, which in Christian theology is called grace, meaning that God freely gives it, not that we deserve it because we have earned it (a theme that also runs throughout the whole Bible).

This proposition meets with scorn and ridicule in enlightened circles. But I remember something that a Jesuit who had earned a Ph.D. in political science at Harvard told me several decades ago. One of his professors there said to him one day, "Father, relax; you guys can't lose." It is time we took those words seriously and stopped trying to keep Catholics in the Church by helping them to "solve their problems." The basic problem of our modern culture is spiritual and cannot be remedied by secular solutions.

Getting It All Here

August 2008

If there is no God who created and rules the world, two consequences follow. One is that there will be no divine judgment on how we have lived our lives. And, anyhow, after death we shall not exist to be judged. The end of life in this world is an absolute end. The other consequence is that, whatever we hope to get from our lives, we have to get it here, because there will be no hereafter in which to get it.

In that case, our life here becomes a struggle to get as much as we want and can of what this world offers. The struggle need not be a bloody one, but it is a competition for the goods of this world. For example, a good job, a raise in salary, a promotion, a fine house, the right spouse, an expensive car, an Ivy League university for the kids — all the signs of success. Or, at the top of the ladder, to be another Julius Caesar, a Napoleon, or a Joseph Stalin.

But what is wrong with wanting what the world offers? Well, I recall reading a news report on a young lady who won a beauty contest. A reporter asked her what she expected now. She replied, "I want it all." But did she "get it all"? I don't know, but reading the reports of the break-up of the marriages of beauty queens and rich girls in the pages of the tabloids raises doubts in my mind. (If you don't have a tabloid in your town, come to New York, and if you can't afford the trip here, try Chicago or Los Angeles.)

For the vast majority of humankind (please notice, ladies, that I do not say mankind) ambition does not rise to those heights. I myself was for two years the acting chairman of a college department, and in the rest of my academic life rose no higher in the administrative world.

In any case, getting what we get here, no matter how much it is, we can't keep it forever. No matter how successful we have been, we die, and if there is no God to punish or reward us, after death there is nothing — not even loneliness, just nothing. The world will continue to exist, but we shall not be in it. Nor will those we knew and loved in this world be in it when they die.

In the post-Christian world, many simply accept that as all there is, yet my atheist acquaintances live decent lives with some regard for other people. Many seem to accept "live and let live" as the norm of a good life, and I respect that. But is that really all there is? Or do they avoid thinking about it?

I once was asked to officiate at the marriage of a friend's daughter. Before the marriage took place, I told the young couple that they had a choice between "until death do us part" and "I will love you and honor you all the days of my life." The young man seemed to be uneasy about "until death do us part," so I asked him what upset him. He replied that it "speaks of death."

That may be the explanation of the rejection of the idea of eternal life. People may regard no life but this life as the only one worth living. And, while we all know that we have to die, it is better in this worldview not to think about it.

That is understandable in a young child. A two-year-old's world consists of Mommy and Daddy who love you and care for you, and of visits by uncles and aunts who make a fuss over you. At age two, you do not think of any life more than that. But, alas, we all grow up.

In my way of looking at this matter, going to see God, as the gospels promise us, can be symbolized in this present life by being taken by a friend to see a view from a mountain. You go up high and around a bend in the road, and before you lies a view of startling beauty, so beautiful that you could stand there forever just looking at it.

God is infinitely more enchanting than that, for he is Absolute Being, Absolute Good, and Absolute Beauty.

In one of his letters, St. Paul describes the pagans of his time as being "without faith, without hope, without God in this world." I would not bother arguing with today's pagans if they demand scientific proof of him. But if the choice is between eternal life with God and eternal nothingness, I choose God, for nothing else gives life a lasting purpose and a meaning.

Community

September 2008

The Declaration of Independence, which we celebrate each Fourth of July, is not a part of the Constitution of the United States and therefore not enforceable by the courts. It is a declaration by certain British colonies that they would no longer be subject to the British Crown but would be henceforth an independent country.

But the Declaration is a kind of national philosophy on which, for example, Abraham Lincoln relied in the famous address that he delivered at Gettysburg during our Civil War. Written by Thomas Jefferson, a future President, the Declaration has had a powerful influence on the American mind.

It is particularly noteworthy that Jefferson began by basing the Declaration on the proposition that "all men are created equal" and "endowed by their Creator with certain unalienable Rights, among which are Life, Liberty, and the Pursuit of Happiness." I have no quarrel with basic and unalienable rights. But there is another view, not contradictory but complementary to our American way of thinking about society. It is that man is not only free but is by nature a social being meant to live in a community of communities.

This thesis is developed at length in a contribution by Kenneth L. Grasso to a recent book, *Christianity and Civil Society*, edited by Jeanne Heffernan Schindler (Lexington Books), on which I will draw heavily here.

According to Grasso, the theory he advocates "is rooted in the Catholic tradition's understanding of human nature and society." In it, he says, "there exists an objective moral order, an order of human ends that binds the conscience prior to and independently of our free consent to pursue these ends. Man inherits an intelligible universe created and redeemed by a loving God whose law constitutes the highest norm of human life. This law is inscribed on the very teleological structure of human nature itself."

A society is a unity of order, Grasso continues, rather than a substantial unity. A society is a reality, incorporating a multitude of families, individual persons, and social groups. Society and life in society are basic needs of human nature, without which we cannot develop as human beings.

This given basic order of human life is what has traditionally been called natural moral law. It is not a document composed by some persons and imposed on others, but it is discovered in experience and a growing understanding of human needs (which, incidentally, is not identical with "progressive" ideas).

To speak of society is not to imply something that is composed directly and only of individuals. In the words of the French Catholic philosopher Jacques Maritain, society is "a whole composed of wholes." Among these social "wholes," the most basic is the family, which Pope Leo XIII described as "a small community but a true one."

It follows from this that a large society must be "pluralistic," composed of the communities that constitute it. But it does not follow that the highest or largest level of society creates, contains, and controls all of the lower levels in all of their aspects.

The larger or higher communities are communities of communities. Which level of authority should be conferred on the government of the highest level is a question that the constituent communities decide, as the states in the United States decided by framing and ratifying the Constitution (indeed, this is the same issue that the nations of the European Union are now concerned with).

The question does not concern only political communities, but a vast number of what we call private communities, e.g., families, neighborhoods, villages, counties, states, nations, and enterprises united in various ways under corporations or private associations.

There is, of course, no simple and universal answer to social questions. But the Catholic social tradition offers a general principle in answer to them: It is called the principle of subsidiarity.

A classic expression of it was made by Pope Pius XI in his

encyclical *Quadragesimo Anno*: "It is indeed true, as history clearly shows, that owing to the change in social conditions, much that was formerly done by small bodies can nowadays be accomplished only by large organizations. Nevertheless, it is a fundamental principle of social philosophy, fixed and unchangeable, that one should not withdraw from individuals and commit to the community what they can accomplish by their own enterprise and industry. So, too, it is an injustice and at the same time a grave evil and a disturbance of right order to transfer to the larger and higher collectivity functions which can be performed and provided for by lesser and subordinate bodies. Inasmuch as every social activity should, by its very nature, prove a help to members of the body social, it should never destroy or absorb them."

The Catholic Church, then, is not an enemy of freedom, but teaches a fuller and deeper understanding of it than the highly individualistic idea of it that is now popular in liberal circles. Human beings are by nature free; they are also by nature social and destined to live in communities, and cannot grow and develop without them. Saying this does not answer the swarm of questions that are raised by this proposition, but is a necessary beginning.

Growing Into

November 2008

Since man is a social animal, his life is based on relationships. Some of them are accidental, others are chosen but temporary, and still others have to be grown into; and these last are the ones that are most important in shaping a human life.

Two strangers may happen to sit next to each other on a transatlantic flight. They strike up a friendly and interesting conversation, and sincerely thank each other when they arrive in the U.S.A. But they never meet again, so their temporary association does not lead to a friendship and does not seriously affect either life.

The most important relationships run far more deeply and really shape lives. One of the most basic ones is marriage between a man and a woman, which today is ordinarily a free choice. But if we can rely on what the media report, half the marriages in this country break up and lead to divorce and custody fights.

On the other hand, we have the relationship between brother and sister, which, even if it turns into mutual hatred, does not change the fact that they look alike and have the same physical heritage. But being born of the same parents is not the only source of family bonds. Many of us feel a strong relationship with uncles and aunts, and cousins within the second degree of kinship (beyond which they can marry one another).

The bonds among extended family members are lesser but can be close, as when the family bond leads nieces and nephews to visit aging aunts and uncles. But this physical relationship is not the most important one in human lives. The truly important ones have to be "grown into."

The success of a marriage is not established by pledging "until death do us part," but by husband and wife growing into each other. They don't grow to look alike, but they do grow in knowing each other and in giving themselves to each other. This is a consequence of growing into a unity of minds and hearts.

We tell teenagers to grow up and they do—by becoming taller. But what we really mean is grow into maturity.

We can also grow in love of our country, especially if we have not been made to feel like foreigners. Growing into one's country means feeling, "this is my own, my native land," or at least my adopted one. I was born in New York to Irish-born U.S. citizens and I have that feeling when I hear a Noo Yawk accent.

The deepest and most important love is love of God, our Creator and Savior. We may have been taught about God and grown up believing in him. The Bible teaches us to fear God, and indeed we should or we shall think of ourselves as gods and goddesses. But it is essential to arrive at a belief in God that is a growing love for and trust in him as Absolute Truth, Absolute Beauty, and Absolute Good, to be with whom is the goal and purpose of our life in this world.

To the modern mind, this is nonsense. As that mind sees it, there is no world other than this world, and no life after the one we live here. Therefore, as I have said in an earlier column, in this view of life all that we hope for has to be gotten here before we die.

But if we determine to trust God for everlasting life with him, we must grow into him. Not that we shall become parts of God, but that by surrendering our selfish wills and growing into his will, we shall find peace of mind in this present life and eternal joy in the next one. The lives of countless men and women who have given themselves to God prove the first one, and give us concrete hope for the second.

How do we go about making God's will a central part of our lives? I do not mean to exclude people of other faiths who sincerely try, but for us Catholics, we can make daily prayers for knowledge and strength to do his will, by receiving the sacraments, and by heeding St. Paul's words: "Pray always." This can be done all day long by reciting short phrases such as "Into your hands, Lord, I commend my spirit," and "Holy Mary, Mother of God, pray for us sinners."

About the Author

Francis Canavan (October 27, 1917–February 26, 2009) graduated Lawrence High School in 1935 alongside fellow future political theorists Harry V. Jaffa and Joseph Cropsey. He then attended Fordham University, entering the Society of Jesus upon his graduation in 1939. The Society sent him to St. Louis University, where he immersed himself in the study of Thomistic philosophy, graduating with his Ph.L. in 1944. He then returned to Fordham for his M.A. in political science. It was there, under the guidance of Moorhouse F.X. Millar, S.J., that Canavan discovered the writings of Edmund Burke.

After receiving his M.A., Canavan studied theology at Woodstock College, where he met John Courtney Murray, who became an important influence on his work. Ordained to the priesthood in 1950, he earned his S.T.L. the following year. In 1957, he received his Ph.D. in political science from Duke University where he studied under John H. Hallowell, a prominent political scientist whose work explored the perennial issues of political theory from an avowedly Christian perspective. Hallowell, who became a friend and mentor, directed Canavan's dissertation, which explored Burke's understanding of the proper role of reason in politics.

Over the course of his career, Canavan taught at Regis High School (1944–1945), Canisius College (1945–1946), St. Peter's College (1950–1956), and Fordham University (1966–1988). From 1988 until his death, Canavan was professor emeritus at Fordham. He also worked as a journalist and essayist, serving as associate editor of *America* magazine from 1960 to 1966 and as a columnist for the *catholic eye* newsletter from 1983 until shortly before his death.

Canavan's works on Burke include *The Political Reason of Edmund Burke* (Duke University Press, 1960), *Edmund Burke: Prescription and Providence* (Carolina Academic Press, 1987), and *The Political Economy of Edmund Burke* (Fordham University Press, 1995). In these volumes and his other writings on Burke, Canavan sought to restore Burke to his rightful place among the pantheon of Christian natural law thinkers and to illuminate the Thomistic character of his thought. Leading Burke authority Peter J. Stanlis, in a review of *Prescription and Providence*, wrote that Canavan's work earned him "a very high permanent place of honor among Burke scholars, living or dead" (*Review of Politics* 50, Fall 1988, 746).

Canavan also wrote an award-winning volume on the political theory of freedom of speech, *Freedom of Expression: Purpose as Limit* (Carolina Academic Press, 1984), as well as many essays, both scholarly and popular, exploring the subjects of Catholicism and American culture, contemporary America's search for a public philosophy, and the impact of liberal individualism on American public life.

At the heart of Canavan's essays is a far-reaching critique of the liberal individualist intellectual tradition. Arguing that liberalism's political theory was shaped in important ways by its philosophical commitments (in particular, by its nominalist metaphysics), Canavan maintains that the liberal model of man and society is simultaneously flawed, incompatible with the Christian vision of the human person, and corrosive of the social and cultural preconditions of democratic government. The frequent protestations of its proponents to the contrary notwithstanding, liberalism, far from being "neutral" on the question of the human good, embodies — and seeks to reorganize social life in accordance with — its own impoverished vision of the good, a vision whose most striking characteristics are its secularism, individualism, and moral relativism.

Some of his most important writings on these subjects were collected in *The Pluralist Game: Pluralism, Liberalism, and the Moral Conscience* (Rowman and Littlefield, 1995) and *Pins in the Liberal Balloon*, which consists of his early *catholic eye* essays (National Committee of Catholic Laymen, 1990). Two collections of Canavan's reflections on recovery were published by the Calix Society: *The Light of Faith* (1989) and *By the Grace of God* (2002).

Kenneth L. Grasso

Dr. Grasso, who studied under Fr. Canavan at Fordham University, is Professor and Chair of the Department of Political Science at Texas State University.

Index

Abortion, 1-4, 6, 28-30, 40-42, 49-
50, 53, 64-66, 69, 84, 91, 109-
111, 121-123, 130, 154-156,
166-168, 175-177, 193-195,
200, 205-207, 217-219, 238-
239, 274-276, 286-288, 304-
306, 314-315, 331-333, 337-340
    easy cases, 193-195
    infanticide, 2-3, 40-41
    personally opposed, 1-4
    personhood, 286-288
Absolute Beauty, 299, 367, 372
Absolute Good, 299, 367, 372
Academic freedom, 59, 88-90, 229
Ackerman, Bruce A., 77
After Virtue, 91, 129
Alan Guttmacher Institute, 194,
269
Anchor, Robert
    Enlightenment Tradition, The,
    120
Ancient Order of Hibernians
    (AOH), 226
Anderson, Jeffrey, 303
Aquinas, Thomas, 331, 349
Arendt, Hannah
    Human Condition, The, 71-72
Aristotle, 55, 66, 288, 336, 345,
353
Arnold, Matthew, 253, 307
Aron, Raymond, 114
St. Augustine, 254-255, 299

Bacon, Francis, 131
Beck, Joan, 92
Becker, Carl, 20, 322
Beckett, Samuel, 151
Belloc, Hilaire, 220
Benedict XVI, 341-344. *See also*
    Ratzinger, (Cardinal) Joseph
Bennett, Neil G., 210
Berman, Harold J.
    *Law and Revolution: The
    Formation of the Western Legal*
    Tradition, 223-225
Bettelheim, Bruno, 247-250
Bible, 82-83, 128-129, 158, 199,
    220-222, 247, 317, 336, 360,
    372
Bickel, Alexander, 44
Biden, (Senator) Joseph, 247
Bill of Rights, 339
Black, (Justice) Hugo, 339
Blackmun, (Justice) Harry, 115,
    212, 264, 284, 318
Blamires, Harry, 192
Blumenberg, Hans
    Legitimacy of the Modern Age,
    The, 10
Bork, Robert, 138, 246
Bowers v. Hardwick, 263-264, 284,
    318
Boy Scouts, 281
Brennan, (Justice) William, 232
Brinton, Crane, 118-119
Buckley, William, 298
Burke, Edmund, 15, 23, 26, 143,
    163-165, 274, 306, 331
Bush, (President) George H.W.,
    156, 167

Cahill, Thomas
    Pope John XXIII, 292
Caldwell, Christopher, 308-309
Calvin, John, 50-51
Canon law, 31, 223-225, 333
Carhart, (Dr.) LeRoy, 275
Catechism of the Catholic Church,
    The, 285, 342
Catholic Church, 2, 9, 22-24, 34,
    69, 106-108, 141, 166, 185-186,
    199-201, 202-204, 208-210,
    217, 223-225, 229-231, 241-
    243, 253-255, 281, 284-285,
    293-294, 295-297, 302-303,
    316, 319-321, 352, 355, 360-
    362, 370
Catholic University, The, 58-63

Catholics
American, 60, 67-68, 112-114, 139-141, 165
dissenting, 22-24
Dutch, 49-51
Chavez, Linda, 281
Chinese one-child policy, 114
Christian freedom, 133-135
Christmas, 120, 152-153, 181-183, 216, 252
Church of England, 53, 164
Civil Rights Restoration Act of 1988, 137
Civil War, 47, 80, 245, 338, 368
Clergy sex-abuse scandal, 295-297, 301-303, 310. See also Priests
Clinton, Hillary, 274
Clinton, (President) William, 345
Code of Canon Law of the Catholic Church, 333
Coffey, (Fr.) David, 181-182
Constitution, U.S.
Bill of Rights, 339
Eighteenth Amendment, 333
Fifth Amendment, 245
First Amendment, 73-75, 357
Fourteenth Amendment, 337, 340
Ninth Amendment, 340
Twenty-sixth Amendment, 136
Contraception, 85-87, 314, 319-321, 338-339
Humanae Vitae, 85, 87, 251
Cropsey, Joseph, 218-219
Culture of death, 250-252
Curran, (Fr.) Charles, 73, 84, 85

Dahl, Robert A.
Preface to Democratic Theory, A, 137, 305
D'Alembert, Jean le Rond, 98
Dalin, (Rabbi) David G.
"Pius XII and the Jews," 293
Danforth, (Senator) John C., 244, 246
Dannemeyer, William E., 260

Date rape, 238-240
Declaration of Independence, 232, 273, 368
Death penalty, 13-14
Decline of Liberalism as an Ideology, The, 107
DeCrow, Karen, 125-126
Decter, Midge, 196-197
Democracy, 43, 53-54, 111, 115-116, 136-138, 141, 162, 170, 176-177, 193, 280, 289-291, 363
Democratic Party, 110, 160, 304-306
Dennett, Daniel C.
Consciousness Explained, 251
Descartes, René, 132
Devil, the, 190-192
Dinkins, (Mayor) David N., 226-228
Discrimination, 226-228
Dissent, 34, 49-50, 85, 113, 201, 209, 229-231, 361
Divorce, 6, 53, 67, 84, 91-93, 106, 113-114, 208-210, 217-218, 237, 315, 336, 361
Dodson, Betty
Sex for One, 127
Domestic partnerships, 178-180, 262-264. See also Gay rights, Homosexuality, Same-sex marriage
Dominian, Jack, 130-131
Donahue, Phil, 16, 127
Douglas, (Justice) William, 233, 338
"Dover Beach," 307
Dred Scott, 338
Due Process Clause, 245, 337, 340
Dulles, (Cardinal) Avery, 360-361
Dunne, Finley Peter, 297, 333
Dworkin, Ronald
Liberalism, 72

Easterbrook, Gregg, 36
Easy cases, 193. See also Abortion
Eco, Umberto, 346
Education, 277-279
Egalitarianism, 140-141, 220, 289-291

Eichmann, Adolf, 37, 39
Eighteenth Amendment, 333
Ellington, Duke, 198
Ellison, Katherine, 167-168
Encyclicals
    Humanae Vitae, 85, 87, 251
    Mater et Magistra, 172
    Populorum Progressio, 173, 316
    Quadragesimo Anno, 173, 370
    Rerum Novarum, 99, 172, 281,
    334
    Sollicitudo Rei Socialis (On
    Social Concern), 172, 174, 200-
    201, 235
Engelhardt Jr., H. Tristram
    Foundations of Bioethics, The,
    257
Enlightenment, 17-18, 60, 96
Equality, 15, 35, 43-45, 48, 51, 59,
    62, 72, 78, 80-81, 124-126, 140-
    141, 146, 170, 172, 224, 227,
    234, 235, 245-246, 260, 263-
    264, 271-273, 276, 278, 280-
    281, 283, 289-291, 295, 329
Eucharist, 169
European Court, 262
Evil, 3-4, 17, 23, 31, 82-84, 98,
    108, 134, 157-159, 177, 183,
    188, 190-191, 203, 266, 274-
    275, 314, 319, 331-332, 356, 370

Falwell, (Rev.) Jerry, 34
Family, 2, 56, 66, 93, 178-180,
    188-189, 224, 232-234, 236-
    237, 263, 272, 280-282, 298,
    326-327, 334, 336-337, 346,
    361, 371
Farewell Address, 347
Farrell, Anne, 268
Fatal Attraction, 122
Federalist, The, 14
Feminism
    Friedan, Betty, 146, 352
    inclusive language, 103-105,
    325-326
    Yard, Molly, 193
    women priests, 68

Fessio, (Fr.) Joseph, 211-213
Feuer, Lewis S.
    *Spinoza and the Rise of
    Liberalism*, 94
Fey, Harold E., 69
Fifth Amendment, 245
First Amendment, 73-75, 357
First Things, 195, 294, 320, 360
Fordham University, 214, 301
Foster, (Fr.) Jonathan, 203
Founding Fathers, 47, 335
Fourteenth Amendment
    Due Process Clause, 245, 337,
    340
Fourth Lateran Council, 348
Frankfurter, (Justice) Felix, 245-
    246
Free will, 242, 254, 257, 316
Freedom of speech, 73-75
Freeman, Jo, 110
French Revolution
    Declaration of the Rights of
    Man and the Citizen, 65
Freud, Sigmund, 259
Friedan, Betty, 146, 352
Furst, Gunilla, 271-272

Galston, William, 237
Gay rights. *See also* Homosexuality;
    Same-sex marriage; St.
    Patrick's Day Parade
Gay, Peter
    *Enlightenment: An Interpretation,
    The*, 118, 131, 293
Genetic engineering, 130, 148-
    150, 313-315
Georgetown University, 138, 140,
    196
Goldsmith, Oliver, 70
Good Friday, 146
Graduate, The, 148
Graham, Billy, 180
Griswold v. Connecticut, 338
Grove City College, 59, 137

Haas, Linda, 124
Hales, E. E. Y.

Revolution and Papacy, 1769-1846, 119
Hall, Terry, 256, 258
Hallowell, John, 162
  Decline of Liberalism as an Ideology, The, 107
  Moral Foundation of Democracy, The, 162, 176
Hamilton, Alexander, 14
Hanafin, (Irish Senator) Des, 91
Hartdegen, (Fr.) Stephen J., 103
Hauerwas, Stanley, 178-179
Hayes, Zachary, 215
Hazard, Paul
  Crisis of the European Mind, 1680-1715, The, 118
Healy, Timothy, 196
Heaven, 11, 79, 81, 101-102, 183, 242, 298-300, 350
Hefner, Hugh, 15, 16
Hell, 33, 100-102, 134, 242-243, 300
Heller, Joseph, 295
Helms, (Senator) Jesse, 197
Herbert, Bob, 198
Himmelfarb, Gertrude, 203
Hobbes, Thomas, 112, 323, 329, 335, 346
Hochhuth, Rolf, 292
Holocaust, 292-294
Homosexuality, 46-48, 49, 76-78, 86, 178-180, 226-228, 259-261, 262-264, 314-315. *See also* Gay Rights, Same-sex marriage
Human rights, 111, 288, 318
Humanae Vitae, 85, 87, 251
Hume, David, 346

Inclusive language, 103-105, 325-326
Infanticide, 40-42. *See also* Abortion
Islam, 342, 344

Jefferson, Thomas, 368
Jews, 293-294, 310
Jews, secularized, 293-294
John Geddes Lawrence v. Texas, 340

John Paul II
  Sollicitudo Rei Socialis, 172, 174, 200-201, 235
John XXIII, 292
  Mater et Magistra, 172

Kass, Leon, 319
Kavanaugh, (Fr.) John F., 304
Kearley, Carroll, 345
Keefe, Nancy Q., 200-201
Kenelan, Bill, 211
Kenmare, Lord, 163
Kennedy, (Justice) Anthony, 340
Kertzer, David
  Popes Against the Jews, The, 292
Kevorkian, Jack, 287
Kimball, Roger, 356
Kinsley, Michael, 175-176
Knox, Ronald, 223
Koch, (Mayor) Edward, 46, 228
Krauthammer, Charles, 197
Kristol, Irving, 241, 294

Lambeth Conference, 87
Landers, Ann, 17
Lasch, Christopher, 179, 329
Last Judgment, 100, 128, 134
Law, (Cardinal) Bernard, 297
Lean, David
  Passage to India, A, 37
Leege, David C., 68-69
Lent, 184-186, 265-267
Leo XIII
  Rerum Novarum, 99, 172-173, 281, 334, 369
Levi, Jeff, 140
Levy, Leonard W., 245
Lewis, C. S., 182, 300
  Abolition of Man, The, 150, 251
  Great Divorce, The, 216
  Screwtape Letters, The, 102, 250
Liberalism, 7, 35, 43-45, 61-63, 72, 107, 115-117, 140, 142-144, 160-162, 173-174, 178-179, 197, 217-218, 295, 309, 316, 324, 329, 345-346
Lincoln, Abraham, 370

Lindley, David
  End of Physics, The, 323, 329
Lippmann, Walter
  Public Philosophy, The, 45, 75
Locke, John, 64-65, 286, 335
Lowi, Theodore J., 116-117
Loyal Opposition, 22-24
Loyola, St. Ignatius, 152

MacIntyre, Alasdair
  After Virtue, 91, 129
Mack, (Senator) Connie, 286
MacLeish, Roderick, Jr., 303
Madonna (singer), 240
Madonna, weeping, 322
Magisterium, 22-23, 360-361
Mansour, Agnes, 1
Maples, Marla, 247
Mapplethorpe, Robert, 197
Maritain, Jacques, 369
  Man and the State, 162
Marlowe, Christopher, 292-293
Marriage, 6, 67-69, 76-77, 85-87,
  91-93, 121, 180, 208-210, 223-
  225, 235-237, 260-261, 262-
  264, 269, 273, 281-282, 314-
  315, 317-318, 321, 334-336,
  337, 346, 366-367
Marshall, (Justice) Thurgood,
  205, 337
Marty, Martin E., 100
Marx, Karl, 79, 83
Mater et Magistra, 172
McBrien, (Fr.) Richard, 190, 229-231
McGurn, William, 194-195
McLaughlin Group, The, 190-191
Meier, (Fr.) John P., 95-96
Meiklejohn, Alexander, 278
Merici, St. Angela, 135, 242-243
Methodists, United, 212
Middle Ages, 97, 348
Miedzan, Myriam, 249
Milhaven, John Giles, 85
Mill, John Stuart, 15, 62, 70-71,
  74, 202, 219, 230, 361
  On Liberty, 71, 75, 202, 361
Milton, John

  Areopagitica, 75
Mitchell, Henry, 73-74
Mohler, R. Albert, 320-321
Moral Majority, 34
Morality, 256-258
More, (Sir) Thomas, 82
Morley, John, 50
Murray, (Fr.) John Courtney, 31, 130
Muslims, 25, 342
Mydans, Seth, 166
Myers, (Archbishop) John J., 329

National Organization for
  Women (NOW), 239
Neuhaus, (Fr.) Richard John, 195
Niebuhr, Reinhold, 9
Ninth Amendment, 340
Novak, (Rabbi) David, 294
Novak, Michael, 172

O'Connor, (Cardinal) John, 46,
  109, 190, 200
On Social Concern, 235. *See also*
  Sollicitudo Rei Socialis
Ordered liberty, 142-144

Paine, Thomas
  Rights of Man, The, 363
Palmer, R. R.
  Catholics and Unbelievers in
  Eighteenth-Century France, 17, 119
Papal Revolution of 1095-1122,
  223-225
Pascal, Blaise, 309
Passage to India, A, 37
Paul VI, 87, 173-174, 242, 316
  Humanae Vitae, 85, 87, 251
  Populorum Progressio, 173-174,
  316
Peguy, Charles, 80
Percy, Walker
  Lost in the Cosmos, 106-108, 186
Personally opposed, 1-4. *See also*
  Abortion
Personhood, 286-288. *See also*
  Abortion
Pfeffer, Leo, 63, 293-294

Pill, the, 130, 320. *See also* Contraception
Pius IX, 316
Pius XI
    Principle of Subsidiarity, 173-174, 369
    Quadragesimo Anno, 173, 370
Pius XII, 292-294
Planned Parenthood, 167, 194, 249, 269, 338
Planned Parenthood v. Casey, 338
Plato, 155
Pluralism, 7-9, 62, 88-90, 139-141, 256-258, 283-285
Pollitt, Katha, 155
Polygamy, 224, 232, 284
Popenoe, David, 92
Population decline, 308-309
    State of the World Population 2002, 308
Populorum Progressio, 173, 316
Pornography, 66, 74, 196-198
Positivism, 94-96
Post-Christian, 106-108, 185-186, 210, 367
Powell, (Justice) Lewis, 284
Presbyterian Church, 234
Priests
    celibacy, 49-50, 113, 164, 188-189, 223-225, 310, 352
    clergy sex-abuse scandal, 295-297, 301-303, 310
Private judgment, 360-362
Progress, 52-54, 70-72, 98, 130-132
Progressive, 10, 16, 52-54, 80, 202-204
Protestant Reformation, 343
Protestantism, 9, 294, 360

Quadragesimo Anno, 173, 370

Ramsey, Paul
    Fabricated Man, 251
Ranke-Heinemann, Uta
    Eunuchs for the Kingdom of Heaven, 223

Ratzinger, (Cardinal) Joseph, 157, 203-204, 212, 254, 316
Rawls, John
    Theory of Justice, A , 72
Reich, Robert, 328
Republican Party, 110, 304
Rerum Novarum, 99, 172, 281, 334
Roe v. Wade, 123, 168, 175-176, 205, 263, 274 287, 332, 337-338
Rogers, Will, 192
Roman Empire, 181, 309
Romer v. Evans, 263
Roosevelt, Theodore, 25
Rousseau, Jean-Jacques, 335
Rubaiyat of Omar Khayyám, The, 19
Rubenstein, William, 180
Ruether, Rosemary Radford, 8
Runcie, (Anglican Archbishop) Richard, 231
Russell, Bertrand, 20
Ryan, Alan, 328
Rychlak, Ronald
    Hitler, the War, and the Pope, 293

Sabine, George, 144
Salvation, 220-222, 253-255
Same-sex marriage, 178-180, 262. *See also* Domestic partnerships, Gay rights; Homosexuality
Satanism, 190-192
Schillebeeckx, Edward, 49
Schindler, Jeanne Heffernan, 368
Schlesinger, Arthur, 257
Schmitz, Kenneth L., 346-347
Scientism, 191-192, 341-344, 354
Second Lateran Council, 131
Secularism, 307-309, 322-324
Sermon on the Mount, 31-33
Sexual revolution, 127, 268-270, 319, 321, 355-356, 363
Shaw, George Bernard, 60, 101
Shaw, Russell, 209
Sheen, (Archbishop) Fulton J., 10
Sheppard, E. Z., 345
Siegel, Fred, 160
Silver, Daniel Jeremy, 311
Silver, Lee M., 148-150

Simon, Yves
  *Philosophy of Democratic
  Government*, 162
Sin, 133-135
Skepticism, New, 34-35
Slogans, 79-81
Smith, Liz, 151
Sobran, Joseph, 227
Social justice, 172, 235. *See also*
  Encyclicals
Sola scriptura, 343
Sollicitudo Rei Socialis, 172
Spragens, Thomas
  Irony of Liberal Reason, The, 7,
  72, 192, 323, 356, 363
St. Ignatius Institute, 211-213
St. Ignatius Press, 213
St. Patrick's Day Parade, 226-228
Stephen, (Sir) James Fitzjames,
  230
Stephen, (Sir) Leslie, 230
Stephen, Beverly, 77
Stevens, (Justice) John Paul, 326
Strauss, Leo
  Natural Right and History, 83
Supreme Court, 122-123, 137-138,
  139, 143, 168, 175-176, 180,
  193-194, 205, 232-233, 244-
  246, 263, 274-275, 284, 287,
  292, 314, 318, 326, 331-333,
  337-338, 352
  Bowers v. Hardwick, 263-264,
  284, 318
  Griswold v. Connecticut, 338-339
  Hodgson v. Minnesota, 205
  John Geddes Lawrence v. Texas, 340
  Planned Parenthood v. Casey, 338
  Roe v. Wade, 123, 168, 175-176,
  205, 263, 274, 287, 332, 337-338
  Romer v. Evans, 263
  Sandford v. Dred Scott, 338
  Zablocki v. Redhail, 337
Sweden, 92-93, 271-273
Synod, Extraordinary, 67

Title IX of the 1972 Education
  Act, 137

Truman, Harry, 364
Turow, Scott, 202
Twenty-sixth Amendment, 136

Unger, Robert Mangabeira, 345
United Nations, 308, 349
United Nations General
  Assembly, 234
United States, 6, 16, 43-45, 67-69,
  93, 155, 368

Vanauken, Sheldon, 192
Vatican II, 119, 169-171, 253
Viviani, René, 290-291
Vocations, 169-171, 241-243, 310-
  312

Walzer, Michael
  Spheres of Justice, 97
Wasser, Hedwig, 49-50
Welsh, Jerome A., 84
Wertheimer, Jack, 283, 310
Will, George, 72, 78, 116, 227,
  278, 295, 329
Wills, Garry, 138, 307, 328
Wilson, Bryan R., 108
  *Religion in Sociological
  Perspective*, 108
Women, 55-57, 145-147
Women priests, 68
Worldview, 341-344
World War II, 364
Wright, (Cardinal) John, 213, 349

Yard, Molly, 193

Zablocki v. Redhail, 337
Zetterbaum, Marvin
  History of Political Philosophy,
  124
Zimmern, (Sir) Alfred
  Greek Commonwealth, The, 40-
  41
Zvesper, John, 72